Digital Paper

For Terry,
with long admiration
very good to see you

Digital Paper

A Manual
for Research
and Writing
with Library
and Internet
Materials

Andrew Abbott

THE UNIVERSITY OF CHICAGO PRESS
CHICAGO AND LONDON

ANDREW ABBOTT is the Gustavus F. and Ann M. Swift Distinguished Service Professor at the University of Chicago. He edits the *American Journal of Sociology* and his books include *The System of Professions*, *Department and Discipline*, *Chaos of Disciplines*, and *Time Matters*. He has twice chaired the University of Chicago's Library Board, and he played a central role in planning the university's Joe and Rika Mansueto Library.

The University of Chicago Press, Chicago 60637
The University of Chicago Press, Ltd., London
© 2014 by The University of Chicago
All rights reserved. Published 2014.
Printed in the United States of America

23 22 21 20 19 18 17 16 15 14   1 2 3 4 5

ISBN-13: 978-0-226-16764-0 (cloth)
ISBN-13: 978-0-226-16778-7 (paper)
ISBN-13: 978-0-226-16781-7 (e-book)
DOI: 10.7208/chicago/9780226167817.001.0001

Library of Congress Cataloging-in-Publication Data

Abbott, Andrew Delano, author.
 Digital paper : a manual for research and writing with library and internet materials / Andrew Abbott.
    pages cm — (Chicago guides to writing, editing, and publishing)
 Includes bibliographical references and index.
 ISBN 978-0-226-16764-0 (cloth : alk. paper) — ISBN 978-0-226-16778-7 (pbk. : alk. paper) — ISBN 978-0-226-16781-7 (e-book)   1. Report writing—Handbooks, manuals, etc. 2. Research—Handbooks, manuals, etc. 3. Searching, Bibliographical—Handbooks, manuals, etc.   I. Title.   II. Series: Chicago guides to writing, editing, and publishing.
  LB1047.3.A22 2014
  808.02—dc23

2013050782

To Judi Nadler

Contents

To the Reader

This is a book about how to do a research project in materials you didn't gather yourself. You may find such materials online, or in a library, or in an archive, or in city hall, or in somebody's attic. "Found materials" are unlike materials that you gather yourself, like interviews or personal observations or surveys. Usually they weren't collected for research at all, but for some other reason. You are rummaging around in them because you want to make them answer some question of your own, a question that was not in the minds of the people who gathered them. You hope or want or need to produce a written argument about your research in these found materials.

The present book covers everything necessary to get from your original hazy idea to that final solid output. Most often your project will aim at an academic product of some kind: a course paper, a BA thesis, a master's paper, an article, a PhD dissertation, and so on. Since this is a broad range of things, this book will aim for the middle of the size distribution: a midsize research paper of twenty to forty pages with notes and bibliography. But its approach can easily be scaled to down to smaller projects or scaled up to larger ones.

You might think that such a book would be about how to find things. But finding things is only a part of doing a research project. So while the book certainly covers finding things, it covers many other things besides: different ways to read, how to browse or scan, and strategies for writing, for example. (It also covers how to ignore things, which today is probably a more important skill than how to find things!) All of these activities are part of your larger problem: managing your various efforts so that they result in a good product at the end. The heart of the present book is therefore not the many activities you will do in research, but learning how to manage those activities to get a good result. It's about project management.

Managing a research project in found materials is much the same whether the materials are found in a library or on the Internet, in city hall or in the attic. The same kinds of questions arise: Should I look for more materials?

Why did I think this material is important? Who has thought about my topic already? And so on. So the provenance of the material doesn't matter much. What matters is that the material has not been expressly gathered for the current research, that you need to decide which material to use and what to make out of it, and that you will need to find more material to help you do that making. These problems and issues are the same whether you are working online or in a library, whether your library is a big one or a small one, whether the paper is for a political science class or an English class or a talk to your town's local history society. In all these situations, you are assembling parts and pieces of found data into an argument, and you are creating a document that sets forth and supports that argument.

So this guide is a quite general one. I myself happen to be a sociologist and happen to work in one of the world's great research libraries. But the book's advice is useful across a wide range of disciplines; I have used its ideas to teach students all across the humanities and social sciences. And its strategies for research in found materials will work in libraries of vastly different sizes, not to mention the fact that the immense Internet is available to everyone, and the few licensed databases discussed in the book are available at the majority of colleges and universities.

Colleagues who read the drafts before publication warned me that readers might be put off by the book's calling them to stretch themselves, to aim at research excellence. These colleagues told me to simplify; as one of them put it, "You need to bring it closer to where the students are." But my own experience in teaching is that students writing research papers are eager to find a place better than where they now are. They are disheartened by the seemingly trackless miasma of research, by the formless information world where everything is equally accessible and everything is equally inviting. And once they realize what serious research skills make possible, they want to improve their skills all the more.

So I haven't changed the book at all. It sets forth a vision of a kind of research and also a vision of what makes that kind of research excellent. I believe in excellence in research, and I also believe that excellent research is within the grasp of many students who don't dream that they can do it. It is a question of learning the skills and making the effort.

IT WILL BE HELPFUL TO INTRODUCE MYSELF, YOUR CRANKY GUIDE TO research in found data. Probably most important, my mother was a working librarian during my childhood, and therefore I spent a lot of time hanging around libraries after school. I once tried to count the number of libraries I have ever been inside and lost track at around 150. If I sometimes sound romantic about libraries, no doubt that's one of the main reasons.

Second, I am a sociologist who does a lot of library research. About half of my publications derive mainly from library research projects, on topics like the transformations of the information professions, markets for legal work in the late nineteenth century, the history of scholarly journals, and the funding of library reference tools in the twentieth century. I write articles with lots of footnotes, wax poetic about unusual sources, and so on.

But third, it happens that in my nonlibrary work I have long employed the sequence analysis algorithms used by keyword search engines. I took these up in the early 1980s, long before the age of interactive library tools. I used them to investigate career patterns, since sequences of jobs are no different from the sequences of amino acids in DNA. Moreover, I also used the clustering, classification, and scaling algorithms that information scientists would eventually use to produce wordclouds and similar adjacency displays; for me they were ways to put career sequences into categories. And in addition, since I did work on networks (I have also written about mobility networks among baroque musicians, for example), I also used the network centrality measures that drive relevance orders in search engines. So I have known for several decades the advantages and disadvantages of the computational techniques that are "under the hood" of many familiar library research tools.

Fourth, it also happens that most of my substantive research has been about knowledge systems. I have published books on professional knowledge, on academic disciplines, and on sociology as a discipline. Indeed, as the reader will learn, much of my current research is about the history of library use and the empirical and normative theory of library-based knowledge.

In short, I am a scholar much of whose research has been done in libraries but also one who has worked extensively with the computational techniques that drive the tools available for library research and its digital analogues. And I'm also one whose research has mainly concerned knowledge and knowledge systems. This somewhat unusual combination of expertises has inevitably produced a distinctive kind of book. Most important, my computational experience gives me an insider's view of digital knowledge tools, and my skepticism about them—of which more below—is based not on simple conservatism but on having extensively used such tools in other contexts.

I should say a little too about why I have ended up teaching library/digital research and writing a book that derives from that teaching. Like most of my colleagues, I myself learned library expertise largely by hearsay and experiment. I found that experience quite frustrating. In order to save students from that frustration, I began to teach these techniques once I became a professor. But while I could do library research well, I couldn't teach it well. That continuing failure made me reflect more about my own library research practices. Gradually I saw that I was teaching the wrong thing: the central problem in library work wasn't so much finding things as it was knowing what to look for. And when I asked myself how I knew what to look for, I realized that I actually had no idea how I knew that. It just seemed a magical intuition. But I don't believe in magical intuitions, so I studied my research habits more carefully.

Now we all know that research is supposed to be a linear journey from questions to data to results. But when I examined my own library practices, I found that I went in circles. Each bit of research would recast my questions. Then the new questions would lead to new research, which would recast my questions, which would . . . and so on. At first I thought I was the only scholar who didn't do research in the right order; my colleagues surely had clear questions and coherent research designs! But I started asking them about their designs. And it turned out that they didn't have clear designs either. Most of my colleagues admit quite freely to operating in a perpetual circle between questions and results. The finished logic of our articles and books is a façade, put on after the fact.

Over the next three or four years, I recast my library research course from a course in sophisticated tools for how to find things to a course in how to manage a complicated and often illogical project so that you would always know what was the next thing to look for. I began to realize that skill (or "intuition") in library research is knowing, when you have randomly found something, whether or not you ought to have wanted to look for it.

This is not to say that it is unimportant to know how to find things. Thomas Mann's wonderful *Oxford Guide to Library Research* should be on every researcher's shelf. Similarly, it's important to have a grasp of the more formal ways of writing up your research, and there are many excellent books on that topic as well. But when these topics are treated separately, they don't make much sense. We want finding techniques because we're doing research, and we want to do research because finding by itself is just random surfing. The two processes must support each other, because between finding things on the one hand and writing things on the other lies the vast sea of randomness that any researcher in found materials must traverse. It is the staggering vastness of this sea—made a thousand times more vast by the Internet—that so frightens the beginning researcher. How in the world does one find one's way across? The answers—or at least one possible set of answers—will be found in the book you are holding.

Now of course, you may have heard from some people that there's a revolution in research and that it is easier than ever before. I don't need to tell you that this is nonsense. You know from firsthand experience that research is confusing and daunting, as indeed it has always been. We are no closer to revolutionary improvement in library-based and "found data" knowledge than we were thirty years ago—more likely the reverse. The new tools in fact make it harder than ever for students to learn the disciplines of research, mainly through sheer overload; for students, universal access simply means a thousand times more things to sift through. But research is newly difficult for another reason. Today's students—unlike those of my generation—do not learn novice versions of "research practices" in precollege education. That's not so much because they don't get assigned research papers as it is because they grow up in an Internet world that doesn't have clear quality standards, authoritative reference tools, and so on, as did the high school library of the past. We had guides; you do not. The overload is worse and the guidance is gone. Oddly, the new tools and universal access do make library research easier than ever for those of us who already know the basic disciplines of research, because we have learned how to handle sources that have the vast quantity and mixed quality of the Internet (the *Readers' Guide to Periodical Literature* was the equivalent "overloader" in our day) and so we can make the Internet do astounding and wonderful things.

Of course it's not all wonderful for the experts either. We are annoyed by the perpetual and functionally unnecessary changes in the interfaces of the tools—you'll hear about some amusing cases of those below. But it turns out that these changes have major implications for you, too. They mean that some—perhaps much—of the particular advice I give in this book will be outmoded very soon. The commercial environment means that the tools and sources are perpetually being "improved." As you know well from the experience of the perpetual new editions of college textbooks, most of this improvement is simply arbitrary change to create new opportunities for profit. But it means that random little changes are perpetually taking place in tools, and specific advice one gives today must change next year, even though there has been no real change in the underlying research tasks or how they are actually implemented in the tools. The changes are cosmetic rather than substantive, although in the pursuit of profit they usually aim to broaden appeal, and therefore more often remove research functionality (research is a small market) rather than improve it.

All this churning and change makes the general approach and advice of this book all the more important. The tools will change all the time as they get bought, combined, separated, improved, and so on. But the underlying themes of the book—following quality, maintaining focused questions, reading sources skeptically and critically—will always remain. And they dictate the functionalities that you must seek in a research tool (what kinds of indexing it uses, what kinds of quality measures it has, what real data lies underneath it, etc.). New tools and new interfaces will arise, and you will have to judge them for yourself. I hope that by reading this book you will see the criteria on which you should make that judgment.

In summary, the core tasks of found-data research are as hard as ever, and the core skills of research—rigor, discipline, care, and imagination—remain the same and will remain the same for the future. There is no knowledge revolution—just a new level of overload, a lot of churning, and a lot of hype. More important then than the actual recommendations I make about this or that tool, about this or that publisher, or about this or that type of material, are the reasons for which I make those recommendations. That reasoning sets forth the canons that are essential to real knowledge. And if you learn those canons, you will be able to negotiate new tools for yourself, once my specific recommendations have been outmoded—as they soon will be—by technological and corporate change.

EVERY TEXT SHOULD MAKE ITS DEBTS PLAIN. I OWE FIRST OF ALL AN enormous debt to all the librarians who have helped me through the years. To my mother, who made me help classify and shelve the various libraries she ran, and who taught me the basics of reference work as she had learned them from Laura Colvin at Simmons College. To the many librarians who helped me in my dissertation work: who kept libraries open after hours because they took pity on a hapless student; who let me spend days in stacks that were supposedly closed to all but staff; who remembered an odd work that "you might be interested in." Librarians have helped me in dozens of ways. They are a great profession, and I devoutly hope that those who seek to centralize all knowledge out of their hands receive their final recall notice from the Great Librarian.

The most important librarian in my life, these days at least, is Judith Nadler, the director of the University of Chicago Library. As chair of my university's Library Board, I have worked closely with Judi for seven years. She is a great technical librarian and a superb leader of her staff. Her planning and oversight in building Chicago's new Mansueto Library are a shining example of professionalism, vision, and charisma.

I thank finally the students whose work has taught me so much through the many versions of my library research course. I shall use their work as examples throughout, for which they have kindly given their permission. But more important, they asked the questions that made me realize what I was failing to teach. If this book is successful, it is largely due to their stimulation.

I write this preface in Chicago's Joseph Regenstein Library. I have used many libraries in my life. Some of them were big and comprehensive. Some of them were small but excellent. All have been a pleasure. But I think that this is my favorite. It is a privilege to have been able to work here.

1

Introduction

1. A Manual of Research

This is a manual on how to do a research project with preexisting materials, stored in libraries or online databases. What exactly do I mean by this?

First, this is a manual, a how-to book. It is not a handbook or listing of techniques and sources, as are most books on library research. Such books are organized from the librarian's point of view. They treat different types of searches: by keywords, by citations, and so on. They treat different types of sources: archives, maps, censuses, and so on. In short, they tell you how to find particular things. But finding things is actually a rather small part of research. Finding things is necessary, but other things are more important. So that is my first point: this is a manual on research, not a guide for how to find things in libraries or online.

My second key phrase is "doing a research project." I could have said "doing research." But then you would have thought I meant "finding things." But as I have just said, "doing research" is not finding things. "Doing research" means constructing an answer to a puzzle you have posed. Now you might think that the answer to any possible question or puzzle is out there somewhere in the library or online, and that "research" means finding that answer. But it doesn't. The number of possible questions (and hence the number of answers to those questions) is far larger than the number of "things out there." This is because the answers to puzzles or questions always involve *combinations* of "things out there," and there are obviously many, many more combinations of things than there are things by themselves. So library and online researchers never think that the answers to their puzzles are simply available to be found, even though information relevant to those answers will of course be available—usually far too much information. The answers themselves have to be constructed by combining that information in a particular way: expert knowing. So to avoid the misunderstanding that "research" is just "finding things," I say that we "do research projects," not that we "do research."

An example makes the distinction clear. Take the question of how many lawyers there are in America. If I ask twenty students to go to the Internet and get this number, they bring back twenty different and equally authoritative numbers, running from around 500,000 up toward two million. For the answer depends entirely on what you mean by "lawyer": Graduates of law schools? People who have passed state or federal bar exams? People currently employed as lawyers (whatever that means)? People who have current licenses to practice (before which courts?)? Each of these numbers is the right answer, but only if we are asking a certain question. If we are thinking about the impact of licensing fees on lawyers, we are probably worried about how many people have passed the bar exam (not just those with licenses), because we are interested in whether the fees discouraged some people from applying for licenses. If we are thinking about whether the typical citizen actually understands how courts work, then we are probably interested in the percentage of the population that has ever attended law school and learned there the legal habit of mind. If we are thinking about legal services for the poor, then we are perhaps interested only in practicing lawyers whose practices include personal clients of some sort.

That is, it is our research interest that determines which of the "numbers of lawyers in America" is the right one. A good librarian will help you find them all. But it is not her job to tell you which one you ought to want or even to tell you that there is more than one. That's your job as a researcher. More generally, gathering information relevant to your puzzle is an important part of a research project, but the main problem is to figure out what the puzzle is and what information it requires. Once you've managed that, finding the relevant information turns out to be pretty routine. So just remember that "doing research" does not mean "finding things" in this book. It means posing a research question, gathering relevant materials, and assembling an answer out of those materials.

This brings me to my third key phrase: "stored in libraries or online databases." Despite the digital revolution, conducting a research project using data that other people have stored or gathered is more or less the same kind of activity that it was before. That is because the social situation is the same. You the researcher are an individual with a puzzle that interests you. You seek material relevant to that puzzle in a preexisting body of materials that is large and indefinite, but that may itself be organized, although in ways that are probably irrelevant to your puzzle. This body of materials may have custodians who facilitate access to it (e.g., librarians), but those custodians do not have any way of knowing what your puzzle is. The only real differences in the digital era are that physical libraries are smaller but well organized while the digital world is larger but unorganized. Other than that, the social situation of research is exactly the same.

As for the tools themselves, the main practical differences between physical tools and online tools are that the latter are (a) far more widely available and (b) of lower quality—in terms of accuracy, durability, and associated information. Everyone knows about the vastly increased access of the digital world, and it is a truly wonderful thing. The lowered quality is less known and less happy. Here is an example. My own first book, *The System of Professions*, was published in 1988. There is only one edition, and there is one card for that edition in my university's card catalog (now in the library basement). There are, however, seven separate title entries for it in WorldCat, and a whopping forty different titles for it in the Web of Science (WoS) citation listings. (There are various reasons for this, most having to do with data-entry processes.) To be sure, 80 percent of the citations in WoS are under the proper title. But for all its many virtues, WoS is not close to being perfectly accurate. So there's an upside and a downside to both physical and digital tools.

The dual situation between electronic and physical materials will persist for a long time. There are expense arguments on both sides (books require large buildings, but digital science journals gobble up library budgets). There are access arguments on both sides (digital format permits faster, wider, and cheaper access, but for many kinds of materials there is no viable business plan for digitization). Even at the user level, there are arguments on both sides. Online sources are staggeringly fast for some tasks. They allow some things never before possible. They broaden access immeasurably. But they are of low quality by traditional standards, and they strip out much peripheral information that is essential to library research practice. On the other hand, physical sources (or physical sources with an untransformed online presence—online catalogs, for example) are generally of very high quality. They are rich in the peripheral cues that are crucial to library research. But they are slow for some purposes, and some kinds of searches are impossible within them. Given the two sides, it is no surprise that good scholars shift back and forth between physical and electronic tools all the time. So you must get used to functioning in both worlds.

This then is a manual about doing a research project in preexisting materials, a task for which I shall hereafter use the shorthand phrase "library research," even though nearly all research in found materials involves use of both physical and online materials. These days, most libraries provide much or most of their material through online licensing, so the word "library" covers physical and digital materials in most young people's minds (so my students tell me). The alternative (but probably more correct) term—"found-data research"—just seems too ugly. So we simply have to remember that "library research" does not mean research only in physical resources.

Examples of library projects are library-based term papers, theses, dissertations, articles, monographs, and so on. Of course, there are also "background papers" based on library and online materials, a common genre in the government and nonprofit worlds. But I am not interested in such things. I am writing about research projects that will produce the classic research output: a text answering a particular question or questions.

2. The Nonlinearity of Library Work

The first fact about library research projects is that they are not done in a strict order. You don't start with a general question, focus that into particular questions, then specify the data you need, gather the data, analyze it, and finally write up the result. The natural scientists proceed that way, or at least claim that they do. But in library research, that approach is a certain recipe for failure. Quite the contrary, you will be doing many different kinds of things at once. Only at write-up time will you cast the project into the classical rhetorical form: general questions leading to specific questions leading to analysis and finally to conclusions. You have no doubt read many library-based books and articles. None of them was researched in the write-up order.

Figure 1 gives a loose view of the time spent on the actual tasks of a typical library research project. There are seven tasks you do at some point: design, bibliography, scanning and materials search, reading, maintaining files, analyzing retrieved material, and writing. As the figure shows, you will be doing all seven of these most of the time. You will, for example, start writing things before you have a final, firm design. In fact, you won't have a final firm design until the very end of the project. This explains why most doctoral students write their dissertation's first chapter after writing everything else but the conclusion. You understand what you were trying to do only once you're done, not before.

That library research is not linear means that a textbook of library research cannot be linear. Because you are always doing many different research activities, you cannot read this book chapter by chapter, mastering one aspect

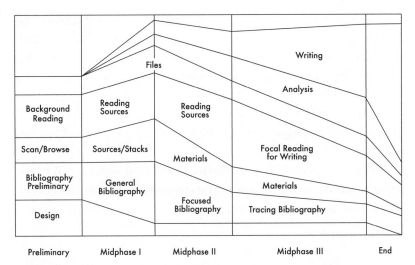

FIGURE 1. Rough timeline for a major library research project

of library research before you go on to the next. For example, you may have to reread the section on overviews whenever you need to do an overview of a new subarea, until you get used to doing overviews. You may have to read and reread the sections on indexing and browsing because these tasks come up again and again in the course of a project.

I have tried to deal with this nonlinearity by going over the basic trajectory of a library research project three times, each time with increasing detail. I give an overview in the next three sections of this chapter. I then present a chapter-length summary in the various sections of chapter 4. And finally I cover the midphase version of each task in detailed task-chapters from chapter 5 to chapter 11. That way you can learn partial versions of basic skills before moving to the next level.

As this "three-times-through" logic implies, then, the book is not to be read straight through. If you do that, it will seem sometimes too detailed, sometimes too vague, never fully organized. That's partly because learning is itself nonlinear. But it is also because the book has to serve many different levels of readers. Some readers know a good deal about physical libraries. Others know nothing. Some readers know one part of the online world. Others know another. Some readers have done serious research before. Others have not. Some are writing course papers, others master's papers, others dissertations. So there have to be simple definitions and explicit explanations for some, but also much more complicated definitions and explanations for others. It may seem strange that chapter 3 explains what "the stacks" are but also explains the financial complexities of EBSCO's thesauruses. That's because some readers need one, while other readers need the other. We should remember that although library research is basically something we do as individuals, it is also something we do alongside other individuals. Each research project relies on prior projects, and all of us rely on the continuous replenishment of our ranks by new and untried scholars. The multiple levels of the book should remind us of that.

Finally, I have tried to explain most terms when they first arise. But if you get lost, there is a detailed glossary at the end of the book.

3. Preliminary

In the preliminary phase, you get started. Note that I don't say that "in the preliminary phase you figure out what you are going to do." You think you figure out what you are going to do. But of course this first guess is only a stab in the dark. You will probably end up doing something quite different. Yet if you wait till you have "really" figured out what you are going to do, you will never get started.

You will do five activities in the preliminary phase. First, you will do design work. Although your plan will change steadily throughout the project, you must start somewhere, and in the preliminary phase, you make your first guess about your design. This means shaping a vague interest into some puzzles and some focused research questions. I am speaking quite literally here: you need one or two clear empirical questions, one or two clear theoretical ideas backing up those empirical questions, and four or five general research questions. Once you have shaped these things into a good three-or-four-page document, you are ready to launch into the midphase of the project. (This will take four or five iterations.)

Producing this design of course requires that you do other things as well. First, you will need to do bibliographical work. Bibliography in the preliminary phase doesn't mean going to Google Scholar and typing in some words relevant to your project. You can do that if you want, but you will get such a big list of material that you will suddenly feel that everything possible has been done already. Your real job in preliminary bibliography is to bypass that needle-in-a-haystack situation and go straight to the needle shop. (Specific advice on that comes later.)

Getting to the needle shop also involves a second activity—browsing and scanning (by eye). Since most of what you find with even the best bibliographical tools will not be useful, you have to scan materials quickly to locate the most useful sources. Note that the usefulness of a given source item isn't a preestablished fact. It is usefulness relative to your project that interests you. Something can be useful to you but worthless to someone else—and vice versa. This is why you have to consider continuously both (a) what your project is about (because that defines whether something you've just scanned is useful) and also (b) what it could be about if you changed the project to one in which the apparently useless source would be useful.

Found material can be useful to you in two different ways. Some materials are primary. This means that with respect to your project they are data. These can be manuscripts, archives, documents, censuses, reports, and so on. By contrast, other material is secondary: it asks roughly the same questions as you do and uses the same kinds of data. Secondary material is other scholarship on your topic.

In the preliminary phase, you will be locating both primary and secondary sources and browsing/scanning them. But most of this work will be with secondary sources. The only reason for delving into primary sources in the preliminary phase is to ascertain whether the primary sources exist that will enable you to do the project as conceived. Obviously, if those sources don't exist, you will need to modify the design, shifting toward questions that can be answered with the primary materials that do exist.

All this means that the three activities of design, bibliography, and scanning/browsing have a particularly dynamic relationship in the preliminary phase. Research questions will be coming onto your list and going off your list with alarming rapidity. Even your basic empirical questions may be shifting.

You will also be doing some real reading in the preliminary phase. By "real reading," I mean reading whole texts at a thinking pace—spending a minute or more on each page. This needs to be active reading, fully concentrated on the text at hand. Think of such active reading as multitasking concentrated onto a single source. In the foreground you are parsing sentences; in the background you are putting those sentences into an understanding of the argument, posing questions to the text, noticing odd references and hints of related ideas and texts, and so on. You will also need to take reflective notes, either by marking up the text itself or by writing separate notes. Such reading is exhausting work and will require five minutes of focused relaxation for every twenty-five minutes of reading. It also requires absolute silence and lack of distraction:

no music, no texting, no chatty companions, no distracting tabs, no notification sounds. Just one open window onscreen or one open book in your hand.

Via this background reading, you start passively learning the terms, the people, the events, the ideas, and the problems that pervade your project. You don't sit down and memorize them; you simply get used to seeing them. It is this passive learning that prepares you to browse effectively. Browsing does not work unless you have things in your head to browse for. And it is through the work of intensive background reading that you begin to learn those browsing "attractors," the newly familiar labels and names that will help you recognize a seemingly random piece of information as something that is worth pursuing.

Finally, you will in the preliminary phase start some files. Whether you use physical or digital files, you need to create a file structure to maintain organized control of your project. You will need a main folder for business matters, correspondence, a to-do list, and a master log of what you have done. You will need a design folder for current and past versions of the design document. You will need a bibliography folder for the bibliography itself and a careful bibliographical log so you don't repeat searches you have already done or fail to do important searches you need to have done. You will need a folder for reading notes and folders for primary materials. Eventually, you will need folders for analysis and writing.

This may sound silly. After all, one way or another you can find everything on your computer. Yes, you can find anything, but it will take time and thought if "everything" is not already well organized with systematic keywords or tags. More important, the organization of your files—along with the concepts that emerge out of doing and redoing that organizing—actually is the overarching analytic structure of your project. Doing the filing is thus a central part of the intellectual work of a project. If you simply tag folders so that you can find them by multiple different means, you are in effect refusing to create and impose an order on your materials; you are literally refusing to think. But thinking about your material is precisely what it is to do research! Indeed, if you want to use database terms, you can think of your final written product as a thoughtful and even authoritative index to a certain set of materials. It is an index from a particular point of view—yours. And the claim you make by writing your final text is that you have a particularly wonderful index to your materials.

At some point, you will begin to feel that the design document has stabilized. It is no longer changing every few days as you do more work. You are now ready for midphase. In my courses, students' design documents have generally stabilized by about the fourth version. Since I require posting and peer comments every week, this means that students are ready for midphase by about the fifth week of the quarter.

4. Midphase

After you've gotten the bibliography started, done the first inventory of primary material, and begun to read the secondary literature, you settle into basic analytic work with your primary materials. Although midphase involves as much multitasking as does the preliminary phase, the dominant activity becomes work with primary materials.

In the first instance, this means actually reading those materials. Only occasionally does one find primary data that is immediately ready for analysis. More likely, you will need to plow through primary sources taking notes, or extracting figures, or searching for indirect mentions of topics or organizations or people. Indeed, you may need to read them simply to get a working sense of the world in which they were created.

The name for this kind of reading and for the analyses based on it is "brute force" (as opposed to scanning and browsing). All library-type research involves a good deal of brute force. You cannot do serious research entirely by scanning, skimming, extracting, and other forms of surface engagement. That works for high school papers, reviews, and position papers. But not for research. Think of Darwin. Darwin was up to his eyeballs in data. Every day he slogged through data on finches in the Galapagos, on the results of cattle-breeding, and so on. Think of Simone de Beauvoir when she wrote *The Second Sex*. Her book assembles and digests whole continents of data. We may remember such writers for their theories. But they spent their days brute-forcing through records, statistics, histories, and reports. That is where theory comes from.

But while you brute-force your way through the primary sources, you will be doing many other things as well. There will, for example, be more detailed scanning and browsing of source materials. You will find that your sources are incomplete, that they need to be augmented by other sources in different places, that adjacent to them in the stacks or connected to them by one web link is some closely related alternative body of primary material that could help you approach your questions somewhat differently. And your primary work will turn up more than new sources. There will also be substantive leads.

As you are reading institutional records new people may turn up whose biographies you need to retrieve. As you are reading newspapers, organizations may appear whose origins, history, and current structure you need to trace. As you compile statistics, new statistical sources may be mentioned that need to be tracked down.

In midphase, you will follow most of these leads, because it is foolish to plow dutifully through all of some primary source when it turns out that everything you needed was aggregated somewhere else. Indeed, one of the arts of library research is that sixth sense that tells you, when you are about to undertake a brute-force task, that somewhere somebody has already done it. But you will also sometimes need the competing seventh sense that tells you that probably nobody did it, and you're going to have to sit down and do it all yourself.

All these new leads in turn demand bibliography, which is ongoing in any case because you will have begun to work with primary materials before you have followed all the leads from the initial bibliographical pass. (Otherwise you'll never get started.) All this new bibliographical work will distract you from the primary sources, which for some of us is a good thing—brute-force work is often boring.

If you need other distractions from brute-force primary source work, there will be plenty of candidates. Interlibrary loan materials may be showing up. A new reference may lead from the manuscript materials out into the published world or to an unsuspected website. Conversations with advisors and peers may provide more and more useful ideas, now that you know what questions to ask in those conversations. At the same time, you will need to resist the temptation to follow all these leads; that is often just work avoidance.

Out of this mixed process of bibliography, scanning/browsing, and primary source work will come materials that need to be organized and analyzed—in a word, filed. You have to pull your materials together, electronically and/or physically. Filing is a key problem for Internet-generation researchers, who are used to just leaving things where they are on the assumption that they can be found quickly if one simply copies their URLs. This assumption is wrong. First, you may not remember where you put the address; second, it may have changed. And if it takes you a couple of minutes to find something, you will in the meantime lose focus on the original thought that sent you looking for that something in the first place. Real thinking and analysis can occur only when the material you are studying can be effortlessly handled: no remembering addresses, no refresh times, no searches, just one thought, one gesture, and you have the material. For this to happen, you must have filed and assembled your material itself beforehand.

Creating such files forces you to invent topics and headings, thereby beginning formal reflection about your data. It forces you to reduce ambiguities in your thinking ("did I think that article was about anxiety or about fear?"), making the judgments and inferences that gradually constitute your analysis. Chances are that the result will be a hierarchical filing system for everything related to the project, from archival permissions to websites visited to bibliographies and to-do lists.

As your material is becoming organized, there will inevitably turn up small analytic tasks that are best done immediately: figuring out the incomes of everybody who worked for some organization, looking at the distribution of votes for a particular measure across the various counties of a state, and so on. Such tasks are best done at once because they have obvious implications for further primary research and because for the moment you are perfectly familiar with the materials necessary to do them. So you do them now. Such "minianalyses" will range from bibliographical essays (which will tell the reader where you've been and where you need to go) to biographies of central characters (always useful and full of leads to related topics) to descriptions of central organizations (necessary to any further study of those organizations) to quantitative analysis of relevant statistics (which may identify other numbers you need to gather and analyze). As you work through the midphase, these minianalyses will pile up in your files. The later ones will more and more resemble written pieces of the final product. Gradually, it will turn out that certain minianalyses seem to go together naturally. Your first sections of the article or paper will probably emerge from taking some of these minianalyses and assembling them as text.

This brings us to the last part of work in the midphase: design. Throughout the midphase runs a common theme—redirection. Bibliography gives you a more detailed sense of what material is available. Reading in primary and secondary sources reveals that some of the original empirical puzzles are uninteresting and others are unexpectedly important. Filing will have forced you to decide on basic categories and to specify exactly what you mean by them. The planning of minianalyses will have forced you to choose actual data to address abstract arguments, which in turn will further specify those arguments. And the results of minianalyses may have challenged your research questions and even your empirical and theoretical questions themselves.

All of this means that you must revisit your main design document on a regular basis in midphase. Students often wonder why: you know what's happening, so why redo the governing document? The answer is that a good project is much too complicated for you to be inside and outside at the same time. It's like being on a roll in a video game. Once it's going well, you go inside it and you lose track of time. The design document provides the necessary outside voice.

Most important, only a clear design document can tell you when you are finished. Video games have levels and ends. But there is no end to research: there are always new things to study, new issues to clarify, new subquestions to ask. Only your governing document contains a specific set of questions whose answer completes the project. Those questions will have changed over the course of the project, as you have adjusted them to the project materials and results. They will have grown more focused, more logically structured, and more coherent. But when they converge, stabilize, and are answered, then you know that you are done.

In summary, the midphase involves all seven activities of library research, all going on at once, in parallel. It is a chaotic but rewarding time. Midphase lasts different times for different projects. For a substantial graduate research paper, it is going to take a minimum of ten weeks, more likely fifteen; for course papers, the time will be less. In my courses, I have students report on their minianalyses every two weeks (you should be doing at least a couple of such analyses every two weeks unless they are very laborious indeed). I also expect at least two "course correction" visits to the design document in that period, the second of which should judge whether the design document is ready for rewriting and transformation into the opening sections of a final paper. That is what defines the end of midphase. (Note that these numbers imply that students in my ten-week course get about halfway through a project; they usually finish in the next quarter. Under a fifteen-week semester system, students can sometimes complete a serious library research project in one semester.)

5. Endphase

In the endphase, you spend most of your time writing. You will now be assembling whole series of minianalyses. The overall rhetorical architecture of the paper is firmly designed and imposed on the existing written materials. This will lead to shifts in both. Just as lightning is the meeting of a ground stroke and a sky stroke, your text results from the mutual adaptation of the empirical work and the design document. If you have steadily updated your design document, you can easily expand it to become the opening section of the paper. And if the paper's rhetorical format calls for a consideration of prior work (a "literature review," as they say in the sciences), this will be easy if you have kept up on your bibliography.

But while you are completing your writing, there are loose ends to tie up: books that came late, via recall or interlibrary loan; articles to chase because you've discovered new people and organizations; websites that have appeared since you began your initial review. You may even have to go through some primary materials a second time because you have found out that somebody or something was more important than you thought before.

But it is also inevitable that there will remain gaps—perhaps quite major gaps—even as you finish writing. You may indeed feel that the writing of the paper is a somewhat arbitrary interruption in the flow of things you are discovering. You will suspect that the paper is nowhere near as good as it should be. Whether or not these feelings are justified, they are unimportant. There will always be gaps in what you know, because there are always more things to study. And every paper is an interim report. Above all, the paper is better than you think. Nor should you be worried about the inevitable fact that you will not use huge amounts of the primary material that you have in fact gathered and analyzed. This too is normal. If you write up all the primary knowledge you have, you didn't get anywhere near enough.

For the serious graduate research paper or for an article, the endphase will take at least five weeks. You will have done substantial writing already, to be sure. The design document has probably been written and expanded into the main framework. The minianalyses are mostly written. But putting them all together, relating them closely to one another, smoothing out the transitions, and then writing all the remaining material that holds them together: those things will take time. New ideas will come as you write, and they will necessitate rewriting, sometimes drastic rewriting. And you will need to allow at least a week for the text to rest (while you do something entirely different) before undertaking final editing.

IN SUMMARY, TO BE A LIBRARY RESEARCHER YOU MUST REMEMBER the two ways in which library research differs from the model of scientific research that many of us have learned so well. First, library research is not linear. It does not go from question to literature review to data search to analysis to write-up. Rather it is massively parallel. You are doing most of its subtasks most of the time. Everything will seem illogical and out of order. But you must nonetheless keep control of this massively parallel endeavor and guide it to a successful final product. And that product will, in fact, make the whole project look much simpler than it actually was.

Second, library research is not mainly about finding things. It is about creating them. The best interpretation of *Moby-Dick* is not out there, under a rock somewhere, waiting in lonely splendor for the fastest Google algorithm to find it. The key to all knowledge is not out there on some ultimate website, if only we could tell it from all the other false websites. Indeed, in the humanities and the social sciences we do not ask questions to which final answers already exist, answers which can be found somewhere. We seek to adjust the questions we can ask and the answers we can find into harmonious writings that explore again and again the subtleties that constitute human existence. It is our pleasure to do this in a rigorous and disciplined way. That is what makes our research academic. But our research is not scientific, for the things we wish to discuss do not have fixed answers. We discover things, to be sure, but their discovery merely opens further possibilities to complexify them.

2

A Library Ethnography

All this talk about "nonlinear research" and "not finding, but knowing what to look for" may seem very abstract. So it is useful to give an extended example. This chapter therefore contains the narrative of a particular research project of mine. Since I know this project intimately, I can show you all the highways and byways. In particular, I can show in detail how question and answer co-evolve. If you don't feel you need such an example, by all means skip directly to chapter 3.

I have written this ethnography from the researcher's point of view. It might be more clever to write in flashbacks, beginning with the conclusion and then gradually revealing where I had begun. That would take the reader's point of view, showing you how a well-formed and polished argument was in fact the product of a (seemingly) haphazard set of research experiences. But it is more important to give the researcher's point of view, since that is the experience you need to understand: how one starts from ill-formed general ideas, follows initial leads amid great confusion, and finally ends with a clear and important piece of research. (If you want to read the final piece, it is "Library Research Infrastructure for Humanistic and Social Scientific Scholarship in America in the Twentieth Century" and can be found on my website or in an edited volume entitled *Social Knowledge in the Making*.)

Don't be put off by all the details and complexities. To be sure, this ethnography describes a large project by an experienced scholar working in an immense research library. But your own project will quickly produce similar details and complexities, even though it's done by someone with less experience and in a much smaller library. You too will become so familiar with your material that you'll seem to your friends to be completely buried in esoteric knowledge and details. Even a fairly straightforward and simple project—if well done—seems a bit magical and incomprehensible to outsiders.

1. Starting Out: Brute Force Plus Two Not-So-Mini Analyses

Like some of my other papers, this one began life as a polemic; I wanted to show that there is nothing very novel about the digital library. In particular, I wanted to underscore (a) that powerful knowledge tools were introduced long before the digital revolution; (b) that one whole family of tools (specialized reference works) was largely absent in the Internet world; and (c) that digital tools were in general of considerably lower quality than the print tools they replaced. In short, I sat down to write a swan song for a beautiful world that I thought was vanishing.

I had already done some writing about libraries. In some senses, I was thus already in the midphase, even when I started the swan song project. Because I was already in midphase, I could move right into primary material.

First things first. If I was going to sing a swan song, I had to describe the swan. That is, I had to create a basic history of library reference tools in the twentieth century—a brute-force exercise. A cursory bibliographical scan had persuaded me that in all probability no such history existed. Everything written about the history of reference tools seemed to be about the virtues of whatever was—at time of writing—the latest tool. Eventually I had to redo and solidify this background check, of course. But for the moment, a cursory scan gave me license to get started.

Luckily, I already knew the proper shortcut for this brute-force project: the American Library Association had published a guide to reference books in multiple editions since the beginning of the twentieth century. From our library stacks, I immediately got the editions for 1902, 1923, 1951, 1976, and 1996, and began creating a master list of reference tools and their dates of emergence. But the numbers and types of major tools were very large. So from the start I had to think about putting them in categories. Originally I used the categories of the 1902 *Guide* itself. But these were changed by 1923—a change that itself told me something about how library research worked in that faraway time. (For one thing, the number of tools in foreign languages plummeted: librarians in 1902 had been expected to read German and French.) But I dealt with this category problem in an ad hoc manner and moved on.

It soon became obvious that I needed at least two other large minianalyses. First, there was no sense talking about tools without talking about users. So I had to estimate the numbers of scholars using advanced research libraries, which I did by using (and augmenting) data on PhD production and by studying membership in scholarly societies. That's an easy sentence to write, but the

PhD analysis took about two weeks full-time, knowledge of four relevant reference tools, and, most important, reconciliation between several conflicting sources of data. It also took some computer estimation. (The details will be discussed in chapter 9.) Getting numbers on scholars' memberships in academic societies was easier, although the data in recent years is very bad: in 1960 the American Council of Learned Societies stopped keeping detailed records of the exact sizes of its member societies, and current sources give divergent and quite dubious estimates. (They're always in round numbers, for example.)

I constructed these two data series because I thought both of them would estimate the numbers of scholars potentially using libraries. But to my shock they gave wildly different estimates—so different that I had to conclude that they were estimating completely different groups. In the 1920s there were four "society members" for each PhD; by 1950 the ratio was close to one to one. Therefore, in the 1920s, most society members must have been amateurs. Thus, because I had sought a second estimate of my library user pool, I had quite accidentally discovered that the real professionalization of academics in America had not come when the main academic societies were founded (late nineteenth and early twentieth centuries), but much later, when the PhDs gradually pushed the amateurs out. What began as "having an extra estimate of something in order to be sure of it" turned out to produce a major discovery. This is a common experience in library research, so common that you always need to be watching for it. Divergent information often means divergent realities.

My second obvious minianalysis was to create a good set of descriptive library statistics: size of the libraries' holdings, numbers of their staff, and expenditures on acquisitions, for example. Here, I didn't have to look hard for the data. The Association of Research Libraries has data from the 1960s forward, and the earlier data—compiled laboriously by a Princeton librarian named James Thayer Gerould—turned up right away in my initial bibliographical work. The "analysis" part of this minianalysis, therefore, had less to do with finding the numbers than with guessing which numbers would be important and how to represent them effectively to a reader. So I ranked the libraries on holdings, staff, and acquisitions and created tables listing, for each of those rankings, the first, fifth, tenth, twentieth, and fiftieth university library. This wonderfully detailed minianalysis (about ten manuscript pages) eventually disappeared completely from the final product for want of space. The paper as finally written requires nothing more than the obvious assertion that "libraries got rapidly bigger." Sometimes, you do a lot of work for nothing.

2. A Brute-Force Adventure

In sum, after a couple of months' work on the project, I had two big mini-analyses nearing completion and on my other front was brute-forcing through the ALA *Guides* to produce a systematic list of major tools. About this time, I decided to undertake yet another brute-force effort, in this case a fishing expedition. My university had once had a library school, and I guessed that its faculty and students must have done some interesting things. So I decided to read the title of every MLS or PhD thesis ever done at the University of Chicago Graduate Library School. I knew there must be wonderful things in those theses, although I didn't know what they would be. Probably over 10 percent of the theses would be useful. I would probably find three or four theses that would be absolutely central. So it was a time for brute force.

The typical handbook on library research doesn't tell you to do this. Indeed, it tells you not to do this, because such a fishing expedition works only on one condition, a condition you won't meet until you are well into your project. A fishing expedition pays off only if you can recognize edible fish when they show up in the net. And you can do that only if you already have in your mind a lot of knowledge about your topic. In this case, all my random knowledge about libraries and all my hunches about how scholars used them were the lines in my net. And I didn't know or particularly care whether my net was going to catch haddock or grouper or sea bass. My random knowledge and hunches meant I would be able to sell them all when I got back to port. So I used the selection delimiters in the online catalog to create an electronic list (600 items), scanned it, marked the names I wanted, and then took a cart down into the stacks and checked out a hundred of them.

I realized from the titles alone that I had found sources beyond my wildest dreams: histories of famous reference tools, ethnographic studies of behavior in libraries in the 1940s, examinations of citation behaviors in a half dozen disciplines, even a complete and detailed analysis of all the books charged out to the university's faculty in May 1956 (by language, by duration of charge, by department, by Library of Congress call numbers!). But rather than diving into these theses now, I would simply use them as needed—as my advancing writing made this or that thesis relevant. Thus, since I was working on my list of reference tools, the first theses I used bore on that topic: a history of the first edition of the *Union List of Serials in Libraries of the United States and Canada* and a study of the 1946 publication of the *Catalog of Books Represented by Library of Congress Printed Cards*. My brute-force exercise had paid off immediately.

3. Specifying and Justifying the Empirical Question

About this time, I also realized that it was time to demonstrate clearly—not just assert on the basis of my initial cursory review—that there was no decent past research on the topics I was investigating. At the start, I hadn't been clear about my puzzle, other than "what were the reference tools that made the old libraries wonderful?" So I couldn't validate my empirical question earlier in the project. Indeed, it is generally the case in library research that we don't actually know whether our underlying puzzles are real puzzles until we are well into the work itself.

But now it was time to ascertain whether I was right that there was no serious writing about my empirical question, which was gradually changing into "how did (do) scholars use libraries?" One might have expected to find this literature in Google with something like the phrase "theory [or "practice"] of library research." But I found next to nothing. Yet that didn't mean that nobody had thought about the problem for which those phrases were my particular shorthand. So how does one locate literature on such an interstitial, nameless topic? (That is always the big issue with keyword indexes.)

I quickly located major reviews of this literature, but not by the methods of the research handbooks. The handbooks realize that trolling in Google or its print equivalent is a waste of time. So they advise you to cruise true subject indexes (things like library catalogs that index the world by human-assigned subjects rather than by passive keywords) in order to find the right heading to locate what one seeks. But in my preliminary bibliographical work, I had tried many possible terms and found that there is no single LC subject heading on library research practice or anything like it. Relevant material was scattered from AZ105 to Z675.U5. So the handbook method would have made me go through the laborious task of pruning the separate long lists produced by all these partially related headings, and then combining and pruning the lengthy result.

I wasn't about to do that. I knew perfectly well that somebody must have assembled this literature at some point for some reason. The trick was to find that summary and find it fast. As usual, the right move was to go backward; if somebody had written that (hypothetical) piece, then somebody else must have cited it. My real task was to find those likely citers and ransack their bibliographies. And I had a lucky outing with WoS. The subject words "research habits humanists"—a long shot that I did not expect to pay off—produced three articles, one of which happened to mention a study of electronic versus physical access to journals, published in the *Journal of the American Society for Information Science*. Without leaving WoS to look at the study itself, I went straight to its reference list of twenty-two items—gratifyingly substantial but at the same time not annoyingly excessive. (These reference lists are clickable in WoS.) Even better, only ten of those citations had titles in the electronic WoS listing, and only four of those looked worth chasing. So I went to the shelves and looked physically at all four (the journals weren't in JSTOR yet, so I had to go to the physical journals in the stacks). Sure enough, two of them were definitive reviews of library-use studies of humanists, one from 1982 and one from 1994. Any later review would no doubt cite them and could therefore be found by using the citation tools in WoS, which (as we'll soon see) allow you to go downstream toward the present as easily as upstream toward the past. Bingo. Total time, ten minutes. Total time saved over the handbook method—probably half a day.

By now I was midway through the project. The demographic and overall library data were gathered. I had found the Library School theses. I was creating longer and longer lists of the reference tools available to scholars as the century passed. For a conference, I had even produced a formal first draft of half of the paper. Producing that draft made two things very clear. First, there was no point in just listing the reference tools. Any idiot could see that the list would just get longer and longer as the century passed. Second, to avoid a simple narration of "one damn thing after another" I would have to create periods. There were four obvious candidates: Before World War I, between the wars, World War II to 1970 (the rough date of the collapse of the academic job market), and post-1970.

4. A Major Redesign, More Brute Force, and Some Brachiation

But suddenly I saw that I was assuming that any reference tool that was available would in fact be used. Was this right? More broadly, I needed to understand what it was like to do library research in 1915 or 1935. Not just what tools were there for you to use, but did you use them? How often were you in the library? In other libraries? Could you duplicate things or have things duplicated for you? All these questions actually emerged from the idea of periods, which had been forced on me by the requirements of the downstream task of writing.

Let me repeat that chain of logic. First, narrative wouldn't work, so I had to create periods. But second, this in turn meant that I needed to take the same view of past library practices that I would take of current research practices if I did a survey. I had to put myself in 1915 or 1935 and ask what it was like to do research at that time.

So I planned to shrink the freestanding demography and library statistics sections (the first two minianalyses). In this new version of my proposed text (and indeed of my empirical question), these things mattered not for themselves, but only for how they set the stage for the actual experience of scholars at successive moments. Moreover, I made a crucial decision related to filing, again something dictated by the exigencies of writing. I created final categories for the reference tools, to replace the ad hoc ones I had evolved from the primary sources themselves. The reference tools analysis for each of my four periods would now be organized around four categories: serial bibliography, book bibliography, archive and document tools, and reference tools proper. But the crowning section for each period would be not demography or library resources or reference tools, but habitus: how had the demography, the resources, and the tools combined to create a world of scholarly practice?

Only after this complete refocusing and redesigning of a paper already half complete did I finally start systematically to read my way through the Chicago theses. But when I started to read through those theses with my tighter trawling net, I found some pretty ugly fish. Everything I could discover about stack behavior in the 1950s indicated that faculty and graduate students were not using catalogs and indexes, even for known-item searches. Nor were they using most of the beauties of my swan, the wonderful reference tools built for them by the H. W. Wilson Company, the ALA, and the library profession. They were just wandering into the stacks and trolling. They were indeed standing in the stacks and reading whole chapters, then pulling something else off the shelf and reading that! There were ethnographic studies showing such behavior in gory detail.

Now it goes without saying that I ransacked the footnotes of these theses for citations. All these long-ago master's and doctoral students had already done the bibliographical work for me, so there was no point in my carefully working through the various volumes of the relevant index for my period, a Wilson index called *Library Literature*, which started in 1923. (I did not yet recognize that my own practice was a clear example of why scholars don't use subject indexes: the work of their colleagues and students provides them with better indexes to important work than can ever be produced by a nonspecialist indexer.) By using those footnotes, not only did I pile up important references, I moreover could and did look up the items that the Library School dissertations did cite, tracing those items in *Library Literature* in order to figure out how the indexers had categorized them. That in turn gave me the proper index headings to use in *Library Literature* if I wanted to get further. These headings would have been completely opaque to me (who could possibly understand how indexers categorized things eighty years ago?!) if I hadn't had the sample references to start with.

Let me summarize the exact logic of this move, because it is most important:

1. I knew by personal judgment that the 600 Library School dissertations simply had to include at least twenty useful dissertations and probably four or five utterly central ones.
2. By a brute-force scan search of all those dissertations, I found a hundred probably useful dissertations, of which at least thirty were important and at least ten utterly central.
3. I carefully trolled the footnotes of the ten highest-quality sources and, indeed, most of the thirty, looking for whatever was interesting.
4. Among those interesting things, I found perhaps ten or twenty utterly central references published in the period before 1940.
5. I then looked up those references in the indexes for the years in which they would have been indexed in order to figure out what indexing terms had been used for this kind of material. If I had gone directly to the indexes, I would most likely have missed these references, because over any substantial period, terminologies shift and indexes shift with them.

It's useful to have a name for this kind of move. I will call it brachiation, the motion of apes swinging through the trees. Library brachiation is like that—you just swing from a primary source to its reference list then to an index then out again via another reference to another primary source and then perhaps on to a specialized reference work and so on.

Brachiation has two crucial qualities. The first is back-and-forthness: some of it goes forward, from subjects to references, the way the handbooks say we are supposed to go, but some of it goes backward from references to subjects, the way we aren't supposed to go. That's what makes it work—it keeps moving upstream, against the indexing, and so avoids becoming overly dependent on assumptions built into everyday retrieval techniques. The second crucial quality of brachiation is that it generally starts in a source that is both close to our area of interest and written by somebody who probably did high-quality bibliographical work. Like most expert library techniques, it free rides on the prior work of certified experts.

Brachiation from the theses took me instantly to several fundamental primary sources: a 1956 ALA catalog-use study, a 1962 Johns Hopkins library-use survey, an MLS thesis I had missed (in my brute-force run-through of titles) on the bibliographical sources used by John Crerar Library clients, and various other formal analyses of library behavior. Because of terminology changes, all of these would have been unfindable in general indexes unless I had known, before I began to search, that they existed and even what they contained.

But those wonderful new sources all had the same substantive message. Faculty and graduate students got their references either from hearsay or from other people's footnotes or reference lists (just as, in fact, I was doing myself). I even began to run across remarks in the broader library literature, which by this time I was reading as well, that made it clear that faculty's unwillingness to use librarians' subject indexes was by this time a standing joke among librarians. (Librarians would say that something was "as rare as a faculty member who uses a subject index.")

Now if faculty and graduate students were getting their research bibliography via hearsay or other professionals' published work, why were they doing this? The answer, at least theoretically, seemed obvious. These sources possessed something that the general bibliographical tools lacked: selectivity. I could therefore infer that the literature—in the sense of all the material locatable and accessible via the general bibliographical system—was already overwhelmingly large by the early 1950s. One had to rely on colleagues to have sifted it. This insight reinforced my increasing sense that overload was a core issue in the development of twentieth-century library research.

But now that I had pushed the date of faculty desertion of the general bibliographical apparatus—my beautiful but lonely swan—back to the 1950s, could it go further back? Surely at some point the librarians and the professors had been of one mind.

5. Theoretical Focus, A Lucky Accident, Some Random Acquisitions

So I found myself back in the interwar period, about which I had already written the section of my paper on the library research habitus. I had written in that section a success story about the new tools of the 1920s—the *Union List of Serials*, the Carnegie *Guides* to archives, and so on. It must have been great being a young researcher with these new tools, I thought. But in reality, I now realized, I didn't know much about actual faculty experience with those tools. Maybe they didn't use them at all.

In my mind the empirical question of "how far back can I push the date of scholars' desertion of the wonderful library tools?" was slowly turning into the more theoretical question of "why and how did the honeymoon end between the scholars and the librarians?" Much later, when I knew what I should have been looking for, I would realize that the answer to this question had been staring me in the face: in the indexes, where I just had to know what the correct headings were; in the books of essays by interwar librarians, where I just had to know which the important chapters were; and even in the academic library surveys, where I just had to know which the important tables were. Many of these things were already sitting on the shelves of my library study by this time; after all, I had about 700 books charged out. But if you don't know what you are looking for, 700 books is about 695 books too many.

This is indeed the heart of the matter. The answer to a library research question is always staring us in the face. Library research is the art of figuring out which of the many things that are staring you in the face is the important one. This is another way of saying what I said in chapter 1: Finding something is easy; it's knowing that you ought to have looked for it that is hard. You search for known items only once you have done all the real work. In the really important cases, you search for known items only once you already know what they are going to say. In short, if we knew ahead of time what the questions were and what books probably answered them, there would be no reason to do the research.

The crucial steps toward my recognition that my true puzzle was "why and how did the scholars desert the librarians?" were, like so many things in library research, the result of very random events. Indeed, this part of the research well illustrates the chaotic experience of midphase.

For an earlier paper, I had at one point gone trolling through the entire Z section of the stacks, the LC classification section on books and libraries, looking for anything interesting. Indeed, most of the books in my library study had come from this fishing expedition, But I needed more space on my shelves, so I started to return the ones already checked out. One item I picked up for possible return was called *A Bibliography of Library Economy*. It had seemed interesting because I had once been thinking of writing a theoretical paper about knowledge as a form of capital. But as I pulled it off my study shelf I idly opened it, and much to my surprise it wasn't about economics at all. It was a general bibliography of library matters. It was in fact the only such bibliography covering the period before 1923, when Wilson's *Library Literature* began. Suddenly I had the right tool in my hands for all the wrong reasons.

Now the reference librarian would say, "Here's another faculty member who would have found that tool if only he had used the subject indexes." That's simply wrong. I would not have found this book if I had searched the many possible headings for bibliographies relevant to my topic. On this book's catalog record, the first subject heading is "bibliography—bibliography," an LC subject category with 275 items in our library and therefore a waste of time to brute-force because of the low likelihood of return. Ditto for the second heading, "library science—bibliography," with its 120 items. To be sure, the third heading, "library science—periodicals—indexes," would have been worth searching, because there were only 6 items. (This ought to have been the first heading, given how the book would be used by any present-day researcher.) So I would have found this book only if I had thought "library science—periodicals—indexes" was the right heading to search. But of course I wouldn't have thought that, because I would have assumed that I already knew the main such source—the later index called *Library Literature*. The real culprit here, as so often happens, is drift of terminology. "Library economy" was simply the 1920s way of saying "library administration." So even my normal browsing self had probably missed noticing this book several times before, simply because I had no idea that there was a time when "library economy" could mean "anything related to running and using libraries."

So I had the right book, at least. Well, I thought, I can start looking for my early scholars on their library honeymoon. What will this book call them, I wondered? Luckily the book had a complete listing of all its subject headings, and a quick scan found an obvious candidate—"Libraries and the Investigator." (Given our contemporary idioms, no contemporary researcher would ever have guessed this subject heading without seeing it written in a list to choose from.) So I started to look through the list of ten or so articles under that heading. Some of them appealed to me, and some awkward work with government documents indexes traced them to the stacks at Z731, which looked full of interesting things that I must have missed on my earlier trolling passes. (Note that I hadn't really "missed" them at all. Rather, my conception of my project had changed so much that now they were useful rather than useless.) There were three early surveys of special collections to add to my lists of general reference tools, and also—of all things—a history of

OCLC, the consortium of Ohio libraries that has morphed into the chief nonprofit organization supporting online library services.

Finding the *Library Economy* book reminded me that I had perhaps missed other, similar things. So some brute-force bibliography was in order. I wandered about a bit in JSTOR; I tried the language and literature journals, constrained to pre-1920, with "library" or "libraries" in the title. For the most part, I found material on school libraries, although there were also some articles on "opportunities for research," organized around particular Italian collections in particular research libraries. (Specialists were apparently advertising their libraries' special collections!) Then I tried the Old Faithful of all print-era reference librarians, the Wilson *Readers' Guide*, now online as *Readers' Guide Retrospective*. I also tried the *Essay and General Literature Index* (*EGL*). But it turned out that (at that point) the online version of the latter was not retrospective, and the online *Readers' Guide* itself was taking endless pauses for screen refreshes. So I went to the physical volumes, whose pages can be turned in milliseconds.

6. A Useful Side Trip: Scholar Autobiographies

One of the things the physical *Readers' Guide* turned up was a 1952 piece by Richard Altick called "The Scholar's Paradise," which turned out to be an interesting riff on his own experiences in libraries. So I suddenly realized that maybe scholars talked about their library experiences in autobiographies—a long shot, but possible. As I mentioned earlier, I had already checked out the ALA *Guide to Reference Books* in order to make my lists of reference works over the century, so I looked in it for reference works on autobiographies, and quickly found not one but two subject indexes to American autobiographies (indexed, among other things, by the occupation or lifestyle of the autobiographer). These indexes led me directly to about ninety autobiographies of scholars in my period. A few days later, I grabbed a cart and charged them all out. While I was at it, I got a list of librarians' autobiographies (not many librarians write autobiographies, by the way). And in the stacks, I also accidentally found some interesting-looking librarian biographies, because they turned out to be in the same LC heading as the librarian autobiographies—Z720.

Two of these librarian biographies revealed a deep debate among early twentieth-century librarians. One was a hagiographical account of William Warner Bishop, czar of the University of Michigan Library from 1915 to 1941, who, I read, had been a relentless "centralizer." (What could that mean?) The other was a biography of Chicago's Pierce Butler, who defended a scholarly ideal of librarianship against his colleague Douglas Waples, an ardent apostle of rationalization and scientization. I had found these two wonderfully contrasted biographies not because I was looking for them but because I was looking at scholars' autobiographies (because of accidentally running into the Altick reference) and had decided that I might as well look for librarian autobiographies, and then librarian biographies had turned out to be in the same LC heading as librarian autobiographies.

I'm underscoring this detail because I want to emphasize that browsing—broadly understood as the productive confrontation between an ordered, informed mind and a differently ordered set of materials—is going on at all levels of investigation at all times. It is not something unusual or occasional. It's like peripheral vision or the virus checker on your computer; it's always running in the background, always ready to pick things up. It doesn't work, however, for minds that don't have anything in them for that peripherally relevant stuff to stick to. This is why the handbooks don't tell you much about it; handbooks are written for beginners. But in point of fact, the best beginning is actually not to use the librarians' general tools, but rather to read carefully some general overviews so that when you do start to use the tools, you already have in your mind some random trolling lines. Browsing and brachiating—not using reference tools in a rational, linear manner—are the heart of expert work in the library.

I began reading the scholar autobiographies, scanning them (by eye) for the word "library." There was useful material in them: not exactly what I needed, but providing great peripheral detail. I learned, for example, that midwestern scholars took summer jobs teaching on the East Coast simply in order to be near major libraries and that Chicago's President Harper promised a new graduate student a private book fund in her particular area of interest. There is no way to look for such wonderful details systematically, in subject indexes. One can only trawl attentively and hope.

7. Systematic Bibliography Upended: The Puzzle Solved

Eventually I decided that it was time, at last, for systematic bibliography. (One undertakes brute-force work only when it is necessary and/or has a high probability of payoff.) I returned to the book that had launched this sideline of inquiry, the *Bibliography of Library Economy*. I grabbed the early volumes of *Library Literature*. Now was the time to follow the handbook method, because I met two crucial conditions. First, at last I knew exactly what I was looking for: anything directly bearing on the details of library use by scholars in the pre-1940 period. Second, after all this other work, I knew that I would now recognize important sources even under their unfamiliar old names—"researchers" were "investigators" and so on.

As I began the brute-force work, I soon ran into the phrase "departmental libraries." For some reason, it began quietly clamoring for attention. Now, "departmental libraries" was a familiar phrase to me. Every academic institution I've known has had departmental libraries. I even recalled some random details about departmental libraries: the centralization of departmental libraries at Chicago in the late 1960s; the enduring importance of departmental libraries in the sciences; the roots of departmental libraries in the seminar libraries of late nineteenth-century Germany. But at that moment, it was as if I had never before really seen what departmental libraries meant in terms of how library research was done. My research diary is clear on this:

> A huge shoe drops as I am looking around here. The topic that I am struggling with is related to departmental libraries. I figure this out as a problem in bibliography. That is, I have figured out that the topic I need to be searching in each volume of *Library Literature* is "departmental libraries." But far more important, I see that departmental libraries are a metonym of the argument I should be making. Departmental libraries were where the scholars wanted to do most of their work—because of the relative density of tools. Everything was at hand, just as it is in the wonder world of the internet. Only, departmental libraries were better because all the good tools and *only* the good tools were immediately in your hands.
>
> Moreover, the importance of the departmental library is analogous to the importance of specialist reference works—limited, but highly ordered and highly particular subindexes of parts of the whole library. Departmental libraries are limited but highly ordered and highly particular subsets of the library collection. It was the librarians' contention that there ought to be one master index, but the research scholars always want partial indexes, indexes slanted their way, organized by their way of seeing the world, not by a generic view from nowhere. They also wanted subcollections, for the same reasons.

I pursued departmental libraries through the formal bibliographical sources. What I found was a long and fierce debate, with diverging views of research between librarians and scholars. The debate withered after the 1920s. At last I had found the end of the honeymoon. But why had the debate ended? Who made the divorce?

Here random personal knowledge produced a lucky guess. I remembered the first departmental libraries I had known—the English and History Department libraries on the top floor of Harvard's Widener Library. It suddenly seemed obvious to me that the entire top floor of Widener had been designed for such seminar libraries; the whole floor was divided into little rooms with shelves on the sides and giant tables in the middle, visible through the glass doors as you walked down the main corridor. And of course I knew the date of the building because it was a memorial to a young man who went down on the *Titanic*. In a flash, I realized that every major university library I had ever entered was about the same age as Widener. In a few minutes I had found, through the catalog and then on the shelf, a history of American university library architecture. This was indeed the ultimate known-item search: I knew what I was looking for and I knew perfectly well what it would say. From the book, it was easy to construct the list: Berkeley 1911, Chicago 1912, Harvard 1915, Johns Hopkins 1916, Stanford 1919, Michigan 1920, Minnesota 1924, Illinois 1926, Yale 1931, and Columbia 1934.

Two of these libraries—Chicago's Harper and Hopkins's Gilman—were collections of departmental libraries grouped in adjacent quarters. But the rest were completely centralized libraries, usually with some seminar rooms scattered in them and provision for graduate student study space in the stacks. This then was my answer; in the interwar period the professors had lost control of the books to the librarians. Oddly, it turned out that the scientists' laboratories had been subject to all the same arguments for centralization, but the scientists had successfully resisted the centralizers. But the humanists and humanistic social scientists lost the battle, and thereafter their research and their teaching were physically broken apart. No longer would faculty and graduate students rub shoulders daily in offices and seminar rooms immediately adjacent to a departmental research library with both basic and specialized reference tools as well as a substantial monograph collection. From now on, doing research meant going to another building, in which faculty might or might not have office or research space. It meant working with general and specialized reference tools now mixed into a huge general reference collection. It meant seeking monographic material mixed into an immense main stack. The days of running down the hall and quickly bringing an important reference tool to one's desk were over.

This then was the big discovery. The divorce between scholars and librarians required the scholars to develop new research practices to deal with the centralized, massified libraries that were forced on them in the 1920s and 1930s. This discovery had indeed been staring me in the face: in the indexes, where I only had to know that the heading to pursue was "departmental libraries"; in the essays of prominent interwar librarians, where I only had to know that the important topics were centralization, physical buildings, and departmental libraries; in the library surveys of the time, where I only had to know that the important tables were those specifying where the books and reading rooms were physically located. All those things were obvious in retrospect. But it is foolish to imagine that I ought to have seen the importance of departmental libraries ahead of time. In actual practice, I discovered that importance only by complete immersion: by trawling in the lean places, browsing in the rich ones, and brachiating around in circles from primary to secondary to bibliographical sources. Only by immersion could I understand which of the many things staring me in the face were the important ones. Indeed, even the underlying puzzle—how and why had the scholars diverged from librarians in their views of research—had emerged only gradually over the history of the research.

All the rest now became clear: the move to specialized reference tools, the refusal to accept the librarians' "scientific" approach to research, the development of brachiation and the heavy reliance on peer specialists. After this discovery, I entered the endphase. I had gradually developed all the pieces of the project, in a series of parallel researches that facilitated each other. Then, over a short time, here in late midphase, it had become clear how all those pieces went together. I had only to write them up.

8. The Finished Argument

Let me now provide—by way of contrast—the result of this long and chaotic process. This makes a coherent, four-period story out of all the pieces: the demography of scholars, the growth of libraries, the habits of reference tools, the move to centralization, the emergence of overload, and so on. The story has the transparent, easy structure that so overwhelms the beginning researcher. But, as I hope the previous section has made clear, that easy structure is an appearance. Puzzle and solution have been developed side by side.

IN THE FORMATIVE YEARS, BEFORE THE FIRST WORLD WAR, THE entire PhD cadre of library researchers in all fields probably numbered about a thousand. Most library research was done in a handful of universities, all of them in or near the great library cities of Boston, New York, Washington, and Chicago. Professors and graduate students did research side by side in departments that had their own office space and, most often, departmental libraries that were immediately at hand. Acquisitions for departmental collections were in faculty hands.

These scholars worked in a surprisingly rich reference environment, some of it in the departmental libraries, some in the central collection. In periodical bibliography, the *Readers Guide* and its scholarly equivalent the *International Index* date from this period. Book bibliography was more chaotic, undermined by the lack of a national classification standard. But on the plus side most American libraries had agreed (unlike their continental counterparts) to follow Dewey's lead in "relative shelving," which meant that physical browsing by subject—an immense research advance—was now possible. (Books had previously been stored by size or by order of acquisition.) As for archives and document bibliography, US government documents had better indexing then than they would at times later in the century, and comprehensive lists of special collections were already available. In specialized reference, however, the future was less evident. The dominant works were typically European: multivolume, foreign-language works combining bibliography with scholarly summary.

In the interwar years, this scholarly world changed radically. The number of scholars expanded steadily, to about 10,000 or so by the Second World War. Nonetheless, disciplines remained small enough—typically numbering about 1,000 to 1,500—for faculty to know virtually everyone in their field. They could know all dissertations going forward across their discipline should they wish to, and, indeed, could in practice read virtually all new work in their discipline should they so desire. Although PhD production remained centralized in the great library cities, library research began to trickle out to the major universities of the Midwest and the West, where professional historians invented "local history" as a way of surviving their banishment from the great East Coast libraries.

In the interwar, the research habitus of faculty changed radically as they lost their bid to retain departmental libraries. They were defeated by university librarians armed with the twin rhetorics of on the one hand scientific management and efficiency and on the other hand liberal education and its preference for generalism over "narrow specialism." Departmental libraries survived but only in centralized settings, where they were of much less use to faculty. Faculty lost most of their role in acquisitions, although they retained—as they would for the whole century—the right to lob occasional sarcastic critiques at librarians' acquisition policies.

The reference infrastructure took several big steps in the interwar. In periodical bibliography, the *Union List* finally appeared, providing enormous assistance to those researchers outside the great library cities. For books, the period saw the halting emergence of the *National Union Catalog*, the creation of the regional depository catalogs, and a serious interlibrary loan system. Again, the boon for those outside the core was great. For archives and documents, LC began a regular census of manuscript collections, the United Kingdom's immense Public Record Office finally issued a serious guide to its holdings, and the *Document Catalog* continued as a solid index to American government documents.

But the real story of the interwar is the explosion of specialized bibliographies and tools, generated by scholars—or sometimes scholarly librarians—for research use. The immense *London Bibliography of the Social Sciences*, the AHA *Guide to Historical Literature*, and the MLA annual bibliographies are all examples. Each is a reaction to the problem presented by centralization and overload. The similar PAIS *Bulletin* was to be sure produced by librarians, but they were special librarians in a research library setting and their product was aimed largely at the research market. All these tools bypassed mass indexes like the *Readers' Guide* and the *International Index*, which in effect became tools for general readers rather than a first recourse for specialists.

After the Second World War, the system changed again. Academia ballooned. As many humanities and social science dissertations were written between 1945 and 1956 as had been written from 1890 to 1945, and as many were written between 1956 and 1968 as had been written from 1890 to 1956. Academia lost its face-to-face quality and also, in most cases, lost touch with its past; a world in which so much research was appearing so fast inevitably forgot older work overnight. Specialization grew rapidly. It might still be possible to know most of the scholars in one's specialty, but not in the discipline. Similarly one could know about dissertations in one's specialty but not discipline-wide. Indeed, even as a nation-wide dissertation location system finally emerged, dissertations were used less and less as scholarly resources, such use eventually disappearing altogether.

In this period, the graduate education system finally began to decentralize, in part aided by a leveling of library resources. This leveling came partly through the steadily increasing importance of nationally deposited government documents in major collections but also because massification brought more and more libraries to behemoth status. Although early collection differences were never erased, current monograph and general reference collections were much more uniform as spending ratios equalized. This leveled the playing field, especially in the social sciences.

As far as general reference tools are concerned, it was in the 1950s that abstract journals finally began to appear in the social sciences and even the humanities, although the latter were not very successful. A massively expanded *Union List* in the mid-1940s no doubt helped scholars locate unusual materials, and the publication, at last, of a book version of the *NUC* meant that one part of the interlibrary loan process became easier. In the late 1950s the *National Union Catalog of Manuscript Collections* finally began to provide systematic guidance on archival holdings, although as with dissertations, the tool was too little too late; historians had long since turned their graduate students toward local topics and local archives. US Government documents limped along under the miserable *Monthly Catalog*.

Meanwhile, specialized reference tools continued to proliferate. A typical example is the UNESCO-sponsored *Current Sociology*, of which each monthly issue comprised a massive review essay and an equally massive bibliography, both by a specialist researcher. Such tools had begun to dominate research practice. In this period, primary evidence shows clearly that researchers got their bibliographical references from hearsay and from other people's bibliographies and reference lists. By this time, then, the researchers had pretty much deserted the general reference system. They were using things like the *Union List* and the *Catalog of Books Represented by LC Cards* only occasionally, when they were needed in detailed brachiation inside research projects. All their preliminary bibliographical work and a good deal of their focal library research work was done with specialty tools, many of which they owned personally through subscription. It is also in this period that the paperback book emerged, which enormously increased the ability of scholars to own both current and classic texts, with their rich bibliographies.

In summary, this was a period in which library research became a much larger, more decentralized enterprise, and in which library researchers completed their emancipation from the main core of reference and bibliographical tools, which they henceforth used only when absolutely necessary. The further evolution of those tools was thus in many ways irrelevant to scholarship itself.

As a result, when the 1970s brought the social science and arts and humanities citation indexes, library research scholars were not particularly interested. These were indeed universal indexes, quadrupling the coverage of the Wilson bibliographies and replacing nonspecialist human indexing with automated KWIC indexes in a kind of race to the bottom. But most library research scholars—I'm an exception to this—never used these indexes at all. They had long since decamped to specialist tools, many of which they owned themselves. (Every economist had an automatic subscription to the AEA's magnificent bibliography journal, for example.) When they needed more bibliography, they went to major recent monographs or to specialist bibliographies.

It is true, however, that the post-1970s world probably brought even those kinds of techniques to their knees. As of 2009, half of the dissertations ever written in the history of American academia had been written after 1982, and a third of them since 1995. It is not clear whether output per scholar has increased much, but when the typical discipline numbers ten thousand or more persons, even the old output rates mean that sheer quantity overwhelms us.

We do still have a few quality indicators. It is easy enough simply to ignore everything published in third-rate journals and by third-rate presses, and many of us do that. But other people's reference lists—even if in high-quality locations—are no longer as good a source as once they were. The number of references in a typical sociology article has gone up by a factor of two in the last forty years, yet most of those additional references are not useful as guides to the literature. The Chicago Library School theses show that across most fields, sixty years ago, a third of references were to a single page in the cited source and another third to some page range. Today, the figure for both together is less than 10 percent. This fact shows that most of the new citations are not substantive but decorative. This destroys their bibliographical utility, which was based on their selectivity and substance.

In summary, then, library research was already in crisis before the arrival of the Internet and the digital library. The mechanisms of that crisis are rooted in processes continuous since the 1920s. The librarians have pushed for centralized reference tools and bibliographic structures, counting on indexing to guide the investigator through the welter that comes with rapid increase of material. Librarians' central metaphors have always been scientific. Their models of successful knowledge systems have been the natural sciences (and in particular chemistry). They have aimed to make the library a universal identification, location, and access machine. The digital library world is in that sense simply the latest version of a quite familiar librarian program.

By contrast, library researchers started withdrawing from this universalist project in the 1920s and gradually erected a system of specialty tools and a set of research practices that enabled them to bypass the inefficient searches that were the only possibility under the universal bibliographical system. By the 1950s and 1960s this alternate system of specialty tools and practices was mature. It could therefore survive the earlier-mentioned race to the bottom, which culminated in the citation databases on the one hand and WorldCat on the other.

THUS WE SEE THAT FROM A NONLINEAR BODY OF RESEARCH—SOME OF it orderly and rational, much of it chaotic and contingent, all of it loosely tied together—has come a clear argument and a straightforward if quite counterintuitive story. And that story reveals a fact crucial to current library debates: the Google project, this research tells us, is very old news.

With good luck, you will have the same experience. Out of a nonlinear, seemingly irrational sequence of research acts will come a clear result. Let's get started.

3 | *Fundamentals*

Since wandering around in unknown lands of knowledge is a crucial part of library research, it helps to consider what to put in our backpacks before we go. As with any traveling, that means thinking about the general qualities of the places we may end up visiting. For holiday travel, we would think about weather, language, accommodations, food, money, local customs, and so on. Those things will determine what clothes we take, which phrase books we buy, how we plan an itinerary. But the library research journey, as I have noted, does not have a well-planned itinerary. It's like going abroad for two months with a fixed budget and fairly loose plans. That means we focus on general things with broad applicability: the equivalents of rail passes, universal phrase books, and all-occasion clothing.

First of all, we need to understand the basics of how knowledge is organized online and physically, both how it is already organized, and how we ourselves can reorganize parts of it. This is the topic of indexing. (The tourism equivalent is not only making sure we have guidebooks, but also that we have some sense of which guidebooks are better for which places and which tasks.) Given that knowledge of indexing, we need next to think about search: not which particular tools to use for which particular purpose, but the properties and possibilities of search in general. (Not which attraction to see, but how to find out about new attractions to consider seeing, and how to get quickly to another country if we're bored.) We will then turn to identifying the products of searches, turning them into the "citations" with which we support our work. (How to take decent photographs!) The chapter will close with two practical topics: first, the details of finding specific kinds of materials (how a typical foreign city is laid out) and, second, quality (how to tell a good tourist attraction from a phony one and when to trust—or not trust—other people's reviews).

In summary, this chapter is about fundamentals: indexing, search, citation, location, and quality. These are matters that are important in library research, no matter where in particular it takes us. The chapter includes both basic and advanced versions of these fundamentals, since it makes sense to consolidate all this material in one place. So you may need to skip a bit if you run into things that seem too simple or too advanced.

1. Indexing

To retrieve information you must use indexes. To organize your own project you must create an index. For these two crucial reasons you need to understand indexing in some detail.

An index entry is something that identifies another thing, thereby "indicating" it. The thing indicated may be a page discussing a particular topic, an article using a given method, a website on a certain subject. An index as a whole (or, for short, "an index") is simply a list of such entries, indicating topics within a particular range of material. Normally, an index is much more compact than the full collection of things indexed. Indexes thus help us find our way in a world of abundance.

You have grown up with the Internet's concept of indexing. Internet indexing is based on actual words, rather than on the concepts those words denote. It makes the rather radical assumption that words are identical with concepts: one word, one concept. On that assumption, we can create a passive index that arises simply through word use; any word that is used becomes an index term. You know well the problem of this kind of indexing. It produces large lists of irrelevant material. That's because you are looking for concepts and ideas, while the Internet indexing is just giving you words.

By contrast, we can also create active indexes, where someone decides what are the best labels by which a given item can be indexed. On the Internet, such active indexing is called tagging; people decide on particular but personal words to use as indexes. Because these are their words, they are word-concepts, not simply words. In Internet terms, a "real index" would be a disciplined and regularized tagging system, in which a single set of agreed-upon tags was consistently and systematically applied to material analyzed conceptually by readers and users. Sound like a fairy tale? Not at all—that sentence describes the standard index of the predigital era.

There are two main strategies for creating an active index. The first associates items into more and more general categories. In such a "hierarchical classification," things are indexed by the name of the various higher classes of which they are a part. We are all familiar with this from the Linnean classification of living things. In a hierarchical scheme, each item has only one index location, which is indeed why LC indexes this way: a physical book cannot be in two places at once.

The second general indexing scheme associates with each item not a concentric set of labels, as in hierarchical classification, but a limited number of potentially unrelated pointers (e.g., tags) that indicate (index) it. An example is the subject headings list of the Library of Congress record for any given book. To be sure, a book has to be in one and only one place in the stacks, and hence it has a hierarchical call number, determined by its first subject heading. But books are generally relevant to more than one topic, and in a traditional card catalog (and in online successors to them) a book is assigned several other subject headings, under which it will appear in any browsing list. This second approach indexes material by "multiple subjects" rather than by concentric groupings. Obviously, it is both more flexible and more informative, although it buys that flexibility at the expense of indefiniteness. A hierarchical index is decisive, but for any particular research purpose, it may well be wrong. A multiple-subject index (sometimes called a faceted index) is less decisive, but more rich.

The ambiguity created by additional subject headings sets a limit on their number. In the days of physical card indexes, books could receive only two or three extra subject headings, because each additional subject heading required another physical card. To move from three to four subject headings per book would increase a library's number of subject cards by one third—an expensive proposition indeed if you have a million-item collection. In the early days of computer catalogs, however, storage space seemed cheap, and so books sometimes got ten or more subject headings. But this meant that for a given topic, a user found far more books, and so had to wade through increasing amounts of what often seemed extraneous material. If a book is mostly about subject X but is occasionally or distantly relevant to subjects S, T, and Z, then most users interested primarily in S, T, and Z won't be interested in it: for them it is just another item to skip. Thus, adding more and more subjects does not resolve the problem that a given book is relevant to many different topics and researches. It just moves us toward the long and useless list familiar from keyword searches.

A more important strategy is something called controlled vocabulary. Suppose you were indexing the King James Bible using a computer. You would find that *sorcery* and *sorcerers* are mentioned fifteen times, *magic* and *magicians* fifteen times, *wizards* and *wizardry* ten times, *witches* and *witchcraft* eight times, *soothsaying* and *soothsayers* seven times, *diviners* and *divination* twenty-two times, *wise men* (and women) four times, and so on. A keyword index would send users who asked about sorcery to the fifteen sorcery citations, those who asked about magicians to the fifteen magician citations, and so on. But if you were writing a paper on "Biblical accounts of attempts to influence the natural world via esoteric rituals," you would actually want to find all these lines: not only the lines for *sorcery*, but also the lines for *magic*, *wizardry*, and so on. But you would have no way of knowing every possible word that King James's translators might have used for the phenomenon. For all you know, they might have used *inspiration* or *possession* or even *spirit* to refer to phenomena that you might think are "magical." The relation between an index term and the thing it indexes is not exclusive. You can talk about magic without using the word *magic* (as in "the sorcerer recited a spell") and you can also use the word *magic* without talking about magic (as in "His words are like magic.")

Indexers recognized this problem long ago, and answered it with the concept of controlled vocabulary. A controlled vocabulary is a list of words that have been explicitly defined as indicators of concepts. As I noted above, the keyword indexing familiar from the Internet assumes that the connection between words and concepts is absolute. *Magic* is about magic, and *sorcery* is about sorcery, and we ourselves must remember that the two may actually be two different words for the same thing. But in a controlled vocabulary index, only one of these words would have listings under it. Suppose that word is *magic*. At the word *sorcery*, you would find a simple pointer saying "for *sorcery*, see *magic*." At *wizards* a pointer would say "for *wizards* see *magicians*." All the index entries—whether the actual text used the word *sorcerer* or *magician* or *wizard* or whatever—would be under *magician*. However, if we were indexing a book on a tribe that had both sorcerers and magicians, and the two groups had different practices, there would be separate headings. That is, it is the conceptual nature of the work being indexed that drives the indexing rather than the nature of the words used.

You might think that it would be great if you had such a tool online. But of course, Google and its relatives can't create controlled vocabularies. For the moment, only humans can, although of course researchers have been working on the problem for decades (without much success). By contrast, virtually all humanly created subject indexes are based on controlled vocabularies. The Library of Congress classification system is a controlled vocabulary. The many indexes produced over the years by the H. W. Wilson Company are based on controlled vocabularies. Most important, any proper book index is a controlled vocabulary invented independently for that book.

In short, in the print world, indexing was based on controlled vocabularies. That's why Google doesn't seem wonderful to older scholars like me. It's truly magnificent for long-shot work, but it's useless for basic bibliography. For that, you need a controlled vocabulary index.

Controlled vocabulary is not simply the heart of good indexing. It is also the heart of your own analysis. One of your central analytic tasks is to develop your own controlled vocabulary. You need to identify the twenty or so centrally important concepts and phenomena in your study and create fixed definitions for them. (You need to decide whether you want to lump or split whatever are the equivalents of *magic* and *sorcery* in your paper; you have to decide what you mean by *wizardry*.) Thus, understanding indexing is not just a matter of being able to find more and better things and to do so more quickly. It is also a matter of doing your own analysis.

With the concept of controlled vocabulary in hand, we can now review the main kinds of indexes available online or in print. I begin with the automated ones, which are all online today, although many of them have print roots.

The most important general type of automated indexing is the keyword indexing with which you are familiar. The name is actually a misnomer. For centuries, printed "keyword" indexes have existed to the Bible and other important texts. (That's where I found the numbers above.) They are called concordances, and hence this type of index should be called a concordance index. But the use of "keyword index" to refer to a concordance dates from the 1960s and is well established. (I shall discuss "true keyword indexes" in a moment.)

The great advantage of keyword indexing is that it is so easy that it can be applied to enormous volumes of text at minimal cost, particularly if that text is digitized. It is also true that if the texts are truly digitized (that is, if the original text is represented by ASCII character codes), keyword indexing is absolutely accurate, although with graphical texts read by optical character recognition (OCR) programs (e.g., PDFs), it has more problems.

The disadvantage of keyword indexing is of course that it works on words, not concepts, and most words of any importance appear too frequently to identify a limited number of texts. The result is huge lists of marginally relevant material. Boolean limitations of such searches—combinations of words, exclusion of words—help a bit. But not much. It is true that wonderful conceptual indexing systems could be designed, given the current state of computer science. But they are not widely available, no doubt because they would be very expensive to implement.

There have, to be sure, been some approaches for solving this problem. The most common are visual displays: word clouds, Wordles, and so on. They are produced by algorithms that first create "distance" measures between words or concepts (two words are "close" if they often occur on the same page or in the same sentence) and then produce cluster or graphical displays that retain as much of that distance information as possible. The first major textbooks on scaling and cluster analysis, from which these algorithms derive, date from the 1960s. In the half century since, no one has yet managed to turn scaling and cluster analysis from an art form into a push-button, replicable analytic strategy. It probably cannot be done. You should avoid using any of these "techniques"; they must make many strong assumptions and, as a consequence, are quite unstable under minor data perturbations. Strangely enough, they are useful only if you already know a great deal about your data. Perhaps that's why their widest current use is in market research.

SO THAT'S THE STORY ON AUTOMATED INDEXING. IT COULD IN principle be wonderful, but in practice it is not. Most of the hype about automated indexing concerns potentialities, not actualities. The good news is that there are much better indexing techniques available for most materials. These are found in human-based subject indexes.

Human-based subject indexes, the second broad type of index, are of two kinds. The less common is the "true keyword index." In true keyword indexing, authors themselves assign particular terms under which they want their work indexed; true keyword indexing is author-chosen tagging. Started in the 1960s, true keyword indexing remains fairly common in scientific and psychological journals. It forces authors to choose their audiences deliberately, and thus increases the accessibility of research. Sadly, it never spread to the social sciences and humanities, although there are recent signs of change.

The other and more important human-based index is the "true subject index" with controlled vocabulary. Up until the digital age, this was the standard strategy for all major indexes. There are two basic steps in producing a true subject index. The first is a conceptual analysis of the text; the indexer reads the text and develops an analysis of what the text says, just as if he were an ordinary reader. The second step is to attach this conceptual analysis to a controlled vocabulary, one word per concept. Note that this attaching combines categories like magicians and sorcerers, but distinguishes things like turkey (the bird) and Turkey (the nation). That is, not only are there usually several words for one concept, there are also places where one word inevitably denotes several concepts. All of these are distinguished in a controlled vocabulary. (Wikipedia did not discover the problem of disambiguation!) A system of "see also" and "used for" labels imposes hierarchical and associative structure on a controlled vocabulary index. The traditional book index uses these terms sparingly however; it is not the case that everything is linked to everything. The traditional principle was parsimony: better too little than too much. As a result, the hyperlinking in a print index (via "see also" and "used for" and so on) is quite powerful by comparison with Internet hyperlinking, which takes you quickly into extremely unfocused and often irrelevant spaces. In human indexing, only truly important links were included, because linking was very expensive.

The archetypical example of a true subject index is a back-of-the-book index from before the digital age. Contrary to what you may think, these are not keyword indexes. They were prepared by someone who read and tried to understand the text, who created a controlled vocabulary, and then read the book a page at a time, assigning controlled index terms for each page. All that information was then combined, a few hyperlinks were inserted, and the whole was edited for the back of the book. An indexed page does not necessarily include all of the words that index it in the back of a book. More important, a given page appears in a good book index only five or six times. (I index my own books and aim for a maximum of five index references per page.) That means that a draconian selection has already been made; only very important material is indexed. (No publisher will pay to print a full concordance at the back of the book, and, in any case a full concordance has the Google problem of masses of irrelevant references.) These facts mean that by Internet standards traditional back-of-the-book indexes are beyond platinum. That is why your crucial task in preliminary bibliography must be to find five to ten truly excellent books on your topic. Their indexes will be the best subject guide you can locate. Sadly, many presses are moving to automated keyword indexing at the back of their books. Such indexes are cheap, but useless.

For an ongoing, continuously produced index—an index for a journal, for example—the controlled vocabulary must be decided ahead of time. This was the situation for all the basic classification schemes on which the print library was based: the Library of Congress and Dewey Decimal classification systems, the many Wilson indexes, the print versions of most tools that have migrated to online status, and a majority of encyclopedias and reference books, thesauruses, and so on. All of these have (or had) human indexers who imposed ongoing controlled vocabularies. As usage changes (the nineteenth century's "nerves" became "anxiety" and then "stress," for example), a term and its replacement typically coexist in such an index (linked by "see also") for a period of time. After this joint indexing period, the later term continues alone. This ongoing practice not only enables you to trace your topic back through the differing labels, it also enables you to easily retrieve the history of the labels. Note that this will not be feasible with the online versions of such tools, since those usually dump all the materials into a single dataset searched by "modern" keyword indexes. (So you never see the overlap during the transitional period between index terms.) This is another reason why you often may want to use the print versions of many older tools. They contain much information that the online versions don't: "see also" references, and the like.

The advantages of true subject indexing are obvious. The indexing is more parsimonious and therefore more useful. Since the terms are controlled, navigation is both easier and more consistent once you figure out the basic conceptual layout. The hyperlinking is also constrained, so it too has a high payoff.

At the same time, true subject indexes have some problems. They have a slant on the material—that of the indexer or of the controlled vocabulary. If that slant is not your slant, then they can be very difficult to use. They also make emerging topics less visible. Indeed, in times of rapid conceptual change they can be quite misleading. (For this reason you can never talk about changes in the numbers of articles on this or that topic in an index without carefully investigating the stability of the index terms.)

There are some kinds of materials that are badly served by both digital and physical bibliographical tools. For the library researcher, the most important examples are chapters in monographs and edited volumes. An enormous amount of useful material appears in these, but there is no index to them. (And given the copyright law, an automated version of such an index is a very long way off.) Suppose you are looking for a history of social constructionism in the 1970s. It so happens that I wrote one in my book *Chaos of Disciplines*, but you won't find that through any index except that of the book itself. The book is subject-indexed in my library's catalog under "Sociology—Philosophy" and "Social Sciences—Philosophy." And although the chapter listing includes the phrase "social construction," so also do the records of tens of thousands of other books that don't have such histories. So even if somebody eventually put all books' indexes together, you would then be cruising a huge mixture of different controlled-vocabulary indexes with a keyword approach. That won't help you at all, because the controlled vocabularies will change from book to book.

In short, chapters in books are findable only through citation: through reference to them by other published materials. Since such citation analysis has become a crucial bibliographical tool (for this and many other reasons), I shall consider it in the next section.

Finally, some general advice about indexing. First, there isn't any "real," ultimate index. Two researchers might easily write two equally excellent papers on a topic like "how have movie executives used financial information in making production decisions," but share only a quarter of their references. We can be sure that the periodical *Variety* will be in both bibliographies, but we cannot be sure about much else. In fact, there are many directions in which to take such a topic, lots of possible sources of data and types of approaches. So there is no prefect index.

Second, there is no index from nowhere. The LC classification system is as good an index from nowhere as we have, yet even it is not very powerful. The best indexes are always from a particular—usually disciplinary—point of view. They can afford to be highly specific without losing breadth of coverage because they ignore whole swaths of materials and points of view. For this reason, one of the first things you must do in any project is to locate bibliographical tools created by specialists in the field within which you are working. Those tools will have ordered things in a way that seems natural for you.

As you may already have found, the "view from nowhere" problem also holds for reference librarians. Inevitably, reference librarians take a view from nowhere. They are not specialists. They simply know a lot about the tools themselves. So they will always seem to you to suggest large amounts of interesting but slightly irrelevant material unless you ask them very specific questions. By the time you can be specific enough to make their answers useful, you usually know your area better than they do. At that point, your best advisor will be either your faculty advisor or the library's "subject bibliographer" in charge of your research area. There will be a list of these people on the library's website. Even in a small library, they will know some things that the reference librarians don't know.

Third, don't expect an online indexing system to produce the same answers twice. There are several reasons for this. As new material comes into a database, it inevitably changes the relative "distance" between materials already there and thereby changes the relevance structure. This may change both the ordering and the content of search lists. If OCR is involved, there is the further problem that algorithms are updated continuously, and hence may change their results. Moreover, as new material is added, the algorithms—which train and retrain themselves on the material in the database—will change their behavior. In my experience, for example, historical newspaper database queries are not replicable after a couple of months have passed.

Even changes of font in the underlying texts can disrupt such tools. My student Brian Cody was once looking for articles on block grants in the Lexis/Nexis government database. He found no such articles in the 1950s, although there were plenty in the 1940s and the 1960s. Of course, it couldn't possibly be true that there were no articles about block grants in the 1950s. After careful work, Brian found out that the federal government changed its font around 1950, and that if you put "blook grants" or even "blook giants" into the search string for the 1950s, you would get many hits, all of which, needless to say, contained not the phrases "blook grants" or "blook giants" but the phrase "block grants."

2. Search

Obviously, search is a different matter in physical and digital tools. So it is useful to cover them separately.

A. PHYSICAL TOOLS

By "physical indexes" I refer to all indexes that were born physical. Because of the ceaseless sale and purchase of these sources, and the ceaseless changes in name and minor functionalities that accompany those sales, it can be hard to trace the remnants of these physical sources online. Indeed, the names of several of these sources have changed during the time since I first drafted these chapters. But it is worth your while to find them, because the print sources were substantially more accurate and better indexed than the online versions.

The category "indexes born physical" includes such things as online catalogs that were produced from card images (that is, nearly all library catalogs online). It also includes the physical-era Wilson bibliographical tools mentioned earlier: the *Readers' Guide*, the *Library Literature*, and so on. It includes the pre-2000 materials in reference tools like *Historical Abstracts* and *Sociological Abstracts*. In most libraries, the physical versions of most of these tools will still be in the stacks. For subject browsing, they are usually better—and in most cases faster to use—than the online versions. Finding such tools born physical is easy. Consult the last print edition of the ALA *Guide to Reference Books*, edited by Robert Balay and published in 1996. It will be in the reference department, and it will list them all.

Search in physical resources is very much shaped by twentieth-century library practice. Librarians aimed at a uniform, exact mode of characterizing particular items (descriptive bibliography, as it is called). Although there were multiple competing systems before the eventual triumph of LC, all systems had the same goal: exact, precise classification; suppression of spelling and other "unimportant" variations; portability across settings (LC sold its cards to thousands of libraries); stability across time. The core concept was what was called an "authoritative record." In the computer era, this has become the MARC (machine-readable cataloging) record.

The searcher in physical tools must therefore remember that librarians imposed various rules on their sometimes disorderly charges. The first is that authors' names are always listed last name first. You won't find John Adams at "John Adams," but at "Adams, John." Most digital resources consider this order nonintuitive and hence use the "proper" (i.e., modern Western) order. The old ordering had its own little problems—how to handle *de* in "Manuel de Falla" or *van* in "Ludwig van Beethoven"—and different libraries handled these in different ways. But the main rule is fixed: last name first, then pre-names expanded to full names even if initials were normally used ("Eliot, Thomas Stearns" not "Eliot, T. S.") Generally in old catalogs initials were handled with cross-reference cards ("For Eliot, T. S., see Eliot, Thomas Stearns"), but these were not often brought into electronic versions of the old catalogs. Remember that non-Western names often place the patronymic first and that names originally in non-roman alphabets may be subject to different romanizations at different times. So if you are looking for non-Western names, be sure to check both orders in either new or old sources. (I recently found the youthful BA paper of a famous Chinese scholar who attended Reed College by checking the college's online catalog using the wrong order in the old romanization.)

Second, physical indexes ruthlessly regularized spellings. Shakespeare, whose name exists in several dozen variations, was everywhere William Shakespeare, even if the title page of the book involved bore "William Shaksper." Cross-reference cards guided the unwary. This created some havoc with the Scots (some MacDonalds spell the name "McDonald"), which in turn caused alphabetization issues. (Many old indexes had the Macs and the Mcs together before Ma, for example. Or again, styles of alphabetizing Spanish have changed over time: the *ll*- words used to be listed after all other *l*- words.) This could also be an issue in matters of anglicization. Classical writers, for example, were generally anglicized ("Horace," not "Quintus Horatius Flaccus"). Diphthongs and diacritics caused predictable problems (German umlauts became appended *e*'s as in *Muenchen*). But once you figure out an index's spelling of a particular person or item, you can be sure you will find everything available for that person or item in one place. (I will note the one exception to this below, when discussing WorldCat.)

Third, regularization causes problems of disambiguation. There are quite a number of John Adamses (twenty-seven in my university's online catalog, in fact). In traditional indexing, dates of birth and death were used to disambiguate authors. This is very helpful, as such information is seldom available in indexes born digital. Disambiguation of titles was more complex, and physical indexes were not particularly good on that. If you were interested in a book called *Hope*, you had to look at each of several dozen cards to find the monograph or periodical you wanted. In browsing, you will encounter this problem as well.

Fourth, the most important regularization applied to subjects. As I noted earlier, all physical subject indexes were based on controlled vocabularies. By far the most important of these is the Library of Congress classification system. You can find the entire system down to a reasonably specific level at the LC website (www.loc.gov/catdir/cpso/lcco, last time I looked). The LC Authorities record system governs master lists not only for subjects but also for authors, organizations, and anything else that appears in an item's MARC record. It is updated daily and is online.

At some point in your project, it will be worthwhile to go find your library's copy of the six huge red volumes that contain the entire LC subject heading system—the whole shebang, as we used to say. When you seek your topics of interest in those volumes, you will inevitably find new terms to search, even if you have studied an area for decades. That's because the choices made in a controlled vocabulary are not always obvious, and if you don't guess the right term, you may miss a lot of material. As my earlier example from the Bible showed, just because you don't find lots of entries on "sorcery" doesn't mean the indexed material contains nothing on sorcery. The word *magic* may be used for the general category under which such material appears. So if you don't find much on a topic in a classic subject index, try some synonyms and don't be afraid to consult the giant LC red volumes, which contain complete cross-referencing of all possible terms.

Fifth, most physical subject indexes (and in particular the LC classification system) follow the principle of "specific citation." In LC, an item is classified as specifically as it can be classified. If it is about the medical profession, it will be listed under "Physicians." This is true even if it is universally regarded as one of the classic works about professions in general, and you might therefore expect it to be at HT687, the heading for works on professions in general.

Moreover, an LC index category includes only the matter at its own level, not the materials from the subcategories under it. If you are browsing, remember that no browser for LC (or any other such system) includes all the subcategory material when you browse the main heading. If you browse the seventy titles under "Professions" in my university's catalog, they will not include anything from "Professions, United States, History" unless the catalogers have specifically added that general topic to the more specific ones in the book's MARC record. You are getting only the general material about professions, not the books about the history of professions in America. (Otherwise, you would get thousands of books under every general category. This restriction is designed to facilitate browsing.)

It is also important to remember that controlled vocabularies change over time but that classifications of items generally do not. I was once searching for a definitive history of scholarly publication in the United States. I completely missed Donald Bean's splendid 1929 book *American Scholarly Publication*. Why? I had searched for material on university presses and scholarly publishing in the stacks by cruising the Z230s and Z280s, which are the relevant LC headings. But Bean's book was at Z471 ("Publishers and Publishing, United States"), because those other headings hadn't been invented in 1929. This shows that it can sometimes be useful to use keyword indexing as well as browsing in indexes and physical sources, for of course I would have found this book using the keyword side of my library's online index.

These then are the basic constraints involved in using indexes born physical: name order matters, spellings are regularized, disambiguation is generally present in the record, and subjects are governed by controlled vocabularies. Most indexes follow the practice of "specific citation," so you need to cover all relevant levels of works. Adjust your search strategies to those constraints, and you will find these tools powerful indeed. If you want further details—or if you just want to witness the virtuosic exactitude of physical-era librarians—go to your library and find a copy of *Anglo-American Cataloging Rules*, published by the ALA in 1967. I guarantee that you will be astounded.

B. DIGITAL TOOLS

Equally powerful, but in quite different ways, are digital tools. Digital tools are of several kinds. If an index is truly born digital, then it does not have any errors produced in the input process. A search algorithm is passed over the electronic version of the text. It spits out the keywords and the page numbers, and a cleanup program neatens up the result. Absent a defective chip and a dirty primary document, there is simply no possibility for error. Many "digital" tools, however, were not actually born digital. They involve "digitization" of graphically represented physical materials. Typically this is accomplished by optical character recognition (OCR). As I noted earlier, OCR can introduce a fairly large number of errors, a fact that has distinct consequences for the researcher.

Still other digital tools are combinations of preexisting physical materials, which may have been themselves digitized by scanning or in other cases by direct input. OCLC's WorldCat is the important example. WorldCat was produced by a collaborative venture in which libraries contributed their records to a consortium collection, which then repackaged them as a composite catalog. Since the great research libraries were cautious both about the cost of conversion and about the imponderability of the catalog's future, smaller libraries (with fewer resources and consequently weaker cataloging) went into the OCLC system first. Since cataloging differed locally, variability in records was built into WorldCat from the start. When the big facilities finally joined, they uploaded only their own less common items, choosing to save money by downloading existing records for anything already in WorldCat. So their own strong cataloging did nothing to strengthen the system. As a result WorldCat contains lots of meaningless variation, in particular containing hundreds of thousands of separate records for what are in fact identical items.

Some characteristics of digital tools are simply the opposite of physical ones. First, on the matter of names. Since the tools are nearly all driven by keyword indexes, and since early users were mostly Westerners, names generally go in the Western order. This creates no problems for Western names, but creates difficulties with Asian and other names that put the patronymic first. Some of these were reversed by some catalogs during the mid-twentieth century, and many Asian academics currently in the West use Western order for their names as authors. So you will probably need to search both orders in the keyword environment, just as in the physical one. As for middle initials or middle names, some digital tools omit them automatically (e.g., when you enclose a name in quotes); others apply them. You have to discover which approach your particular tool is using.

As in physical sources, romanization causes problems for names in Russian, Chinese, and other non-roman writing systems. You should always consult a specialist or a librarian on sources coming from non-roman scripts. Typically, prominent figures and institutions have standard anglicizations as well as romanizations, but things get very counterintuitive once you move away from the well-known figures. (The *Anglo-American Cataloging Rules* have instructive advice, but they do not govern the digital world as a whole.)

Second, by contrast with physical searching, digital sources do not regularize spelling. This could be easily accomplished using sequence alignment algorithms, but checking for errors would be very expensive, so the vendors of digital reference works leave it to you to check alternative spellings. Remember this, particularly if you are working with sources that have been through OCR with its randomly induced spelling variations.

Third, outside of places like Wikipedia, where the problem has been recognized, disambiguation can be a major problem in keyword indexes because there are no dates or other information to distinguish between people. Thus, there are 893 entries for the author keyword phrase "John Adams" in my library's keyword catalog. But if I look at the author browse list, which contains a strict representation of the cards themselves, I find that there are only twenty-seven distinct people named "John Adams," and the total of their author entries is not 893 but 412 items. The keyword side of the catalog is providing the other seventy-nine distinct people, who turn out to be all the John Adamses for whom there are known middle initials and names. (These are not counted on the browser side.) These people provide the other 481 items of the 893 total. The seventy-nine can be distinguished online by initials and names, but the twenty-seven cannot be so distinguished, except in browsers that retain the dates of birth and death. In short, disambiguation in online keyword indexes can be very complicated, just as in print indexes.

Finally, keyword indexes do not have controlled vocabularies. This is both a strength and a weakness. On the one hand it means that librarians haven't decided ahead of time what goes where. There is no conceptual structure coded into the index terms used. On the other hand, it also means that the user must produce a broad range of possible terms for any given concept. It means that historical drift in terminologies is concealed even more than in controlled vocabulary systems. Because of this problem, I recently had an undergraduate student who thought that the problem of sexual abuse did not really exist before the 1980s, because there were no articles about it. But of course the search strings "domestic violence" and "child molesting" produced a depressingly large harvest.

There is a special problem that plagues tools that have migrated from physical to digital and in the process have combined several prior indexes. A good example is the amalgamator *19th Century Masterfile*. Such tools have mixed dozens of different controlled vocabularies together. But of course there is no reason the different indexers would have chosen the same controlled vocabulary, so the tools mix apples and oranges and kiwis. For fine work, then, you are better off working with the individual tools. For a first pass, however, such amalgamated tools can be very useful.

Another word about migrated controlled vocabularies. A number of digital tools continue to have "thesauruses." What this probably means is that the physical tool that they have superseded at one time had a controlled vocabulary. Whether that vocabulary continues to evolve or even to be applied is another matter. You can't trust the vendors to have kept applying it, for it means an immense effort in microcoding. And you can be very sure that if they don't apply it, they won't admit that in public. So unfortunately you have to assume that any online, migrated-to-digital index is a keyword index, the dumbest index possible. Even the ones that promise thesauruses probably don't deliver them.

Since keyword tools generally produce immense lists most of whose entries are useless, those who develop them have created sorting mechanisms to bring the useful material to the top. Most of these "relevance" sortings are themselves useless. Relevance is decided by what the networks literature calls centrality measures. Essentially, these take the total list of everything your search returned, look at the citation network between the items (or sometimes the common terms network), and define a measure of "centrality" on those pairwise distances. Highly central things are high on this measure and appear first in the list. (These measures mostly derive from the sociological literature on human networks like gangs, high school friendship groups, and so on.)

Relevance is thus entirely determined by the search string itself. Twenty different investigators, for twenty different reasons, could use that one, identical search string and would all get the same listing of "relevance." But obviously, the "relevance" cannot possibly be the same for all twenty different investigators. In fact these lists aren't "relevance" ratings at all. They are centrality ratings. That's why they are unhelpful, particularly if your project does not concern the dominant (i.e., central) problems researched by those people who happen to use this particular search string in these particular sources. Indeed, you could change your search string slightly and find that two articles which were adjacent in the old relevance list are far apart in the new list. In short, don't use relevance listings as guides to quality. Use the date orderings (most academic fields think that recent is better) or the citation orderings (at least they are real popularity contests rather than fake ones), especially early in your work. Dates and citation rates don't change when the search string changes. (There is more on quality later in the chapter.)

As for tools that involve OCR, I have already mentioned their strengths and weaknesses. As the "blook grant" story shows, you cannot trust any source based on OCR scanning to be exhaustively accurate in anything like the way the original sources were accurate. But for many or most purposes, this does not matter. Much of library research is "satisficing"; we aim to get enough data to make a solid assertion, but we can't expect—it is usually impossible in any case—to get every single thing. If you are in satisficing mode, as scholars often are, then you're fine with OCR-based sources. If you must really have everything, then do your searches several times over, on different days.

All of these issues with digital sources mean that you should usually try to discover, before using any tool or database, how it was generated. Make it a habit to go to the About tab on the website. Look for the words "scanned in," which means the source is OCR. If the About discussion claims that there is a thesaurus, see if you can figure out where it actually came from. For example, EBSCO's thesaurus appears to have come from Whitston Publishing Company, which EBSCO bought in 2003. Since Whitston itself was founded in 1969, its system could be a conceptual or a purely keyword system. There is no easy way to tell, and it is quite likely that EBSCO itself doesn't know. Now that EBSCO has bought the Wilson tools, they should in theory reconcile the two different controlled vocabularies (Wilson and Whitston). They aren't likely to do so, however, because the process would be immensely costly.

A note about Boolean and other advanced searching: As any reader knows, different tools have different rules. Everyone allows *A and B*, but some read *A and B or C* to mean *(A and B) or C*, while others take it as *A and (B or C)*. These are different sets. The varying uses of *not* are similarly worrisome. Also, some tools automatically treat your search string as delimited in quotes (that is, they search only for the phrase). Others automatically treat the words separately. As a searcher you have to remember to figure out exactly how each tool works. There is no standard.

Finally, and most important, you can't assume that any given tool works the same way it did the last time you used it. Programmers make their livings by making tools "better" and "more intuitive." So expect lots of meaningless change in tools. Anything you have not used for several months may suddenly have acquired new habits, particularly if it has new owners.

3. The Citation

Whether you use physical tools or digital ones, you are aiming to acquire something called a citation or reference. You can dump this into software like Endnote if you like, but if you do that too often, you'll just find yourself with yet another huge list of partially relevant material. I myself do not use bibliographical software, largely out of fear that I would quickly amass a personal bibliography of tens of thousands of things that looked interesting. I do my bibliographies from scratch for every piece. It keeps me honest. It is also more fun.

A. AUTHORS

Having a citation means having enough information to locate an item without fail. This will almost always include an author. Sometimes this won't be a person or persons, but an issuing agency; librarians have fairly rigid rules about how organizational authorship works, but I confess that I don't understand them. I just know that you have to be very careful about organizational authors. "American Library Association" as author is not the same as "American Library Association" as publisher or "American Library Association" as subject.

An example from the *Anglo-American Cataloging Rules*—which explains organizational authorship in detail—is useful. On organizational changes of name, for example, *Anglo-American Cataloging Rules* tells us that a catalog should include cards like the following for any organizational name change, at all the various names involved:

> PENNSYLVANIA STATE UNIVERSITY—The name of the Farmer's High School was changed in 1862 to Agricultural College of Pennsylvania; in 1874 to Pennsylvania State College; in 1953 to Pennsylvania State University. Works by this body are entered under the name used at the time of publication. (ALA 1967: p. 114)

That is, there would be four cards, at the four different names, each point-ing to all three other names. If your library still has its card catalog, you can find information like this throughout it. If not, too bad. Almost none of this information was carried over to the online catalogs; it was too expensive. And there is no automated way to discover—much less deliver—this information.

Note too that like organizations, individuals sometimes change their names. Don't expect classification systems—online or off—to catch those changes. My friend Margo Anderson, who wrote the history of the American census, is the same person as Margo Conk, who wrote the history of American occupational statistics. For such name changes, you are on your own.

B. TITLES

The second thing you need is an item title. For a journal article, this is the arti-cle title, not the journal title. For a book it is the book title. From the librarians' point of view, the Statement of International Cataloguing Principles guaran-tees that a book has one title—the "uniform title"—that governs cataloging in all languages and formats. So all copies of a novel appear under one title what-ever their language; the King James Bible appears under "Bible"; and so on.

Many books have subtitles. Practice varies on whether they are necessary for citations. I never bother with them, but occasionally publishers insist on my using them in publications, and I have to go back to find them.

Titles are problematic in two cases. First, in the case of annual reports and such like: regularly issued documents may sometimes have annual sub-stantive titles. (The USDA yearbook used to have annual titles like *Climate* or *Water*.) Some libraries will file such items under the substantive (temporary) title, others under the permanent title. If you're lucky, there will be cross-references to guide you, but for the most part these disappeared in the conver-sion to digital. Hopefully, uniform title rules will take care of most of these problems, but you can never be sure. Another implication of this problem is that you will miss many useful things if you browse long-term serials like monograph series simply by the running, permanent series title. The Bureau of Labor Statistics monograph series is in fact a continuous collection of liter-ally thousands of wonderful books and monographs. But few if any libraries index it by individual title. You have to find such gems through government documents indexes or through other people's citations of them.

The much more problematic case for titles is the situation where the per-manent title has changed. With periodicals, this happens through acquisition or simple renaming. Sometimes these will be mentioned in electronic records (look for the words "continued by"). And for any periodical published before 1950, there's the six-volume *Union List of Serials*, which has a complete history of virtually every serial item in existence to that point.

The most difficult case of title change involves government documents. These change their names all the time, through restructuring of government agencies, random retitling, merger, and so on. The *Union List* has a fair number of ongoing government series. And a good card catalog—if you can find one and figure out how to use it (alphabetization is a complicated business in an author/title/subject card catalog)—will have a large number of cross-reference cards revealing the history of this or that government agency and its serial offerings. Some digital tools now contain quite a lot of this information, which is a good sign. But the underlying point is that titles—of serial items especially—change disturbingly often, especially in government documents. So you need to be very careful in following them.

Deciphering changes of title is something librarians do well. They understand the MARC rules, and we scholars don't. All you need to remember is that titles are often problematic and that the difficulty you may be experiencing in resolving a citation or finding an item may be related to a title difficulty. If you think so, head to the reference desk.

C. LOCATIONAL INFORMATION

The next items in a citation give the locational information itself. In the case of a journal article, this will be the journal title, year of publication, volume number, and article pagination. These are necessary to find the item online or on the shelf (unless you are simply clicking through from some other source) and are also necessary for your reference list or bibliographical footnotes. Note that if the journal's title has changed since the article was published, the citation uses the title as of publication date; it does not change. In the case of a book, the locational information comprises the location and name of the publisher. You don't need any of this information to find the item in the library, but you will need it for your reference list or bibliographical footnotes. Since you will probably not be citing more than a quarter of the items you peruse in the course of research, there's a temptation not to bother with recording the locational data; you can always get it later from the catalog.

D. OTHER INFORMATION

Beyond author, title, and locational information, you can ignore the many other things listed for books in the catalog records: subjects, pagination, size information, ISBN, and special remarks. They aren't necessary for scholars—only for librarians. Indeed, the main decision you need to make about citations is how much detail to keep. Keeping detail is time-consuming, and if like me you are always eager to keep moving rapidly through the sea of potentially useful information, minimizing citations is often useful. Particularly when items are long shots and when I am doing my preliminary-phase bibliographical work, I don't even bother with authors or titles for books. I just make a list of call numbers and head for the stacks. With journal articles, I often take only the volume and pagination. After all, if chances are low that I will use the material, why bother with the details? On the other hand, if something is good, then I'll print it (if it is an article), or I'll charge it out (if it's a book). In both cases, I have the citation information automatically. Sometimes I get caught and have to find something a second time, but I've saved a huge amount of effort in the meantime.

4. Location: Actually Finding Items

Our librarians recently told me that in a library instruction class they found that many students literally did not know how to locate an article that was not available online as a single click from some familiar web page. So here are some notes on how to retrieve items in the library or online.

It is best first to say something about how a library is physically organized. There are four parts of a library that matter to you: reading rooms, stacks, circulation, and reference. You already know about the reading rooms, which are probably where you study or work. The books themselves are all located in something called the stacks. The stacks are organized by Library of Congress call number (or Dewey Decimal call number in some smaller libraries), but changes in the collection over the years mean that it is very unlikely that the call numbers follow some absolute logic from one end of the library to the other. There will be a stack map somewhere, and you will need to study it.

Beyond the reading rooms and the stacks, the library has two other crucial places. One of these is the circulation desk, where you take stack materials to check them out. Checking materials out is "circulating" them. When a book cannot be checked out for some reason, librarians say it "does not circulate." (In many libraries, physical periodicals do not circulate.) A few giant libraries don't allow undergraduates in their stacks—a relic of the bad old days. You may therefore have to file a "paging form" at the circulation desk, and the book will eventually be brought to you. This is also how many large public libraries operate their stacks—for everyone, not just undergraduates. And it is how nearly all big libraries in Europe operate, as well as the Library of Congress.

The final crucial place in the library is the reference desk and—if they exist—the reference shelves or stacks. The reference works are the guides to the rest of the library, and I will emphasize them throughout this book. As I have already remarked, the American Library Association *Guide to Reference Books* is the single most important book in the library, just as its online version is the single most important online library tool. Note that while many reference works have gone online, many have not. In the former case, the physical resource may now circulate, which can be very helpful to you. You can have the physical version all to yourself. In the latter case, prepare to be surprised: the print era had many spectacular reference tools.

Somewhere near the reference books will be the reference librarians. These people are helpful, smart, and knowledgeable. They are experts at finding things, and if you are having trouble with that, they are the place to start. They won't tell you what to look for, although like books, indexes, and other materials in the library, they will often guide you to material that may not be exactly what you want but is worth following up all the same. One caveat: unless they are over forty, reference librarians probably won't know much about physical reference tools. Most of their users work purely online, and they perforce have moved toward their clientele. So don't expect younger reference workers to guide you through the physical reference world. You will have to learn that for yourself.

Given this physical layout, we can discuss how to find things. Books are easy. They are generally in the stacks listed by call numbers, usually LC. There will be a map somewhere telling you which call numbers are where. As for the numbers themselves, up to the decimal point, LC call numbers are quite simple. They start with one to three letters. (Don't ask me why they are still said to be "call *numbers*.") In the stacks, these letters behave in exact alphabetic order, with single letters preceding two-letter combinations. These initial letters are immediately followed by some numbers. These numbers behave just like the integers.

Then there's a decimal point. All the excitement in LC happens after the decimal point. (Think of this as level 99 in the library research video game.) After the decimal point (or after the first decimal point if there are two) may come a number. If there is such a number, then it behaves just like a decimal fraction (.6405 lies between .640 and .650). Such a number is the sign that LC had to subdivide a classification category that was getting too full. After this number, if there is one, comes another decimal point. (If the category hasn't been subdivided, then there is no such number and you're at the first and only decimal point.) This decimal point is followed by what are called the Cutter numbers, after the man who invented the system. Sometimes these signal subdivisions of a topic, which can be geographical (U5 usually means United States) or substantive (H94 means HTML). At other times they signal subtopics, which are sometimes handled by this mechanism instead of decimal subdivision. The last Cutter number (or the only Cutter number, if there is only one) gives a representation of the author's last name, using its first letter, followed by some numbers that behave like fractions again. (Cutter numbers are what enable LC to find infinite new space for new books; think of them as fractal generators.) Hence, my book on professions is (in our library) HD8038.U5A6150: H for Social Sciences, D for Industries, Land Use, and Labor, 8038 for Professional Workers, U5 for United States, and A6150 for Abbott (they must have expected a lot of writers beginning with the letter A!).

I myself have found that life contains enough difficulties without having to master Cutter numbers. I work in an 8.5-million-item library system and have gotten along quite successfully without that knowledge. (I had to relearn the system in order to write the preceding paragraph.) I merely get myself to the proper position in the stacks indicated by the stuff before the decimal point plus any numbers immediately afterward. Then I just look around.

Online there are a variety of places to find books, some of them legal, some not. It is fairly easy to find copies of major classics online in a variety of formats. What is harder is to ascertain the provenance and warrantability of those texts. Some fields—ancient literature for example, and English literature to a considerable extent—have put a good deal of effort into digitizing major works. Others have not. So it is wise to check with a bibliographer or reference librarian at the start of your project to ascertain whether there are substantial relevant online databases of books and whether those databases can be trusted. Remember that the situation online changes very rapidly. Although your field may not have had such resources a year ago, it may have them now. Subject bibliographers are the people who know about such things. Use them.

Journals are a little more complicated. Print journals are sometimes categorized by call number but in many libraries are collected in a single alphabetical collection. All the issues of any particular journal are in one place in either system, typically bound into annual volumes for safekeeping. Once you have found the run of the journal, just follow the citation (which will give the year, the volume number, and a page) to the article. Scholarly journals almost always have annually continuous paging, so issue numbers are not used. The appearance of an issue number in a citation means that the numbering starts anew in each issue. It also usually implies that the journal is not a scholarly one.

Finding journals online is very easy at this point. Go to JSTOR and find the item. If it's not in JSTOR, then hopefully your library has placed a clickable subscription link on the title card for the journal in the catalog. If it hasn't, then the library may have an "electronic journals" page containing all its subscriptions. If finding an article is infinitely hard, then it is unlikely that the article is important. Most BA-level papers have no need to go beyond JSTOR, at least for secondary materials.

Government documents are a realm of their own. Many of the US government's documents are now online. This is one area in which the online system is far ahead of print. Unfortunately, large quantities of federal documents (especially agency documents) as well as virtually all state and local documents remain undigitized, in the never-never land of "govdocs" as it is always called. There is a SuDoc (Superintendent of Documents) classification system for US government documents, but it's been years since I met somebody who really understood it. If you are lucky, the catalogers of your university will have cataloged the government documents with the general collection, by subject in most cases and by issuing agency in the case of long, heterogeneous series. If you are not so fortunate, and your project involves a lot of government documents, go to the government documents department of the library— there probably is one—and ask for a personal tutorial. No one can understand govdocs without serious professional help.

I have several times mentioned another form of material—"series." True series are quite rare at this point. There are many current university press "series," for example, but they are in effect just editorial and publicity frameworks, not actual publication formats. The monographs in them are all issued and cataloged as separate books. But particularly in the late nineteenth and early twentieth century, many universities issued series: The *Johns Hopkins University Studies in Historical and Political Science* and so on. These consisted of published dissertations (dissertations had to be published in those days) which may or (more likely) may not be cataloged individually in a university's catalog. Where there is one volume for each monograph, catalogers may have treated them as separate volumes. More commonly, however, they are cataloged as series without any internal listing of contents.

There are a number of strategies for finding such things, which can be a very rich resource indeed. One of them is to surf to the catalog of a library that (like Chicago) cataloged most series as individual documents but located them under the general series call number. For example, *Admission to American Trade Unions*, by French Wolfe in 1912, is a book that provides a magnificent cross-sectional portrait of American unionism. In the Chicago catalog, it has its own author and title records, but carries the call number of the Johns Hopkins series above (H31.J6) and the designation "ser. 30, no. 3." By using the Chicago catalog, you can at least see the contents of these old series. It may turn out that your own library has the series but never bothered to catalog the internal items. Given the huge amount of publishing done in series in the first part of the twentieth century, it can be worth going to another library's online catalog to locate such materials. That's one of the wonderful things about the current digital environment: you can use other university's catalogs.

Otherwise, the usual way you will encounter series items is in other people's bibliographies or in handbooks or specialized bibliographical reference works that explicitly aim to comb such literatures. (Literary studies has the *Annual Bibliography of English Language and Literature*, for example, which has routinely cataloged series volumes.) Then your problem is simply to figure out how your university chose to locate the series volumes (some locate them as alphabetized serial publications and others locate them by call number). Once you discover that, you've got your item.

Here let me break frame and insert a salutary story. It turns out that there *is* a universal index to series. After I had written the preceding paragraphs and while the copyeditor was working on the production of this book, I was working on another project and discovered something called *Books in Series, 1876–1949*, from R. R. Bowker Company (1982). It has complete indexes by author, title, subject, and series. This last-minute discovery just goes to show that we're all always learning new tricks, and, more important, that the print era produced nearly every reference tool imaginable.

Back to business: Beyond books, articles, and series, materials can be very hard to find, because libraries' practices vary widely. For things like maps, films, CDs, DVDs, and other such materials, your university is likely to have a special staff member who will guide you.

5. Quality

In a library research project, all primary materials are equally useful to you. As long as they are relevant to your question, issues of quality do not arise. With secondary materials, however, it is quite different. As you know well already, there is a lot of bad material to be found online. The print world has somewhat more stringent standards and some of them are formally enforced. But probably the more important difference is that there are money costs to publishing in print, and this fact dissuades a large group of less serious authors. Yet despite the standards and the costs, print libraries also contain plenty of weak material. You must therefore learn to assess quality in both digital and physical environments. To do so, you need to understand how secondary material is produced and finds it way online or into the stacks.

The organization of the online world is obvious enough. Anybody can create a website about anything, and the giant search engines will return a list of websites using any set of keywords you specify. That list will be ordered according to a relevance ranking, which, as I just noted, does not indicate quality but is more like a popularity contest. As you will recall from high school, sometimes such contests really do pick out the best or most interesting or most likely to succeed. More often they just pick out the centrally located people. So search engine rankings are not reliable guides to quality. Neither are claims of authority. Many sites on the Internet of course claim to have more authority or greater quality than others, but there is no general or authoritative way to judge these claims. As a result, most of us troll the Internet using simple heuristics like ".gov websites are probably more authoritative than .com websites" or "self-interested websites are less reliable than disinterested ones" or "organizations I have heard of have more trustworthy sites than organizations of which I am unaware." But the reality is that none of us really has a solid way to judge authority or quality online, and at the same time there is no threshold of quality that must be met to publish online.

The print world, by contrast, has longstanding systems for maintaining authority and quality. In many cases, these systems have in effect migrated online as the materials they produce have migrated online. And the print world has a subset—academic knowledge—that is formally organized to produce relatively high-quality and authoritative knowledge. Academic knowledge is generated by communities of scholars who share concepts of rigor and who submit their work to the judgment of peers. So you can assume that any book from a university press has been "peer-reviewed" in this manner. You can also assume that any article in an academic journal has been peer-reviewed. (You can tell an academic journal by its list of "consulting editors" or "advisory editors": these are the more active reviewers. Another sign is that academic journals have few or no advertisements.) And the vast majority of online academic material (everything in JSTOR, for example) has been peer-reviewed.

By contrast, articles in nonacademic periodicals, as well as books from commercial publishers, have generally not been peer-reviewed in the formal sense, although of course such items will have had other kinds of review, appropriate to their ultimate use, and may have seen peer review as well. It follows that, in general, articles in nonacademic journals and books from commercial publishers are less trustworthy and of lower quality than the articles in academic journals and the books from university presses.

The process of peer review is simple—I'll use the journal case as an example. An author sends a possible paper to a journal's editor. The editor selects three or four relevant peers to read and judge it. Typically, he will choose one or two of the journal's consulting editors plus some others. These reviewers send their private judgments to the editor, along with more extensive and particular comments for the author. The editor then reads the paper, as well as the referee comments, and makes a judgment. The judgment is then sent to the author, along with the detailed author advice from the reviewers. In peer-reviewing, the author never knows who the reviewers are. The reverse is not necessarily true. In the "single-blind" system of peer review, the reviewers know the author. In the "double-blind" system, they do not.

In the humanities and social sciences, most papers are turned down, as are most books proposed to university presses. Not surprisingly, the most prestigious journals and presses have the highest turndown rates (approaching 90 percent). Knowing this, authors generally send their work as high in the prestige system as they think reasonable, but often end up publishing in a lower-tier journal than the journal to which they first submitted.

The peer-review system is far from perfect. There's a lot of randomness in the choice of "peers" to do the reviewing, and editors can sometimes be arbitrary. But it's far ahead of having no quality judgment other than a popularity contest among an unspecified population. So you are well advised to use the information produced by the peer-review system and the academic prestige structure that it both sustains and enforces. (We'll return to the topic of popularity contests when we discuss citation rankings in chapter 4—they're the academic equivalent of relevance rankings online.)

Exasperation with peer review—particularly with the fact that it can mean waiting a long time for reviews and eventual publication—has led to various forms of temporary publication. Working paper series are common in some fields (economics, for example). And several online forums have emerged for such work-in-progress (Social Science Research Network, for example). None of this material is formally peer-reviewed. The papers that appear in such places are therefore self-published. To be sure, the fact that this self-publishing is by licensed academics does create an implicit suggestion that it is more likely to be high-quality than is self-published material by nonacademics. But it needs always to be recalled that working paper series, papers deposited with humanities and social science research amalgamators, blogs, personal websites, and so on generally contain material that has not seen peer review. So you should be careful with it. In the book trade, self-published books (which are quite costly to the author) are said to be "vanity-published." The name indicates what scholars think of them.

In summary, there are very serious differences of quality in the secondary material available to you, whether online or in the library. There is no general guide to quality in secondary materials online. But for physical materials (and such physical materials as have migrated online), there are distinct markers of quality. First of all, there is the definitive marker of peer review. Second, there is a loose prestige hierarchy of journals and to a lesser extent of publishing houses. These hierarchies are not by any means sharply defined, and they vary by scholarly subareas. But as a novice scholar, you should take every advantage of these quality indicators when you can. The most obvious rule of thumb is not to bother with any secondary materials that are not peer-reviewed. The only exceptions are those occasional "crossover" academic books which so combine scholarship and popular appeal that they are published by trade publishers: Robert Putnam's *Bowling Alone*, for example. Such books will be quite obvious, when they exist. But other than that, sticking with peer-reviewed material is the best choice for a researcher just starting out.

THESE THEN ARE THE FUNDAMENTALS OF IDENTIFICATION AND location, the true nitty-gritty. To go back to the travel metaphor, we've packed the backpack. Now it's time to buy an open ticket, get on the train, and start thinking about where we might want to go. In library research terms, you have to know what you are looking for, if you are going to have things to locate. And figuring out what to look for is the real subject of this book. So let us turn to the preliminary phase of true library research.

4

The Preliminary Phase

As I noted earlier, library research means doing many things in parallel. So in this preliminary chapter, there are sections on design, bibliography, scanning/browsing, reading, and files. You must start all these things at the same time. But each of these sections will later have a full chapter expanding the discussion here and showing how these aspects of the project change in the midphase.

1. Design

Research design consists of four things. The first are the puzzles, which set the agenda. The second is the conceptualization, which specifies the situation that you are researching. Third are the research questions, which address the puzzles for your particular situation. Last is the your program of research, the "action list." This list comprises the research activities that—if you perform them—will find the things you need to answer the research questions, which in turn resolve the empirical puzzle, which in turn solves the theoretical puzzle and therefore provides the payoff that justifies the research.

A. PUZZLES

Let's begin with puzzles. A library research project is seldom of the form "What exactly happened in, at, or during a given time period, place, event, etc." Quite aside from whether such decontextualized description is possible, it is an uncommon aim in library research. Rather, every library research project has at its heart not one but two puzzles. One of these is empirical, the other theoretical. The empirical puzzle is always of the form "Why should it be (or have been) that blah-blah-blah?" The theoretical puzzle is an abstract question or questions that we can judge, test, clarify, or advance by solving the empirical puzzle. Of course, any given empirical puzzle bears on several theoretical puzzles and vice versa. But you will have a particular pairing.

Empirical puzzles are often easy to focus: "Even though psychiatry started as the profession of mental hospital superintendents in the 1880s, there were almost no psychiatrists working in mental hospitals by the mid-twentieth century. Why?" (That was the empirical puzzle of my PhD dissertation.) The theoretical puzzles are often harder. After all, why does it matter that psychiatrists deserted the mental hospitals? The best way to find your theoretical puzzle is to ask: "To what question is study of my empirical puzzle the (or an) answer?" or "What broader issue will my study enlighten?" or "What is my empirical puzzle (my case) a case *of*?"

For most undergraduates and beginning graduate students, finding theoretical puzzles is the hardest part of research. Yet you must always have a theoretical puzzle, because it is the alternative theoretical accounts of your empirical situation that specify what you need to find out. For example, if psychiatrists are pushed out of mental hospitals by bad working conditions, then the hospitals with bad conditions should empty first, but if they are pulled out by attractive communities of fellow specialists in large cities, then hospitals near those cities should empty first. To know whether push or pull factors were stronger one has to research both working conditions and communities of specialists.

If you have only an empirical puzzle, you can just go on and on doing research about it. But if you develop theoretical puzzles, you get more specific research questions. One theory thinks the empirical puzzle is explained by one set of things, the other by another. Your actual research questions are thus provided by the list of things necessary to evaluate the alternative theories.

Sometimes, we have merely implicit alternative theories, as in the paper whose writing was described in chapter 2. In that paper, I began with a purely descriptive task: what was the history of reference tools? But central theoretical questions soon emerged: why did faculty do research the way they did? (In particular, why did they not use the indexing tools and central resources that the librarians thought were so important?) The descriptive paper thus became gradually reorganized around a theoretical issue, and ultimately around the professional warfare between scholars and librarians over whose concept of research was preferable and why.

Beginning researchers will find it best to have two real alternatives from the start. Otherwise the temptation to fall back into pure description or mere illustration is too great, as in "A Bourdieusian Interpretation of American College Classes in the 1950s." A researcher is not in the business of simply putting someone's labels on some new situation. He or she is posing empirical puzzles and advancing theory by answering them. The theory does not have to be elaborate or fancy. Don't worry about that. Just have two real alternatives. It's no good doing a paper about gender relations in twentieth-century retail stores if you know ahead of time that patriarchy is the thing that makes the situation the way it is. If you know that ahead of time, the data are merely illustrative, and there's no point—other than aesthetic—in retrieving them. Rather, one should test patriarchy against age or education or something like that. Then if it wins, it wins over a real opponent, not a shadow.

In short, do not start on a project, even one that seems very, very interesting, without having a sense of what is peculiar, what is worth studying, what is consequential or important, about the case or situation or data you are studying. Your theoretical puzzle is your guarantee that the project can be finished; it will be over when you've answered the theoretical question.

On the other hand, at the outset your puzzles should not be (and in fact will not be) tightly specified. As we have seen, most library projects are shaped by data, both by unforeseen constraints in data availability and by discoveries in the data itself. So it is not good to have a puzzle that is too closely specified too early. Remember, too, that the puzzle isn't waiting somewhere to be discovered. It is something you see in the social world. You are making a picture out of random jigsaw pieces. And there is no picture, ahead of time, on the box. (There is more about puzzles in chapter 11.)

B. CONCEPTUALIZATION

Once you understand that something is puzzling, you need to create for yourself an analytic description of the social situation surrounding that puzzle. This is more or less a newspaper reporter's "who, what, when, where, and how." ("Why" is so important that it gets separate billing as the puzzle itself.) This conceptualization of the situation will change gradually as you work. Things that didn't seem relevant become important, while what at first seemed important may fade. You need to be self-conscious about these changes, rethinking your conceptual model of your research object from time to time throughout the project. But most important, you must be clear about that object at the beginning. There are five basic questions to ask.

First, who are the actors in your setting, your dramatis personae? You just need to list them. Some of them will be particular individuals, some will be types of individuals, some will be organizations. Watch out for various kinds of reification. Suppose you are writing about the history of babysitting. "Babysitters" are not really a conscious group like a church or a company; they're simply a category of workers. And the overwhelming majority of babysitting is done by two demographic categories—girls in their teens and grandmothers. So you have to think about "teenage girls" as among your dramatis personae, but also introduce grandmothers as another important category. Note that organizations—in this case, private day cares, crèches, and employers' day-care services—may be important actors also.

Second, what are your actors doing? What are their routine activities? Some of these will be relevant, some not. With the rise of grandparent child care, one crucial action might be geographic mobility (a huge proportion of Americans end up settling near their parents, which helps child care), but you also have to think about routine activities. What kinds of babysitting do grandparents actually do—is it for parents' "big night out," or for a week off here and there, or just covering day to day?

Third, you need to think about the "whens" of your situation, from daily and weekly rhythms to major historical events. In a study of the history of babysitting, the move of mothers into the labor force is obviously important, but so also is the rapidly changing communications technology that allows caregivers to contact parents anywhere, anytime. Whether you are doing historical work or not, there is always a complex temporal structure to what you study. Be clear about it from the start.

Fourth, you need to think about scenes and settings, about "where." The history of babysitting has become a story about in-home versus out-of-home, about geography. Often a situation concerns multiple geographies. My dissertation on psychiatrists involved the geographies of the state mental hospital systems, of the states themselves, and of the large cities with their elaborate medical establishments. There are many levels and scales to whereness.

Finally, how do your actors understand what they are doing, and what are their symbols and images and ideologies? This last question does not involve the way *you* think about the situation, but the way that *they* think about it. Do they have special languages for it? Do they record their thoughts and feelings about it? What are their general approaches—formal and informal, linguistic and pictorial? What are their slang and their rituals? Obviously, you will not understand all of these things at the beginning. But by posing this question early you provide yourself with a list of sources to check. Those whom you study are one of your most important sources, and you cannot study them without understanding how they think of themselves.

Once you figure out some answers to these five questions, you have a basis for moving ahead in the project. You will be changing those answers throughout the project: amending, refocusing, and shifting them. But the answers that you create at the beginning will probably end up providing the first structure for the analytic files you create. They thus profoundly shape your final product.

C. RESEARCH QUESTIONS

The puzzles and the conceptualization combine to produce some focused things called research questions. These are the questions you must answer from the data to solve the empirical puzzle and make in turn an advance on the theoretical puzzle. Like the puzzles, these research questions will become more and more focused as you go along. The typical dissertation might have three big empirical puzzles and three to five general research questions flowing out of each one. An MA paper—typically around thirty to forty pages—is going to have one big empirical puzzle and three or four general research questions.

Here are three setups (with one example of a research question for each) from my recent classes.

Project A

Empirical Puzzle: Why is it that despite the fact that the famous pragmatist philosopher George Herbert Mead published dozens of professional articles in his lifetime, his current reputation rests almost entirely on a posthumous book made up by combining two sets of lecture notes from his courses?

Theoretical Puzzle: Do scholars shape their legacy by what they actually write, or is it shaped for them by their successors?

Research Question: What was the order of presentation of concepts in Mead's lectures year after year? Did it change? If so, how and when?

Project B

Empirical Puzzle: Why were different kinds of rules used to act against prostitution and drug use in Thailand, and in particular why was the AIDS crisis addressed by rules about condoms but not about brothels?

Theoretical Puzzle: Does the making of different kinds of activities into "social ills" reflect different kinds of state-making?

Research Question: How and by whom was enforcement of rules about condom use in Thai brothels actually accomplished?

Project C
Empirical Puzzle: Given that the Committee for the Comparative Study of New Nations at the University of Chicago (CNN) seems to have been a major force in the lives of its participants, many of whom became quite famous, why is it invisible in historical writing about academia in the 1960s?

Theoretical Puzzle: Are there kinds of intellectual entities that are not schools or paradigms or institutes? What might they be?

Research Question: How did the CNN present itself to the university, to potential funders, and to the academic community at large?

Each one of these questions specifies a bunch of actual research to be done: going to the university archives on G. H. Mead and listing the order of a certain set of concepts; going to Thai sources and figuring out how enforcement actually worked; going to archives, writings, and biographies and finding out what the CNN said about itself. When those tasks are done, we know these researchers will be able to answer part of their empirical and theoretical puzzles, because they'll have successfully answered one of the research questions flowing directly from those puzzles. That's the task of research design: to take the puzzles and the conceptualization and turn them into a list of researchable questions. Of course they will change. About half of my students' PhD dissertations have finished with research questions quite different from those with which they began. That's the nature of research. As it turned out, the first and third projects above grew smoothly into major papers. The second project changed completely, partly for want of data, but mostly because the other "social ill" investigated—opium—proved so much more rewarding vis-à-vis the main theoretical question that the student switched her dissertation topic almost completely.

Despite such changes, however, you must at any *given* time have clear research questions. Otherwise, you just drift. Your list of research questions will not be very specific at first. But you should try to make it specific as early as possible. You must continually work with it, improve it, and focus it, or you will become lost in details.

For every general research question, you should have four or five specific research questions. This distinction between general and specific questions is important but not obvious. In the examples above, the question about the order of certain concepts in Mead's lectures is a pretty specific question. It's likely to be one part of a more general (and in this case descriptive) research question: "How did Mead's lectures change over time?" One could look at content, order of terms, types of examples, and so forth. But the second research question mentioned above—about enforcement of condom use—is actually a quite general one. It needs to be broken down into subquestions involving the possible enforcers, the types of data bearing on enforcement, and the specific arrays of data that could answer this question. There are likely to be several different pathways of enforcement, and the data on them may be in quite different places. So they must be listed as separable questions and hence separate tasks, or they won't get done. The third research question above is also fairly general. For one thing, it involves three quite different audiences for the Committee's public presentation: the university, potential funders, and the academic community at large. And there will have been several different avenues of communication for each. That means this is a general research question, which needs to be further specified into researchable subquestions.

As these examples make clear, getting the general research questions can seem easy. In fact, it is all too easy to come up with vague and useless general research questions (e.g., "How did the Committee on New Nations present itself?"). If a research question doesn't tell you what to do tomorrow when you enter the library or go online, it is not specific enough. Turning the general research questions into specific ones is therefore the crucial task of early design. As you do a library project, you need to evaluate your progress on your specific research questions all the time, every week.

This is why you must always maintain a design folder. It keeps the project on track intellectually. Otherwise you can end up doing weeks and weeks of "research" and end up simply having found out a lot of interesting stuff, but being no closer to a written paper than when you started. This is the single most common problem with both graduate and undergraduate library research projects.

D. ACTION LISTS

The action list is the current to-do list. It follows immediately from the empirical and theoretical puzzles, the conceptualizations, and the general and specific research questions. The specific research questions should bring you pretty close to particular things to do. But library research is not a linear process. Thus the task list itself must be a fluctuating thing. Any task on it may advance several specific research questions at once. As you move into the midphase, action lists are dominated by what I earlier called minianalyses: studies of particular topics that will become paragraphs and pages of the final result. But in the preliminary phase, the action list simply sketches the tasks that will enable you to settle the design document. Chief among these are preliminary bibliography, early scanning and browsing, and file design.

All this means that you will inevitably find yourself going over things—sources, bibliographical tools, copied material—more than once. This is not inefficient; to the contrary, it is very useful. In the second and third passes you will be looking for different things because you have more new ideas in your head to associate with what you are reading. Efficiency is not an advantage in library research. In fact, it restricts the browsing and multitasking on which library research thrives.

At any given time in the project, there must be a design document containing the current versions of your empirical and theoretical puzzles, your conceptualization, your general and specific research questions, and a current action or to-do list. In the preliminary phase, this design document will change rapidly. For an article, chapter, or paper, it will take about five iterations, over as many weeks, to shape it into a document that can see you through midphase. For a larger project, such a design document—in effect a dissertation proposal—will require a couple of months and several rounds of feedback from advisors.

In midphase, you will revisit this document on a regular basis—every couple of weeks for a major paper, every month in a longer project. (Chapter 11 will take up this review in detail.) You must continually update the design document so that it corresponds with where the research has taken you, and so that its plans for the future are plans relevant to that new position, not to the old paper that you may have originally planned.

Not until endphase does your project escape from the design document. At that point, the emerging written text takes over project control. You will then reenter the world of linear argument. Until then, you will be in the nonlinear world of library research.

2. Preliminary Bibliography

In preliminary bibliography you orient yourself. Having begun to conceptualize the situation (above, section 1.B), now you seek basic descriptions of it.

A. OVERVIEWS AND REFERENCE TOOLS

Overviews are a reasonable way to get started, both at the beginning of a project and in the midphase when some subproject brings you to an area you don't know well.

The key to overviews is always the ALA *Guide to Reference Books*. Since this tool exists in a constantly updated online version as well a dated print edition of 1996, this is perhaps as good a place as any to say something about physical versus digital with respect to reference tools. I myself switch between physical and digital resources on the criteria of speed and quality. In general, print versions of reference tools are much faster to use, if they exist. The physical document "refresh time" (the physical version of "refreshing" is page-turning) is much faster than the refresh time online. Also better is the amount and organization of the material you see accidentally while finding what actually interests you. The density of things on a single page—far greater than that online—makes it much faster to scan through large numbers of sources. (Online sources are often heavy with chartjunk: meaningless or redundant information, ostensibly for reader convenience, but in practice requiring so much scrolling as to slow your scanning to a crawl.)

These rules about physical and digital apply to the ALA *Guide* as well as to other reference tools. I personally find the print version both faster and more informative. (It's dated, but most of the enduringly important reference tools were already in existence in 1996.) Moreover, if your topic is any distance in the past, the old print guides are especially useful because they contain past tools that were removed from the *Guide* as time passed. (Later generations produce—and use—new tools that do not necessarily duplicate all past information.) This steady pruning occurs both online and in the successive print editions. For example, there exist detailed by-author indexes to all the fictional characters in English literature. But these disappeared from the *Guide* in the 1970s. Yet of course if you happen to need an index to characters in English literature (the equivalent of the Internet Movie Database), those are all still sitting on the shelves somewhere. So it can often be worthwhile to use the earlier print versions of the ALA *Guide* as well as the online one. (You can even check out an old print edition and have it all to yourself.) As noted earlier, Robert Balay edited the last print version, in 1996. Just glance through its listings for your topic area. For any topic, a reference tool or tools exist that can vastly accelerate your research, and the ALA *Guide* will locate that tool for you.

Given that most overviews will be found either in encyclopedias or in handbooks, you can also use a good library catalog to search for overview reference works. Just use advanced keyword search in the catalog's subject index, specifying your subject and adding a search term for the following specialized subtopics: *encyclopedias, handbooks, directories*. (These words should appear in the subject field, since they are part of the LC subject classification.) But remember that books are cataloged as specifically as they can be within the LC system. Often, therefore, the most useful general reference source for you is not at the level of specificity where you begin in the catalog, but well above it. The best overview of the medical profession, for example, may well be in a book on professions in general (because a review in a general source will be shorter and more succinct). But such a book will be cataloged under *professions*, not *physicians*.

There are online tools for general reference. As of this writing, Reference Universe and Oxford Reference Online seem to be the best of these. The first is a tool to find tools. But its interface is awkward; the online ALA *Guide* is clearly better. The second is a metacrawler that sits atop the vast body of reference material published by the Oxford University Press (OUP), which has long been one of the major publishers of print reference tools. That the interface is full of irrelevant chartjunk is a problem you are probably used to. And to the extent that the things "crawled" are older print tools, the tool is a good one. So Oxford Reference Online can be useful. But to the extent that it points you to online and newly published print tools you face more general problems that exist with such tools.

To understand the problems with newer and online reference tools, it's helpful to examine the new economics of libraries. In the twentieth-century print era, publishers and librarians were a sleepy and conservative lot, and the indexing market was dominated by the quiet and beneficent monopolist H. W. Wilson, Inc. By contrast, there is now intensive competition between publishers, aggregators of journals and subscriptions, and providers of online reference and indexing services like EBSCO. This competition has had large effects on scholarship, but particularly malevolent effects on reference tools and overviews. Because the main problem in modern research is overload, overviews are very big business. Vendors have very strong and for our purposes problematic incentives. The first incentive is to subdivide the areas overviewed. This segments the market (providing more sales), but thereby reduces the utility of the tools. (As of this writing, there are in fact 401 Oxford

University Press books in my library's catalog with the words "Oxford Handbook of" in their titles.) The second incentive is to skimp on quality. Metacrawlers and new reference works actually contain much low-quality work. The unsigned articles are never written by senior experts. Graduate students write many of the smaller articles (and even some of the larger ones). This is because there is no professional reward for writing such review pieces, so real experts write overview and handbook pieces only if the article requested is a long one, if its location allows serious influence (a major handbook by a high-prestige publisher), and, most important, if it is signed. The third perverse incentive is the temptation to refer only to other tools of the same publisher, even if another publisher's tools are preferable or better for a given purpose. In sum, there are real problems with many current reference tools; they are driven by markets, not knowledge. So be careful where you look for overviews.

I should point out that similar problems are endemic elsewhere in modern knowledge; the publishers are not the only culprits. For example, many an academic journal is now requiring authors to refer to other articles published in that journal, merely so it can raise its "impact factor" (a citation measure) in the WoS databases, and in turn raise its subscription fees and profits. Or again, when Sage Publications briefly owned *Sociological Abstracts*—which indexes all sociology journals—they apparently changed the "Easy Print" facility in that tool so that it worked only for Sage journals! It wouldn't print journals from other publishers. I found this restriction by accident one day and informed my librarians. They in turn informed CSA, the firm that had acquired *Sociological Abstracts* when Sage had wanted to sell it. It turned out that the new owners had no idea that this restriction existed in the software, even though they had owned it for two years.

All of this means that if you can find and use tools from not-for-profit operations like ALA, JSTOR, and OCLC, you can always assume that because of the deformations induced by the profit motive, those tools are preferable, other things being equal.

On Wikipedia, there are strong and divergent opinions. It is rapidly becoming a more centralized and authoritative work. Some of the more important articles are now "locked" (the article on the sun, for example) so they can't be trashed. On the other hand, so central an article as that on Bayes's theorem featured an edit (last time I looked) saying "fixed a few formulas that were not displaying; don't know if they are correct." That's not very comforting. As for articles in two of my own areas of expertise, a recent glance shows that the article on William Isaac Thomas contains numerous minor errors and omits crucial bibliography, while the article on professions is so interesting in its weakness that I once wrote an article about it ("Varieties of Ignorance" in the periodical *American Sociologist*). Overall, Wikipedia is useful for a first pass at something, a quick orientation, or a reminder if you have forgotten something. But for nothing more. Its average quality is well below that of the print encyclopedias it replaces.

A final concern with all online and some print overviews is migration, which caused the Sage/CSA snafu I just mentioned. The commercial "information providers" have an enormous incentive to import material of unknown provenance and to migrate old material forward without editing or revetting. Even the free tools are subject to this pressure: now that the monumental eleventh edition of the *Encyclopaedia Britannica* is out of copyright, large portions of it have been imported into Wikipedia without further ado. It was a magnificent reference work to be sure, but it is very dated, particularly in its historical discussions.

With for-profit sources, the pressures are greater. The last time I checked (July 2013), the article in the online *Encyclopaedia Britannica* on sociology was by R. E. L. Faris, who trained in the 1920s and died in 1998, and William Form, who trained in the 1940s and is no longer active, although still alive. It was a fine article for its day, but internal evidence suggests that that day was some time ago—probably the 1960s or 1970s, with a few citations added in the 1980s and 1990s. The article is certainly not a viable overview of sociology today.

Reference works and overviews are full of such migrated information. For many years during the print era, the *Encyclopedia of Associations* simply republished old information on organizations if they had received no new information in a given year, a practice they now claim to have stopped. But all that erroneous information is out there in the print versions and probably will soon be digitized and widely available. Needless to say, no one is going to go back and correct it.

As consumers, we have little defense against such migration errors. But make it a habit to check the provenance of the information you use, particularly online. You will discover that most online reference sources make that provenance very hard to find, and that once found, it turns out to be much less solid than the site's claims and appearances make it seem.

At the end of the day, therefore, there is no question that the best overview source for most subjects will be a recently issued handbook from a good publisher with an editor at a relatively well-known university, at least half of whose articles are written by scholars at similarly well-known universities. Handbooks always have contributor biographies, so it is very easy to check on these things. If you have doubts, ask your advisor for a judgment.

If you cannot find an excellent handbook, you have to turn to the periodical literature. In most of the humanities and social sciences, the "review article" format does not exist. There are to be sure annual reviews for the various disciplines, but their contents are uneven. They do not continuously go over the major areas of a field, since the size constraints on articles permit only cursory reviews of an area of any substantial extent. So the articles are often a little quixotic. Nonetheless, annual review volumes are always worth checking; they do have good pieces.

After all this depressing news, it is a pleasure to say that there is a quite straightforward way to find the core peer-reviewed articles of a field. This is what chapter 1 called the needle shop, your way to avoid the haystack of Google. This technique starts with a basic word central to your research. Suppose you are studying a social movement. You want current reviews of that area. You use "social movements" as a topic search string in WoS, constraining your search to the past ten years because you want a current review. You rank the results by level of citation, putting the most-cited articles first. As of July 2013 you got 9,196 studies. That's too many! So restrict (*refine* is the word in WoS) the list to your field—let's suppose it is political science. There are now 848 pieces, and the second-most cited one is a review by Paul Burstein of the impact of public opinion on policy—a topic dead center in social movement studies. The reference list of Burstein's article will produce other important studies (at this point in your project, "highly cited" can proxy for "important"), and the list of articles that cite Burstein will produce more highly cited pieces. Suppose you were a sociologist. You would restrict the list to the 1,844 sociology articles, which, in my view, is still too many and too unfocused. So I would go back and insist on "social movements" in the title, not just topic (topic means anywhere in the title, abstract, etc.). This is only 1,167 articles, not 9,196, and the sociology restriction limits it to 399. The third of these is a general theory of social movements (by Elizabeth Armstrong and Mary Bernstein). It turns out that this paper starts with a short review of the whole field.

Two minor caveats. Do not restrict the "type of material" to *reviews* in your WoS search. In WoS, *reviews* usually means book reviews. Also, in general do not search for articles with the word *review* in them, unless you're a psychologist. Most humanities and social science overview articles do not use that word. On the other hand, if you have too many articles in your list, then by all means use the requirement of the word *review* in the title as a way to thin things down. The central point is that it is absolutely certain that any important scholarly area has recent reviews and summaries in the periodical literature. You find them by knowing that they tend to be highly cited. The citation level will identify a universe of important articles; you then choose the best-looking among them in terms of their titles and promise of further information, and use their reference lists and footnotes as your guide to further work. Given the current state of the reference world, you should employ this citation strategy quite early in your project.

In summary, there still are distinguished overviews and reference works available, even if they are hard to find among the junk. It is worth looking for two or three of them. As I have noted, the ALA *Guide* is always the place to start your search; you just need to vet the sources you find there, checking the contributors' biographies and current positions. But use the WoS citation strategy to identify current and influential articles. (For reasons I'll explain shortly WoS is preferable to Google Scholar for this task.)

B. BIBLIOGRAPHY PROPER

You should begin a preliminary bibliography on your topic at once. You will be adding to it throughout the project and you will also be removing things from it throughout the project. (But don't throw things too far; I generally keep rejected bibliography in a file somewhere. Otherwise, you can find yourself rediscovering the same old blind alleys.)

For the starting bibliography, for a thirty-to-forty-page (MA-sized) project, you are aiming at something like ten books and twenty or thirty articles, all of high quality. This will at least get you oriented in the literatures related to your topic. Eventually, you will have two or three times this much material in your bibliography.

You are aiming for quality, not quantity. This means that you should rely most on bibliographical tools that have quality controls built into them. For example, your own university's catalog is better than WorldCat, simply because the acquisitions bibliographers in your library will have made quality judgments in choosing what appears in it. The material your school owns is likely to be better in quality, more important in substance, and more widely used in practice than the material it does not own. That's why that material was bought.

Another key to quality judgment is duplication. A source that shows up in many places is likely to be better than one that does not. This is all the more true if the places it shows up are themselves of high quality; first-rate journals, books from good university presses, and so on. (I will discuss how to identify those things shortly.) Remember that the democracy of knowledge lies in the fact that everyone can publish; there is no democratic right to have your publications admired. Although there are exceptions, it is roughly true that the more widely cited and discussed a source, the more important it is relative to other work of the same kind. And importance is for your purposes an acceptable approximation to quality. As the project progresses, you will form your own more specific quality judgments. But in the preliminary phase, you should assume that broad visibility indicates importance.

(i) Where to Look for Preliminary Materials

The place to start your search for preliminary materials is your home university library catalog. Now that you can easily use any online catalog in the US, the truly sophisticated might choose a relatively small library—250,000 volumes, say—for their initial bibliographical search, because its quality selection will be sharper than at a place with many millions of items. But you may also want to go to a large library online catalog, check the relevant subject listings, and look specifically for anything listed with the word *bibliography* after it. As I have noted, these are items that may already have done your work for you.

With luck, a catalog search will find you a couple of books that can serve as an entry to the entire area. Because books (particularly good books) are written by smart authors who have spent a lot of time on their subjects, they can give you far better guidance into a topic than anything you can produce for yourself. A central aim in preliminary bibliography is to find such crucial books. They will themselves have long bibliographies, perhaps even bibliographical notes. Be sure also to look at the index of such a work; you can identify the major authors in the field by their long entries in the index of a serious overview.

After the catalog, your next recourse is basic periodical indexes. Most students begin with Google Scholar or JSTOR. The quality structure of the former is bad. It is built on the same voting-structure analysis of relevance as the Google indexes generally. But because the algorithm ranks a given source by its level of citation in widely dispersed literatures, it tends to emphasize the citation opinions of the biggest literatures. But these big literatures may not be the ones in which you are interested, and so their ratings of sources may be irrelevant or even wrong for you. The problem is exacerbated by the fact that Google Scholar cruises websites as well as peer-reviewed literatures, which weakens its quality judgments considerably from the start, because websites are not peer-reviewed (WoS citation rankings are overwhelmingly based on peer-reviewed material). The lesson is simple: don't use Google Scholar.

Preferable to Google Scholar is JSTOR, since it contains only the cream of the academic crop (although that too is declining as JSTOR admits more and more journals—it began with the highest-quality sources). JSTOR is particularly useful because it contains the articles themselves: it is both an index and a collection of the material indexed. Moreover, it is nonprofit, and hence has no particular axes to grind.

Although for cutting-edge scholars JSTOR's coverage can sometimes be a problem, for the vast majority of students, JSTOR's limits are an advantage. An article in JSTOR is much more likely to be important than an article on a comparable subject that is not in JSTOR. You should use JSTOR to find the major articles you need to get started. Then you can use the reference lists of those articles to find anything you might need outside JSTOR.

But JSTOR lacks any measure of importance or impact. For this, one must use WoS. I myself therefore do most of my bibliographical work in WoS, usually adding one specialty-area index. For me this is often *Historical Abstracts* or the American equivalent (*America: History and Life*), because of my research areas and periods. (In my studies of library scholarship I used *Library Literature* instead.) But you might be using *Art Abstracts* or something else depending on your topic of interest. WoS is a very broad tool, covering all the literature you could possibly want to see, while the specialty index will focus you on immediately relevant things. The utility of always having WoS in the background is that you can use its citation ordering facility to produce rough quality judgments, which are especially useful early in the research process. WoS also has considerable historical depth (mid-1970s) at this point. Remember to select out the natural science portion of the database before using it. (Select only the humanities [AHCI] and social sciences [SSCI] citation indexes.) Otherwise, there will be a lot of needless stuff.

Finally, virtually every topic in the world has had a dissertation written about it, and you can find them easily. The basic tool here is *Dissertation Abstracts*, now online as part of the ProQuest system. But don't read all the way through somebody else's thesis early in a project. It will make you certain that your project has already been done! Nonetheless, feel free to pillage any dissertation's bibliography.

Do not go to WorldCat early in a project. Anything you want in the preliminary phase will be at your local university library, which will have a friendlier and better index. Moreover, you can physically browse the shelves near the material you locate. WorldCat has a high junk-to-quality ratio, a weak indexing system, and a truculent interface. Moreover, a surprising amount of the library information in it is wrong, as you will find out if you try to rely on it. It's a useful tool, but only for long shots, alternative editions, and the like. Use it later in the project.

(ii) Bibliography Rules of Thumb

Often, someone has already done the bibliography for you. The trick is to find that somebody. One approach is to search the heading "bibliography of bibliographies" in the ALA *Guide* (and the *Guide* also has "bibliography" subsections for hundreds of its topics). If the topic you are studying antedates the Second World War, you can consult the amazing print tool *A World Bibliography of Bibliographies* from 1940 (the last version was in the mid-1960s). In the old print version of the ALA *Guide*, you will find far more subdivided (and therefore faster) classification of the "bibliography of bibliographies" heading than is available online. This is yet another case where online is slower. Note finally that detailed bibliographies used to be routine assignments in library schools, and your library's stacks for the call numbers above Z5051 are probably filled with useful bibliographies on every topic under the sun.

Doing bibliography involves multiple sources. Because of this you should expect to go to the library to do it, especially after the initial stages. Even at the start, you will probably need to look at books to see if they are actually worth reading. Google Books does not contain enough information for you to make this judgment sensibly; you can judge a book far more quickly if you are holding it in your hand than if you are laboriously paging through it on screen. Probably more important, cruising the shelves enables you to combine locating sources with judging their quality, since you can scan a range of books far more quickly as physical artifacts than onscreen. A worn binding means an important book. A famous colophon on the spine means high quality. A huge thick volume means unnecessary detail. More generally, once you are really moving ahead in a project, you must work in the library itself, because bibliographical chains will bounce in and out of the print materials, and you can't afford to wait till you get to the library to follow a chain. You have to keep swinging along.

Note that you will not at first actually read most of the things you find. Read them only enough to find new directions to move in. But by moving through lots of sources quickly you will also be gradually filling your head with the terms, the names, the concepts, and the issues that dominate your literature. Just let them become familiar faces. Then they can serve as attractor points for further browsing.

In the end, you will look at three to four times as much material as you need in order to find a given number of sources listed above. You need to have looked at forty books to find ten good ones, a hundred articles to find twenty-five good ones. They're not all going to be locatable in the same indexes. It is a good, not a bad, thing to use multiple indexes. All indexes—print and electronic—have their peculiarities and lacunae. Multiple searches make up for that. And remember that more is not better in the realm of bibliography. Quality is far more important than quantity.

(iii) Quality Criteria for Bibliography

Quality means different things for primary and secondary materials. For primary materials, quality means quality as data. That involves things like closeness to the original events or happenings of interest (are primary materials verbatim from the scene? reports of reports? recollected? hearsay?). But most of your early bibliography is secondary, where quality means something different. Quality in secondary materials refers first of all to the expertise and authority of the writer, second to the general acceptance of that expertise by third parties, and third to the relevance and detail of the source with respect to your particular topic of interest. In short, high-quality secondary materials are those that are written by recognized experts about things that are of immediate concern to you.

I have already given some basic rules for quality in bibliographical tools. The best bibliographies are those developed by specialists in fields, and these are most commonly found in the back of a first-rate book or in the reference list of a first-rate article. But there are also fields (e.g., English literature) that have annual bibliographies developed by specialists. Such bibliographies can be found through the ALA *Guide*. As for the rest, human-indexed tools are better than keyword-indexed tools. Tools that are found in the ALA *Guide* are better than those that are not. Older tools are usually higher quality than newer ones. Online tools with lineages going back to the print age are better than purely digital ones.

Once we move out of tools and into actual secondary materials, we can get more specific about quality ratings. I already noted that peer-reviewed materials are higher quality than non-peer-reviewed materials, but also that there are prestige hierarchies in academia, and that you are wise to take advantage of them. So here are some simple rules for judging all kinds of secondary sources, bibliographical and otherwise.

For books, the first indicator of quality is the publisher. Loosely speaking, much of the best work comes from the top publishers, in part because of peer review itself but largely because authors themselves believe this to be true and submit their work to the most prestigious press where they think they can pass peer review. So the top publishers have more work and better work to choose from. The top publishers do vary considerably by field. It is therefore best to ask your advisor to list the best relevant publishers for you. But in general you can assume that university press books are of higher average quality than commercial books, and that university press books from the great university presses are mostly of very high quality in the view of the contemporary disciplines involved.

But these are only rough rules, and rankings will vary a good deal from discipline to discipline. All the same, any expert library researcher has a working status list in his or her mind when wandering in the stacks. As an example, here's mine, which like everyone's is idiosyncratic, because it is governed by my own interests and areas of work. For me the top six publishers are California, Chicago, Oxford (although nowadays they publish a lot of junk, too), Cambridge (which also overpublishes a bit), Princeton, and Harvard. Of the commercial presses in the social sciences, Norton is for me the only really distinguished current publisher. Thirty years ago, Basic Books, Academic Press, Aldine, and Free Press were very serious publishers, but not today. In particular fields, however, I know well that other presses are extremely important in areas that interest me: North Carolina and Hopkins publish much important American history; Illinois and Temple publish lots of important labor history; Minnesota is tops for French theory, Cornell for large areas of literary theory. The Brookings Institution is important in political science. And I often remind myself that there may be other strong specialty lists that I don't know about.

As for the other end, for me Routledge, Sage, and Palgrave are today's high-volume bottom feeders. I find most of the enormous amount they publish pretty weak. Praeger, Lexington, Erlbaum, Greenwood, and Westport are similar. I know that all of these presses do publish some truly excellent and influential books, but I also know that I'm likely to have heard of such books or seen them cited elsewhere. I also know that quality rankings definitely change over time. Half a century ago, Routledge & Kegan Paul, as it was then known, was a very distinguished publisher. Similarly, in the 1920s, first-quality academic work was routinely published by commercial presses. So remember that any quality rating is merely a first guess.

Your main problem is that you will easily find ten times as much as you can possibly read. You need quality information to guide you. So ask your advisor, early on, who are the good publishers in your area. Seek their books first if you're overloaded with material. If you're not overloaded, then use what you can find and get the most out of it.

A direct indicator of quality in books (or at least of their importance) is their use. To figure this out you have to see the book physically and judge the level of wear and tear it has had—the more the wear and tear, the more important the book. This is another reason for cruising the stacks. Note also that recency is not necessarily a proxy for quality. Often, it is a proxy for trendiness. I return to this theme below.

For periodicals as well as for books, the top ranks vary by field. Often, in a particular area, the best journals are not discipline-wide journals—however prestigious—but specialty journals of various kinds. (Thus, in sociology, the second-tier generalist journals like *Sociological Forum* are not as important as the top specialty journals like *Demography* or *Social Studies of Science*.) A fast way to guess journal quality, when you don't know anything about it, is to look at the citation levels in the "Journal Reports" section of WoS. (This is conveniently found in the top line of the home page.) It takes some work, but you can find a complete listing of journals in your field of interest, and you can sort it by citation level. A journal that is not in the top 20 or 30 percent in total citations is unlikely to be important, unless it is the main journal in a hyperspecialized field. You should master the names of the prestigious journals in your research area very early in the project. You are wasting your time if you stray too far from the top.

Note that citation metrics systematically underestimate the importance of those journals that are mostly cited by books. There is still no effective indexing of book citations. Remember too that Google Scholar trolls websites as well as real scholarship and thus is not as reliable a guide to citation importance as WoS. As for the metacrawlers that operate on top of Google Scholar, you should avoid them absolutely. They are filled with software errors that are perplexing and even amusing. The last time I looked, the tool "Publish or Perish" didn't think my book *Chaos of Disciplines* had ever been cited outside the biological literature. The truth is almost exactly the reverse!

Bibliographical work inevitably pushes backward in time. A source can cite only those things which are available when it is written. This means that after you have gone through a couple of rounds of bibliography, you may be earlier than you want to be. Citation indexes are the way around this problem. I will cover this use of them in the next chapter.

(iv) A Note on Primary Materials

While doing the preliminary bibliography, you should locate the major primary materials that are relevant to your project. Primary materials often take a long time to find. They are usually not well indexed. You tend to find them by accident, which means you should allow maximum time to find them. So you should start looking for them very early.

If you are looking for archival material (manuscripts, unique holdings, institutional records) you should go to ArchiveGrid. But beware—the interface of ArchiveGrid is very cumbersome and has a high junk-to-quality ratio. It can therefore occasionally be faster to look at the old print tool (the *National Union Catalog of Manuscript Collections*), which has cumulative printed name and subject indexes and now has an online presence. Remember that important archival material can appear not only in collections of your focal subjects, but also in collections of people who wrote to or heard from one of those subjects, so you need to search widely and diversely. Often the best guide to manuscript materials will be in the source note or appendix of some recent monograph in the area. Make it a habit to cruise the stacks for such books: it's probably more efficient than working with ArchiveGrid.

If you are working on a problem where you expect substantial amounts of primary material to come from a foreign country or be in a foreign language, you must at once get an appointment with a faculty area specialist who can explain the major repositories and sources. You cannot find such things alone. However, do not make this appointment until you've done the basic bibliography, read a bit of secondary literature, and clarified your problem. An area specialist will do more for you—in the limited time he or she has—if you've already learned some basics on your own.

If you are working in government documents, your primary materials must be found by assiduous bibliographical work. The Serial Set (that is librarians' name for the basic American congressional documents) is fully indexed online, so Congress is pretty easy. These indexes, however, are generally based on OCR algorithms, with their usual problems. But national administrative documents (at least before 1975) are not as well indexed as congressional ones. As for state documents, you're on your own. Some states have developed excellent online indexes. Others are appalling. Remember that issuing state agencies change with bewildering rapidity and that names, content, and sizes of reports can vary even over two or three years.

Your primary materials may also be institutional information—histories of companies, circulation of journals, addresses of voluntary organizations, lists of movies—or they may be various kinds of statistical data. For all of this, you start with the ALA *Guide*. This will lead you to serious reference sources that provide pathways to all of these things. (Yes, there are general guides to statistical information—the US government has a statistics portal, for example.)

3. Browsing and Scanning in the Preliminary Phase

As I have said, browsing works because it brings together two sets of information—one in your head, the other in the material. In order for some fact to seem important in the source you are browsing, you the browser have to know a lot already. This requirement has profound implications for the timing of browsing activity in a project. Except for seasoned researchers working in areas they know somewhat already, straight browsing is not an effective way to start work on a project. For most of us, heavy browsing is a midphase exercise. At the beginning we are laying systematic groundwork: puzzles, research question, ground-staking bibliography, and so on. At the end we are closing out the loopholes and leftovers. In the middle, we tend to know the terms and have lots of data issues in our heads. That is what makes browsing most effective.

Because browsing is heavily dependent on what is already in your head, concentrated, long periods of work are more productive than short bursts. I myself do best on projects when I am working on them full time. Of course, most of us can't work full time on a given project. But three whole mornings a week is better than six two-hour blocks, for example.

While browsing is relatively unimportant in the preliminary phase, scanning is central. In the section on bibliography above, I noted that you should always keep moving. That presupposes that you scan. By scanning, I mean that you retrieve from the text itself only what seem to be the most important facts, such as names and major references. By moving quickly, you will possibly run into them again, and after a little while, you will begin to know on your own—from sheer repetition—what are the names and references and so on that are important. Scanning means using your short-term memory to bootstrap your way to a better knowledge of a field.

Preliminary scanning is mainly concerned with finding extremely relevant and central texts and identifying them by sheer repetitive discovery. Your aim is to avoid reading in detail, to capture about four times as much material as you actually need, and then to choose among those things at leisure, when you can compare them with each other. As with browsing, it is best to scan in long stretches, because like browsing, scanning depends on recognizing minor cues in lean spaces, relying on short-term memory that will probably be gone by tomorrow morning.

4. Reading

Preliminary-phase reading has a dual quality. On the one hand, you use it to learn about your topic. On the other hand, you use it to learn about the literatures on your topic. You begin to see the different dimensions of previous analyses. You see different interpretations. You see possible disagreements.

What should you actually read in the preliminary phase? Not much. Most of the preliminary phase will be spent scanning things, trolling, racing through various different bibliographical tools, all in search of the basic bibliography noted above. But while you are doing the initial bibliography and locating primary materials, you should be actually reading the major secondary sources relevant to your project. These should turn up quite early in the bibliographical work. Make a reasoned choice as to which are the most important and read them cover to cover. There's no need to overdo this. If there are ten of them, read the three or four best cover to cover, and scan the rest carefully. If need be, you can read the rest in detail later.

By the "best" sources here, I mean the ones with the most information and the least political opinion and other baggage. For example, if your background knowledge of an area or period involved in your project is not good, you may need to find an old-style basic history or survey of the period or area in order to master the fundamentals. Contemporary survey histories and area studies are often very theory-heavy, not to mention strongly political.

Handle with care or, preferably, go back to earlier scholarly work. Earlier work may be excessively narrative, slightly conservative, a little sexist, and overly focused on elites of all kinds. But it will tell you some details about what actually happened. Much recent history does not.

An important reason for reading the background and basic secondary material quite carefully early in the project is that—just like scanning—this reading starts putting facts and people and organizations in your head that will serve as contacts for browsing. This means that relevance is another important criterion for those works that you read early in a project. Cast your net wide, but not too wide. You want your ten core books to cover your area like a set of fish scales, not to be disconnected and far apart. At the same time, you don't want them to be about exactly the same things. Learning how to judge such relevance is crucial to library research.

As I have said earlier, there are moments in library research when brute-force methods are required, when you have to "read all the things that refer to X," or when you have to "list and analyze all the sources related to Y." But there is no need whatever for brute force in the preliminary phase. You need to do bibliography and a lot of it, but don't use brute-force approaches, even in bibliography, much less in reading. They are only used when you have narrowed a topic or a task to a point where the effort involved in brute force will pay off because most of the items searched will be important.

5. Files

You need to record somewhere all the things you have found and all the things you have done to find them. These files need to be able to grow sufficiently to manage a medium-size research project. You need them partly for a simple record. But the main payoff from careful filing is to free your mind from the task of remembering where everything is. Then you can use your mind to think, to browse, to analyze. Do not for a second imagine that you will remember all the things you need to remember to run a substantial project. Even young memories can't do that. So file things; then you can forget them with impunity.

You may note an underlying theme here. With respect to most tasks in library research, imposing an arbitrary if limited structure on your materials is always preferable to leaving them unorganized. Thus, in cataloging, the LC cataloging system is better than a universal hyperlink index (because any given book can be indexed too many ways). In indexing, a controlled vocabulary of fixed terms is better than a fluctuating, hyperlinked indexing system for the same reason. So too in the matter of files. A fixed, hierarchical structure is better than leaving materials in one place and relating them via relational database tables.

For any given library project, you should expect a folder system to look like the following:

- Master folder
  - (Bibliography subfolder—likely to split out of master)
  - (Ideas subfolder—likely to split out of master)
  - (To-be-filed subfolder—likely to split out of master)
  - (To do—likely to split out of master)
- Design folder (contains all drafts of the design document)
- Log (A list of what you have done)
- Published material folders (as necessary)
- Primary data folders (as necessary)
- Analysis folders (as necessary)
- Writing folders (as necessary)
- Final text (and hopefully publication correspondence!)

Here are the basic rules for running such a system.

1. Have a main folder that includes all the basic business related to the project except access documents (e.g., for archival materials) and Xerox orders, which go with the material that they cover.
2. Have one main bibliography folder. Otherwise it is very easy to duplicate bibliography. A way to avoid this is to dump all your bibliography into one giant personal database, as do most students and many of my colleagues. But I think it is best to separate this by project, at the least. Also, you will need to keep the bibliographies of minianalyses (of which more later) separately, in the folders for those analyses.
3. Have one design folder.
4. For primary materials, have folders in which you break out subfolders for ideas, to-do, to-be-filed, and (possibly) bibliography as necessary. Always be able to find everything quickly.
5. In creating analysis folders be careful not to lose provenance information (where it came from) on any primary material.
6. Use common sense. The purpose of files is to enable you to forget about the details in order to focus your mind on data-gathering, analysis, or

whatever; to open your mind to browsing, free-association, and multi-tasking. So be as detailed as you need to achieve that end, but no more. There's no point wasting time in unnecessary elaborations.

It is wise always to be dynamically working with your research files. Even indexing is no substitute for wallowing in your data all the time looking for things and deciding how to reclassify. This wallowing gives you a profound knowledge of your data. It forces you continually to think about where things fit and how they go together. It also produces continuous browsing insights, random connections, and new ideas. In that, it is just like the surfing around from index to index that is good bibliographical work.

It's not wise to rely too much on any form of ongoing indexing. It is possible to make archival or source notes as a long text list of unfiled blips on the computer (or in some qualitative database software), putting keywords ahead of each blip. But you may not come up with the right keywords ahead of time. And in any case, the more times you have simply read through all your data, the more you will figure out. I have had a number of students who have used indexing software, but it has not seemed to help them; rather it has bogged them down in pseudoscientific minutiae. Indexing is only a supplement to your thinking, not the main attraction.

My students take eagerly to the idea of physical files. They say it's because they can see the project growing before them. I think it is also because physical files lack the frightening, elusive infinitude of digital ones. Once again, the constraints imposed by physical reality—bulk, cost, weight, accessibility—force us to exercise more judgment. Do we really need one more article copied? One more handbook entry downloaded? One more reference list copied? The move to physical materials makes us exercise more judgment. And judgment is what knowledge is about.

6. Some Concluding Notes

A few final words before you start out. Keep good records of what you have done. In a given session you might get only partway through a source or bibliography. Remember to note down exactly how far you got, or you'll redo work when you come back (or worse yet, miss some part of the primary source). Careful records will also save you time in the final written bibliography and footnoting. Even in a long historical paper, the footnotes—no matter how detailed—will take very little time if the records have been very carefully kept throughout the project. The same goes for personal connections. All of this should go into a comprehensive log—essentially a detailed diary—recording your research work.

Keep scratch paper or its electronic equivalent around. Once you start to live and breathe a project, ideas will show up at all times: while you are showering, during a meal at a restaurant, during a conversation with a peer. Jot them down on something and throw them into the to-be-filed folder. You will forget them unless you write them down or email them to yourself.

That's enough advice for one chapter. Design, bibliography, scanning, reading, and filing will get a project started. You do them all at once, not sequentially. You're like a dog chasing its tail. Don't worry. All of these things will gradually settle out into a functioning project. Just get them all going and have confidence.

After about five iterations, your design document will have stabilized, and you will know enough about sources and research questions to be able to plan the actual analyses that will answer your questions. At this point, you are ready to enter midphase. Midphase has the same five activities as the preliminary phase (design, bibliography, scanning/browsing, reading, filing) and adds to these two further activities: analysis and writing. The subsequent chapters cover these various activities as they unfold through midphase. Because they can come in a variety of orders and combinations, I consider them in a more or less arbitrary order. Moreover, this problem of various orders means that it makes no sense to discuss the overall flow and regulation of midphase—the issue of midphase design—until we have understood more about the activities themselves. But if you want to get a quick sense of how the various parts of midphase flow, you may wish to look ahead to the first part of chapter 11.

5 | *Midphase Bibliography*

I begin my chapters on the midphase with two warnings. First, remember that these midphase chapters are not sequential. Do not read this chapter on the assumption that you should complete your bibliography before going on to scanning, reading, indexing, analysis, and so on. Second, throughout these midphase chapters, I will from time to time repeat advice already given earlier. The same things are no less true in this middle phase of the project, but they may have different implications and we all need to be reminded of them in any case.

1. The Changing Nature of Bibliography

When I first taught library work, my students' problem was finding materials. Now their problem is ignoring them. This overload happened because in the old days costs forced selectivity. Libraries could not afford to buy everything, and so they selected by quality. Indexing sources could not afford to index everything, so they indexed the top-quality sources first. As a result, beginning researchers simply didn't find a lot of peripheral work. And as it happens, much of that work wasn't worth finding—that's why it was peripheral. After all, scholars themselves send their better papers to better journals, so some of the quality gradient follows from personal selection. But that selection is then strengthened by the more stringent refereeing at the top-prestige journals and publishers.

Today, by contrast, availability is not an indicator of quality. The average student can quickly generate a huge mass of relevant bibliography, most of which is mediocre at best. Yet viewed on a screen it all looks the same. On screen, the thick paper, precise production, and detailed copyediting of the elite presses now look little different from the double columns, garish fonts, and numerous errors of the lesser publishers. Even those unobtrusive correlates of scholarly quality—which were once used by researchers seeking quick indicators of quality work—are gone.

Because of all these changes I have changed my advice. I no longer emphasize systematic and exhaustive bibliography. I now recommend locating a small, high-quality bibliography at the outset, then relying heavily on the further references within those sources. Chapter 2 showed that this is in fact how scholars have always worked. You should do the same.

The current version of this strategy rests on citation patterns, and there are to be sure well-known disadvantages to that approach. Scholars "pile on" to particular citations because of mere convenience, or because those citations coined a useful phrase, or because they are in highly visible locations. For the expert, yes, these can be problems. But for the student, they are not. Taking advantage of prior expert work is always your optimal strategy.

Pillaging other scholars' bibliographies has the disadvantage that it takes you steadily backward in time. An article refers only to things written before it, most often several years before it. So you will need from time to time to come forward toward the present. You use citations for this too. It's very simple. You use WoS to find the most heavily cited piece or most perfectly relevant piece in your current bibliography. Then you use the "Cited Reference Search" facility of WoS to find the list of more current papers that cite that piece. Then you rank *those* papers in order of the number of papers that cite *them*. Somewhere in the top five to ten will be some obviously crucial recent articles. (There may also be some very highly cited articles that are not relevant, which would take you in a new and less useful direction. Disregard them.) If those newly found crucial articles are current enough for your purposes, then you're done. If not, then choose the top two or three of them and repeat this strategy until you get up to the present. (You may end up with a lineage of very highly cited pieces, which will show you the history of research in your research area.)

Remember finally that bibliography can be seductive. Ponce de León spent his life looking for the Fountain of Youth and hence failed to live. You can spend all your time looking for the ultimate, perfect article, but such an article doesn't exist. In fact, the ultimate, perfect article is the one you will write.

2. Midphase Bibliography

A. THE TRAJECTORY OF BIBLIOGRAPHY.

Although bibliographical work is continual throughout a project, its type changes as you move along. In the preliminary phase, you locate a few good background works, identify the central books and articles in the research literature, and assess the availability of primary sources. You must set the quality bar very high; using weak material early in a project is costly, because it is misleading.

In the beginning of the midphase, you begin to fill in the holes. The background section of your bibliography should be mostly complete. Indeed, you should have read these works by now. Note that most of them are not going to appear as references in the final product, be it article or thesis. They are just to orient you to the background and needn't be cited unless they influenced you decisively.

On the other hand, the main substantive section of your bibliography will change considerably in midphase. You should by now have read the major articles identified in the preliminary phase and taken from them a clearer sense of the most influential papers. But you will have missed a few of these, and, at the same time, other pieces will turn out to be less important than you thought, in part because your puzzles will be gradually changing. As you constantly purify your list of the really important work, you will also identify why it is influential: because of its theoretical scheme; because it contains important data; because its interpretation was the first and therefore determining account. So your bibliography should be increasing in size, but also becoming more clearly categorizable and more clearly "tellable" as a historically evolving literature. At this point, also, it is wise to start annotating your bibliography: short decisive notes of twenty to thirty words are enough.

A first-rate found-data research article in my own field of sociology seldom has more than a hundred necessary citations. (Some such articles have two hundred citations, but probably half of those are decorative.) You don't need a bibliography of five hundred items for a good library research paper; rather, you need the right one hundred citations. So don't be afraid to throw things out of your bibliography. (As I said earlier, keep them in a "dead bibliography" subfolder so you can don't "discover" them a second time.)

Early midphase is therefore the time for brute-force bibliography. Now is the time to sit down for two hours with the online catalog and check every single reference under thirty or forty headings. Sometimes, this will be in connection with a minianalysis responding to a particular research question. Suppose you are writing on the reception of the book called *The Kallikaks*, by H. H. Goddard, a famous (some would say infamous) text in eugenics. Early in your project you will have to slog through a large library's online catalog under headings like "eugenics" with the search restricted to English-language sources before 1930. At Chicago, that search produces several hundred items, and among them, it turns out, is a five-hundred-page bibliography. A student writing on art critics in New York in the early twentieth century will have to slog through the "Art critics—United States—Biography" section of such a catalog, and, as it turns out, the Chicago catalog produces a dissertation on New York critics in the period 1900 to 1939, whose bibliography will save the researcher a lot of time. In brute-force bibliography, therefore, you are not just simply building lists of primary and secondary sources. You are also making sure that you have found the major preexisting bibliographies.

The brute-force bibliographical work of early midphase will prevent you from being unpleasantly surprised by decisive, central sources later in the project. And at the same time, it produces a horde of useful references to follow. Don't follow them all. Use your design to discipline your working bibliography. And if it is easy to locate copies of these intriguing papers online, you should always look at their reference lists. Scan these for neglected treasures. And of course any bibliographies that you turn up should be inspected carefully and thoroughly.

Finally, in the early midphase, you need to make sure of the primary sources you need. In the case of things like archives and newspapers that are not widely available, you must—if you have not already done so in preliminary work—identify what you need, where it is, and what are the conditions of access. In the case of government documents, you should have begun to dig into the online materials and, if you are working in a period or country where print is the only available indexing, you should have started to brute-force your way through those indexes to identify the crucial documents.

If your project calls for archives, newspapers, or government documents (especially state documents and non-US documents), it is possible that you may have to make a trip to sources. You want to plan such trips as early as possible, in order to schedule your visit well. You do not want to be delayed in later midphase because you can't get to certain primary materials until some far-future time.

In the center of midphase, bibliography shifts again. By now the project is breaking up into a series of loosely connected minianalyses. Each one of these will have its own focal bibliographical needs. These are not likely to be general-search, cover-the-waterfront efforts. Quite the contrary, they will be focused efforts to answer particular detailed questions—just-in-time bibliography. You will find yourself returning to indexes you have used before, but with new search terms and new controlled vocabulary. Your bibliographical work turns from brute force to brachiation. You don't stop to evaluate everything at each stage but move on swiftly in search of the particular bibliographical gem you need.

All these bibliographical leads will pile up in the folders and subfolders related to some particular minianalysis. Don't bother to merge them into the main bibliography. For the most part, bibliographical work that emerges out of minianalyses will just clutter up the main bibliography. The overwhelming majority of the bibliography you gather in this middle period—even things that seem very important at the time—will not appear in the reference list of the final product.

You can, however, merge this minianalysis bibliography into the main bibliography if you use an online bibliographical software system and retain some mark on the record identifying it as relating only to a minianalysis. But otherwise the main bibliography will fill up with unused material. (For example, in the paper whose writing is discussed in chapter 2, I ended up citing only six of the thirty or more papers on departmental libraries that I had found and copied.) This "necessary only for the moment" quality holds even more for the interim works—the trees you swing through on the way to some ultimate bibliographical reward. Just file those and let their memory settle into your brain for the next project. When the time comes you will find yourself saying "I remember, there was some book that listed all the major people who had ever worked in the Library of Congress, so I could search that for Mr. Q . . ." And in a few minutes you will find that book, even though you don't remember its title or authors, simply because you remember having seen it and vaguely recall what it said.

In late midphase, writing begins to dominate the research process. At this point, bibliography becomes extremely focused. You are now looking for particular things to justify particular points in the text, and even then you look for them only when you don't already have them in the main or minianalysis bibliographies. In this late bibliographical work, you may well be revisiting sources read earlier. You may be verifying citations that you didn't fully record before. You should also be starting to establish the actual reference list for the final text. Depending on your software, this can be a little or a lot of work, but bear in mind that the final published bibliography is likely to contain a maximum of from 10 to 25 percent of all the citations you have ever gathered. Your minianalysis folders should be full of things you noted down but did not have time to follow up. If they aren't, you didn't do enough work.

B. STANDARDS AND PURPOSES

It is still sometimes taken for granted that the ultimate criterion of bibliography is exhaustiveness. This is implicit in sources like WoS that pull all sources together, as it is in things like JSTOR that contain journals that range from the truly excellent to the less than mediocre. But today any scholar knows that no bibliography is exhaustive. Even a subfield like "sociology of work" would have an exhaustive bibliography of thousands of items per year. There will therefore inevitably be sources, and probably important sources, that you miss.

The criteria of a good final bibliography today are rather

1. that it contains the vast majority of truly important sources on a topic; this means 80 to 90 percent of them;
2. that it contains a substantial sample of middle-importance materials, a sample large enough to provide evidence from all major areas involved in the project; that is, distribution of sources is particularly important in the middle-quality level;
3. that it not contain any real junk;
4. that it contain enough relevant material to justify persuasively any minianalysis that you choose to report; that is, the bibliography should be deeper in areas where you have gone into detail.

Remember that bibliography has not one purpose, but several. These are symbolized in the three different versions of your bibliography. The first is your master bibliography, which consists of all the references you have identified. The second is the smaller list of things that you have actually examined for longer than a few minutes apiece—your effective bibliography. Then there is the actual reference list of the final text. The ratios of these things will be drastic. The effective bibliography is probably less than half the length of the master bibliography. The published reference list will be less than half of the effective bibliography. It is often less than 10 percent of the master list, and probably less than 5 percent if you count the dead bibliography of irrelevant and low-quality material.

These different parts of the bibliography serve different purposes. Most of your bibliography is purely for you. It orients you to the field. It makes you feel confident in saying things like "Most scholars think X," even though your text may cite only one or two examples of that scholarship. Having an oversupply of bibliography also makes you confident that new references would not produce huge surprises.

Similarly, background works are just for you. The reader is going to assume you are expert about the general area of your research. It is up to you to guarantee that assumption, even though you don't give citations to prove it.

As for the final, written reference list of the paper, what is required in that list is the following:

1. anything directly quoted in the paper;
2. anything that is the sole source for a piece of information in the paper, or in its tables, figures, etc.;
3. any primary or secondary material mentioned by name in the paper;
4. enough other secondary material to justify your appraisal of the literature to the reader.

Obviously, the main place for flexibility here is number 4. Most modern scholarship is moving toward overkill. Some monographs now have "bibliographical essays" listing more sources than could actually be read in a decade. Usually these appear without page citations, which is a clue that their real function is not intellectual but decorative.

In summary, the real purpose of the reference list is to persuade readers that you are a trustworthy analyst of sources. But it also should allow them to replicate any particular piece of your work, in particular any minianalysis. This means that your citations of primary materials must be scrupulous. In particular, your citations and reference list should ideally not contain any "second-hand" citations: citations of primary material as reported by a secondary source. These can appear only when you have failed to verify the primary data despite serious effort, and then they should be noted by the phrase "as reported by," so that the reader knows that you have not verified the primary data. Citing a source is claiming that you personally have seen it.

C. BIBLIOGRAPHICAL ROUTINE IN THE MIDPHASE

(i) Search

In the midphase, you should start moving beyond basic sources like JSTOR and WoS. New indexes are invented often and, much more important, old ones are perpetually increasing their coverage of earlier and earlier years. As I have said, do not assume that you know the coverage of a source. That something is called *Sociological Abstracts* does not mean that it will have every journal that could possibly interest a sociologist. Also, don't assume that coverage is continuous for all periods even if that is implied or stated by the index. For online sources, read the fine print on how the index was developed.

Remember, too, that the proprietary tools will foreground the proprietary journals of the same firm.

Get to know all the major indexing tools in your area. As I said in the preceding chapter, remember that tools change often, without telling anyone about it. I myself am a conservative, and so rely on WoS heavily, because it doesn't get "improved" (i.e., "made user friendly," i.e., dumbed-down) very often. But you may choose your own bibliographical tool. Just don't use Google Scholar, because its rankings are partly based on non-peer-reviewed material. That's like deciding the answers to the calculus test by a popular vote that counts the fraternity brothers along with the math majors. You don't want that.

(ii) Routine

Of course you need to keep a bibliographical log in the midphase, just as you keep a log of all your library research work. This is all the more important since the bibliographies of the minianalyses will be separate from your main folder. Do this by hand or in a text file. Do not rely on your browser's history file. History listings are excessively specific and quite uninformative, as you know well. So keep simpler records: what indexes you used on a given day; what search words and phrases you employed; where you stored the results and, broadly speaking, what they were. This enables you always to know what you have already done (so you don't repeat it).

Second, develop a single standard format for references. This will typically be your own discipline's form, although most bibliographical software will switch citations from one to another. But if you haven't got a clear disciplinary standard, the default in the social sciences is the *Chicago Manual of Style* (University of Chicago Press) author-date format (unless you're a historian) since this (or some close variant of it) is becoming standard in most scholarly journals. For example:

Mead, G. H. 1934. *Mind, Self, and Society*. Chicago: University of Chicago Press.

Boyd, M. 1989. "Family and Personal Networks in International Migration." *International Migration Review* 23:638–70.

In history and the humanities, the standards are the *Chicago Manual of Style* notes/bibliography system or the MLA (Modern Language Association) style. You may of course use software to impose these standards, but you will often be scrawling references on paper in the stacks (copying them out of the bibliography of some book), so having a standard personal format is wise. I am not always careful about this, and there is nothing more annoying than having to redo citations in the late endphase, when you are completely bored with the project.

As I noted in the discussion of disambiguation in chapter 3, you can get away with using only authors' initials most of the time, but not always. It may be useful to get the full names in case you need them. Not having first names could sentence you to vast amounts of unnecessary work if you use a large-scale online catalog: there are many authors in the world named "Smith, W." and even "Smith, W. R." Some other cultures are even more name-concentrated. There are vast numbers of M. Cohens, K. Lees, K. Yamaguchis, and X. Zhaos. And you don't even want to think about the Kims. So keep the first names when you are working with common patronyms. (As of this writing, WoS is mixing initials and full names, creating a lot of unnecessary chaos.)

Finally, as your bibliography piles up, it becomes more and more important to categorize it. If you want to retain multidimensionality, you can associate several keywords (i.e., from your own controlled vocabulary) with each item. But do not let your bibliography become a giant undifferentiated list. Follow a simple rule: if you have more than six items in any list, break it down into subcategories. This rule is usefully applied to folders, terms, and many other things as well as to sections of a bibliography.

(iii) Facts to Remember

In the midphase, you will become ever more reliant on real subject indexes, which you will examine carefully, as opposed to keyword searches that you will scan rapidly. Where are these true subject indexes? First of all, as I have said before, in the backs of books. Electronic keyword indexing of books is only just beginning now. So you can assume that nearly all books from good presses through 2005 are well indexed. That means that they have controlled vocabularies developed for the book, cross-referencing to take you to the correct vocabulary terms if you don't guess them at first, and a page-by-page reading for importance and quality. The older the book, generally, the better the index, at least back to 1960. Certain presses also tend to have excellent indexes, while others do not, as you will learn. In the early twentieth century, many fine publishers (e.g., Oxford) did enormously detailed but very flat indexes in which each index term refers to only one or two pages, and the index is just a huge list of seemingly unrelated terms. Not everything old is wonderful.

The second place for real subject indexing is of course in the reference lists of the best articles on your subject. You already know this, but it is important to state it once again. Article reference lists don't use controlled vocabularies, but they do contain implicit categorizations, because they cite certain texts for certain purposes. Careful reading will reveal these implicit categorizations.

There are also some reference tools that remain truly subject-indexed. Last time I looked, *Sociological Abstracts*, for example, had a controlled vocabulary and a human staff that read and assigned terms. The Wilson indexes once had such indexing, although with the recent sale to EBSCO one can't be sure whether it continues. In chapter 4, I noted that well-indexed bibliographies of specific subjects were standard assignments in library school in the old days, and the LC Z classification (from Z1000 up and especially from Z5051 to Z7999) is full of such bibliographies. Some disciplines (English and economics, for example) also have annual lists of subject-indexed bibliography. You should look for such tools very early in midphase. They exist for nearly everything before 1980, often by the dozens. Even more recently, you can find review articles and other centralized bibliographies. Make sure you look for them. They will save you immense amounts of work.

Once again, you find these things either through the online catalog of your library (using your subject plus the word "bibliography" in an advanced search of subjects, that is, LC headings, not keywords) or in the ALA *Guide*. (Return to chapter 4 for more detail on finding bibliographical tools.) An example makes clear how important it is to do systematic bibliography. In chapter 4, I mentioned a student studying the evolution of regulation of sex work in Thailand. Although she could not find any bibliographies, I was positive there would be detailed preexisting bibliographies, and sure enough it turned out that there was (from 1977) an annotated bibliography of bibliographies on Thailand, covering 205 bibliographies in Thai and various Western languages, edited by Donn Vorhis Hart. Interestingly, I couldn't find it in our catalog via some of the obvious keyword searches. I found it only through the advanced search facility, using *Thailand* and *bibliography* as subject keywords, because I hadn't happened to see this heading in a pure subject browse (which is my preferred mode because you get so much useful peripheral information.)

This example embodies three important lessons. First, don't assume that a source isn't there just because you don't find it on a first try. All indexing and access systems have their peculiarities, and for important materials like bibliography of bibliographies you should try several strategies before you accept that a given type of source does not exist. Second, if you find the right thing but for the wrong (typically earlier) period, that earlier source may identify ongoing bibliographical resources that continue into your period of interest or—more likely—will identify important substantive works that you can use as the seed citations in a "cited references" analysis in WoS, finding present-day works that cite these important earlier works.

But the third lesson is the most important. It involves my sense that there had to be a relevant bibliography. As you become more skilled at library research, you will develop the sixth sense I mentioned in chapter 1: the sense that "wait a second, there has to be a source on that"—whether a bibliography or a reference work or a dissertation. Very often, students will come to me and say, "There isn't anything on X." And I'll say immediately, "That can't be. There must be at least two or three dissertations on that and probably a published bibliography. It's just a problem with your search terms or the tools you are using." You need to cultivate such a sense. Of one particular thing, I can assure you: with a total of about 300,000 dissertations in the humanities and social sciences since the late nineteenth century, it is pretty certain that there is a dissertation about virtually any topic you can imagine. Their quality may be mixed, but their authors will have done a lot of bibliographical work that may be useful.

3. Brachiation

Brute-force bibliography tends to come earlier in the midphase. In the main midphase, most bibliographical work will take the form that I identified in chapter 2 as brachiation. It moves quickly back and forth between sources and indexes, relying on high-quality prior work, but also taking many long-shot guesses. Brachiation is also how bibliography works in minianalyses. Here is an example from my own work, from a paper on the sociology of work and occupations. (I keep field notes on my library work to provide examples for my teaching; this is one such.)

1. I am in the middle of writing a handbook chapter on the sociology of work. One of many subtopics is job tenure. So I am in need of a series of

numbers on how long people stayed in their jobs at any given point in the US in the twentieth century. Given what I know about labor statistics, I doubt that this statistic will exist in consistent format over a long period.

2. Sure enough, this figure isn't in the *Historical Statistics of the United States*, either the new *Millennial Edition* or the 1976 *Bicentennial Edition*.

3. I have, however, happened on some of this so-called tenure information (during early midphase, when I was working on several parts of the project at once) in a 1922 book, which I had found because it appeared in the notes to the employment series that do happen to appear in the *Historical Statistics*, which weren't quite about job tenure (typical total time in a given job), but rather about turnover (percentage of people leaving a given job in a given year). The 1922 book had data on both, and I wanted to move to tenure, because I liked the measure better for my theoretical purposes in the chapter.

4. My RA had found a book called *On the Job*, about whether job stability had decreased 1980 to 2000. So I decide to use information on stability (the reverse of turnover) as a proxy for information about current job tenure, but continue looking bibliographically, off and on, for more precise information.

5. I suddenly remember a famous article on careers by Harold Wilensky, which I had found at some point while doing brute-force bibliography but then had forgotten. I am reminded of it while reading an *Annual Review of Sociology* article on careers for another part of the research. That article happened to mention the Wilensky piece.

But because the annual review piece reminds me of the Wilensky paper, I go back to it, and it refers to another paper of Wilensky's, which turns out to have a complete list of all the studies available to him (in 1960) on "whole career" information about individuals. There are only a dozen. The most recent has data to the early 1950s; the earliest has data on the 1930s.

So now, in my search for tenure information, I have something, at least, on the beginning of the century (the 1922 book), the early midcentury (Wilensky), and after 1980 (the book *On the Job*), but nothing for the glory years of the economy from 1950 to 1975.

6. Unwilling to wait any longer, I start writing the section of the paper that involves tenure and decide that my interpretation will focus precisely on the disappearance of tenure information, which I will attribute to a

shift in theories about social mobility: the rise in stratification studies of the Wisconsin status attainment model and the structural equation model of O. D. Duncan, both of which focused on "attainment outcome" (the prestige of latest job), ignoring the process of how people got to that latest job and what kind of a career track (i.e., tenure) that produced overall.

7. Nonetheless, while writing, I glance through articles in the *On the Job* book. One of them has a reference to a study by some people that reported tenure data from 1951 to the 1980s. It turns out to appear in a textbook on the actuarial theory of pensions. Our library doesn't own the latest edition, where these numbers were to be found. But I determine to focus intensely on the bibliographical problem of finding such numbers.

8. So I cruise all the shelves around the earlier editions of the pension text. Maybe some other book will produce what I needed. I pull books off the shelf and scan their indexes and tables of contents.

9. The sixth book I pull down does have something on tenure. (I had become interested in two other books on the way to this one, since they told me other things about pensions that were probably interesting for my paper, but that had no relation to job tenure.)

10. This sixth book is by an economist and so from my point of view it is somewhat overtheorized. But I do note in it a citation to what looks like an interesting paper on tenure by the maverick economist George Akerlof. It's in the *American Economic Review* for 1981.

11. I find the Akerlof article in JSTOR and it proves to have several quite specific references on tenure. Among these are four reports by the Bureau of Labor Statistics that have exactly what I want. I go directly to the stacks and check out all four.

Thus, by a series of a dozen or more steps, some of them deliberate, some of them accidental results of earlier or parallel investigations, I had found what I wanted. I had also discovered a number of things relevant to other parts of the project, and had been reminded of some important theoretical connections I might have ignored.

It is possible that I would have found these four reports in another way, but very unlikely. The indexes to government periodicals are notoriously poor. These particular reports are not indexed in our online catalog as are most government documents. (Maybe they were, however, indexed in the card catalog, which we still have: I should have thought of that.) These four reports were unmentioned in the bibliographies of the *On the Job* book, however, because it is about a later period and itself took the hazard-rate (turnover) approach, which as I noted earlier regards tenure as an uninteresting by-product of other causal forces.

This example shows what midphase bibliographical work is like—continuous, complex, directed, but at the same time quite self-consciously using randomness at important junctures. It is also networked, in that this particular story draws references from other searches and in turn contributes references to them. Such midphase bibliographical work goes on in the background via unconscious browsing, then comes up into the foreground when you need it. You have to be at it all the time: always chasing things, always cruising shelves. Things turn up and your browsing-mind should always be ready to recognize them.

Serendipity is not an unusual, once-in-a-lifetime, even once-in-a-project thing. It is the one constant factor in library research, because you are continuously looking at material close to your immediate focus, but in sources organized by somebody else, with slightly different interests. That's the lesson of the works on pensions that were beside the book I was seeking. In order to recognize these books as useful sources, I had to know there was going to be a section on pensions in my chapter and what would be the issues in that section. One-time, keyword bibliography of the kind facilitated by Internet digital tools will not produce this continuous, low-level generation of important research leads. This is why you have a design and research questions. To repeat yet again, library research is not about finding things, it is about knowing, when you see something, that you are in fact—in some other part of the project—looking for something just like that. You will find that many or most of your most important bibliographical hits are made on the way to other things.

Note too that the brachiation that found these reports led out of a likely source (the *On the Job* book) to one you would never imagine (a textbook on pensions). That source then had to be physically inspected, and I took the opportunity to physically inspect a bunch of physically adjacent books. It was by that random search that I found a passage that happened to refer to what looked like a good further source (Akerlof). This source was then located electronically. Once located, that source produced the references I sought. So I was shifting from physical to electronic and back, from present to past and back, from topic to topic and back. And I was always keeping my eyes open for all kinds of things that happened to be close to the things I was inspecting. The whole process of swinging along through the sources was sustained by my inner confidence that somebody had to have written on the topic of tenure and, indeed, had to have published extensive data on it.

Note also that the final discovery took place when I had already written much of the section on tenure in my paper. Getting this particular topic right turned out to be a cleanup matter. I had to rewrite the section completely, based on what the mid-1960s tenure data actually told me. In fact, reading the Akerlof paper made me think of a new theoretical problem (about time and the measurement of jobs) that was quite important.

Note, finally, the intensely parallel nature of this work. My RA was finding things. I was reading other things. I was stocking up information relevant to other aspects of this project even when I was focusing on tenure, and so on.

Brachiation is thus the very opposite of brute force. It is not done once and for all. It is not based on strict rationality but rather on a kind of Bayesian swinging in the most likely possible direction, and occasionally drifting aside. (The formal name in computer science for this approach is "simulated annealing.") Many of the moves it makes are long shots. Many of its payoffs are tangential—information on pensions, in this case. But eventually it pays off on the main question.

Brachiation is very strongly subject to the rule that bibliography always moves you back in time. Because there are many swings in such a journey, each one inevitably moving backward, you will often need to turn to WoS and its lineages of citations to come back to the present. An important aid in this is the "Related References" facility in WoS. This selects articles that share citations with what you are currently looking at. It is a powerful tool. I wouldn't use it in a brute-force approach, but if you're stuck on a brachiation, it can be very helpful.

4. Selection

A crucial issue with midphase bibiliography is keeping it manageable in size. Some of this I have already covered in chapter 4, since quality judgments are overwhelmingly important at the beginning, when your choices are immensely consequential. But quality criteria bear repeating.

The factors you are trying to maximize in your bibliography are the quality of the thinking, the reliability of the judgments, and the strength of the scholarship on which you will be relying. I take it for granted that you feel unqualified to make any of these judgments. For the most part, so do I. Because I constantly move into new areas, I'm often unfamiliar with the scholars I'm reading. Even a scholar who specializes is constantly encountering new approaches or previously unstudied contexts. So we are all looking for heuristics that enable us to make quality judgments in areas where we have no real expertise.

A. CRITERIA FOR INDIVIDUAL ITEMS

I have already covered some basic indicators of individual item quality in chapter 4. There I talked mainly about venue: the publisher for books and the status or citation level for a journal. For journals, look at total citations, by the way, not at the "impact factor." Most citations in the humanities or social sciences are to items over ten years old, so impact factors—which are determined by citations only to those articles published in the last two or five years—do not make any sense.

There are a few other quality heuristics for individual items. To some extent, author and author location are good indicators. To be sure, the long buyer's market for academic talent in America means that first-rate scholars are spread quite broadly through American colleges and universities. But the academic system, for all its faults, does produce a rough correlation between quality and position, so location of author can be a useful criterion. But remember that younger people are often closer to the cutting edge, and that an assistant professor at a good place is particularly likely to have written something strong, useful, and current. So prefer high over low status and young or middle-aged people over old. For work before 1970, the status of an author's university is probably the strongest indicator: scholarship in the US was extremely centralized at midcentury.

Citation is an obvious quality indicator as well, but as I have noted earlier, must be handled with care. First, citation levels vary very widely by discipline and subdiscipline. You should never compare citation levels across subdisciplines, much less across disciplines. Second, citations are very subject to "piling-on": once a piece gets well known it gets cited by dozens of people who haven't read it. Third, citation is not a linear scale, but a fairly loose order. Citation levels don't mean much when they are below ten or so. But even if you are comparing two pieces each with twenty or more citations, the relation can be indefinite. A piece cited three times as much as another is almost certain to be more important, but a piece cited 1.5 times as much as another is not. Where exactly the line falls between those two cases is impossible to say. Luckily, piling-on means that the truly important citations in a field are very obvious. They tend to have five or ten times as many citations as other articles or books.

Another way to identify crucial articles and books is simply to remember articles that show up again and again in the bibliographies of articles you glance at quickly in the course of other things. You will find that you start to remember certain references. Any reference you start to remember is something that should go into your bibliography.

Some indicators require that you scan or read an item before making a decision about it. Is it well-written? Do you understand it easily? Is the argument followable, plain, logical? Is the author fair and just toward his material, or is his material merely a punching bag for his political or theoretical views? Does the bibliography look (a) cursory, or (b) substantial, or (c) overstuffed? If the item is a book, don't be afraid to read the preface and introduction. While it is true that fools can write excellent books and geniuses can write duds, knowing something about your author's character may help you estimate the quality of his or her scholarship.

For some people, currency is an important measure of quality. Obviously, the date of publication gives you a first estimate on currency, but with books, you need to determine whether the book is a current edition (and if it is a second edition, check whether the references have been updated). Remember, too, that current is sometimes better, sometimes worse. Fields go through cycles. If you want detailed, source-based analysis of English poetry by people steeped in the canon, you don't want to read work published in the last twenty years. On the other hand, if you want to read interpretations attending to race, class, gender, and such issues, that current material is precisely what you need to read.

A special caution is important for web-based sources. The Internet is not a source of record. Websites get changed all the time, whereas the ethic of scholarship requires that your references allow somebody else to trace your route to your conclusions. So in general, a scholarly bibliography should rest overwhelmingly on print sources. In my view, this particularly includes statistical sources, although many of the government sources are now born electronic. You will want to print these, by the way, because the government corrects things silently from time to time. Even with a government website, you can't count on finding exactly the same thing when you go back. The instability of the Internet—both the material on it and the web indexes to those materials—is a real problem for scholarship.

On the Internet more generally, remember the following things. First, anyone can publish. There are no editors, no fact-checkers, no peer review. Second, there is no affirmative evidence of authorship on many sites, nor is there any way to appraise the skills of those writing the material, or, indeed, whether the material was actually written by those who claim to have written it. (Web journals, for example, are rapidly moving toward the XML format, which permits the disassembly and reassembly of texts ad infinitum.) Third, currency is also a problem: the date of a web page can be ascertained, but in most cases the date of the information on it cannot be ascertained. Finally, there is no reason to think sources on the web objective. Even professional academics have a hard time guaranteeing objectivity, and yet they are full-time communities of scholars with institutions like peer review that aim to guarantee the trustworthiness of work. It is pure fantasy to think that loosely organized web-based groups have comparable authority.

B. CRITERIA FOR A BIBLIOGRAPHY AS A WHOLE

More is not better. Technology has made gathering bibliography very easy; indeed technology has made storing bibliography very easy. You can find yourself with five hundred items in Endnote before you know it. As I have said, it is in part for this reason that I do not retain my bibliographies across projects. I generate bibliography for each project anew. Otherwise, I would be drowning in references all the time.

I do keep the library charge slips for all my old projects, for this means that I have some guidance if I need to find a book that I vaguely remember from an earlier project but did not use in the finished product's bibliography. But I don't keep the periodical material in so centralized a form, and I often have to paw my way through old bibliography folders if I'm searching for an article on that basis.

But the most important reason for doing bibliography afresh for each project is that the main results of bibliography come from doing it, not from having it. Suppose some genie could hand you, on the first day you start research, the bibliography that will ultimately be used in your finished product. Would you be able to write a decent piece of scholarship based on that bibliography? No. It is the doing of bibliography that teaches you what is connected to what, that tells you what topics bear on which research problems, that enables you to understand where the boundaries of your project are located, and, above all, that creates the thousand moments of serendipity that produce great research.

Such theoretical and empirical lessons from bibliography are also crucial because together they help determine when the project is done. For bibliography itself, there is a simpler criterion. Once you recognize about two thirds of the important citations in each new source, you are more or less done. If you do not recognize over a third, then you aren't done.

I noted early in the chapter that a good bibliography should be comprehensive but not overly detailed. What does that mean in practice? The published version of the paper discussed in chapter 2 had eighty-nine items in its actual reference list, for a very detailed historical paper of forty-six pages in manuscript. I had probably looked at five times that many particular sources at one time or another in the project. But that's highly detailed work with lots of primary sources. A typical qualifying or master's paper of forty pages is going to have forty or fifty items in the reference list of its final version. But they will all be important and high-quality, and they will stand for the three or four hundred references you have probably contacted at some point during the project.

6

Midphase Scanning, Browsing, and Brute Force

In library research, you can engage your materials with varying degrees of focus. You can glance through them quickly. You can troll through them carefully. Or you can examine everything. We usually think of the latter as "reading," but as every student knows, reading itself can be done with varying degrees of focus: you can scan, browse, or closely read a given text. But reading is a such special practice that it deserves a chapter of its own, following this one. Here I shall consider the varying degrees of focus as they apply to everything in your project that is not a particular text: bibliographies, search tools, databases, reference lists, statistical compendia, and so on.

I will distinguish three levels of engagement—scanning, browsing, and brute force—and I begin by discussing when to deploy each level. Of the three, browsing is the most important, because it most clearly illustrates the theoretical issues that undergird all types of engagement with library and Internet materials. I therefore next discuss the selection of material to browse and then turn to the theory of browsing itself. I then consider explicit and implicit browsing and turn in a final section to the discussion of scanning and brute force.

1. Choice of Search Strategy

Scanning and browsing are both words for "not looking at everything." Essentially, they suggest different levels of not looking. *Scanning* means going through material extremely fast, most often looking for a small number of quite specific things and ignoring everything else. *Browsing* means going somewhat more slowly, with less specific interests. Both terms can be opposed to "looking at everything," that is, to *brute force*, a term that captures the relentless, almost mechanical character of forcing yourself to examine everything, no matter whether you expect results from each item or not. Note that "looking at everything" is no more feasible for professional scholars than it is for you. Professionals themselves have to scan and browse. The question is when to do which one.

Your strategy is determined by the probability of finding (or missing) something good. It is wasteful to brute-force material with a low probability of return. Conversely, you shouldn't scan material that is very rich. Rather, you scan materials with very low payoff: when, for example, only every twentieth item is worthwhile. By contrast, you browse material where you expect a payoff from 10 percent to 40 percent of the items. And you brute-force material when the payoff is 50 percent or better. In that case, it pays simply to look at everything.

The rate of processing in turn determines the type of "filter" you use. By filter, I mean the type and list of things you are looking for. Because scanning is very rapid, you have to watch for very few and very specific things: a particular word or phrase, a small range of dates, four or five important names. Browsing is slower, so you can afford to watch for more things, and to be less specific about them ahead of time.

But your choice of search procedure depends not only on the probability of payoff in the material searched, but also on the worth of that payoff if it comes. Toward the end of a project, it is sometimes necessary to brute-force even low-payoff materials, because the payoff if you do find something is very large or because the loss if you miss something is very large (as when, for example, you have written "There are no studies of topic X"). In such situations, brute force is necessary—like panning for gold in the positive case, like frisking all the suspects in the negative one.

But there is a problem with the gold-panning metaphor, a problem that tells us something very important about searches. Gold nuggets are worthwhile because of the gold market. That is, their value is established ahead of time, by somebody else. But the things that have huge value for you at the end of a project are things whose value will have been created by you: by the care of your research design and by your diligence and good fortune in carrying it out. If you recall chapter 2, you will remember that once I discovered the importance of "departmental libraries," I dropped everything and focused only on that topic. The evolution of the project had made it clear that the history of departmental libraries was at the center of what my project had become (although it had not been at the center of what my project started out to be). So I went back to bibliographies and sources I thought I had already processed and re-searched them by brute force, carefully going through every possible heading under which material about departmental libraries might occur. But the importance of this material was not there ex ante. That importance was created by the course of the research to that point. Put another way, it is the current state of your research that defines whether a given body of material has a high or low probability of payoff.

There is an art to imagining, at any given point in a project, what are the useful places to scan, browse, and brute force. Thus, in my library research course, I have a session on browsing in the fourth week. By this point, the empirical puzzles and theoretical puzzles of most students are becoming explicit. The vague generalities and the unfeasibilities are gone. So I run through the list of projects, and for each student I decide a body of material to browse: a range of shelves in the stacks, a list generated by a specific search string in JSTOR, perhaps a set of finding aids in the archives. Almost always, in a class of twenty, someone finds the pot of gold that makes his or her entire project almost trivially easy. Another half dozen find centrally important material, and beyond them another dozen find at least one or two obvious items that they can't believe they had missed. Perhaps four or five find nothing useful.

That is, by looking at a student's current design document and reflecting for five to ten minutes, I can come up with browsing ranges that produce major payoffs for most of my students, even though they have been working hard on their projects for a month. But how? Certainly not by simply knowing everything there is to know. I'm no more omniscient than the students. But there are strategies for selecting areas to browse.

2. Selecting What to Browse

These selection strategies are of two kinds, reflecting the two things required: (a) to select a direction or area for browsing and (b) to specify a filter and a precise range of materials that will actually be browsed. The directional strategies are the simpler ones. They are driven by the kind of conceptualization I discussed in chapter 4. As I said there, your conceptualization is an analytic description of the situation you are studying, a newspaper reporter's "who, what, when, where, and how." The main substantive strategy for finding an area of material to browse is to make a small move in this conceptualization.

For example, one of my students was writing about why production of tea in China remains highly traditionalized, whereas tea production in India is highly rationalized. With that puzzle, obvious areas to browse would be tea sales (marketers and sellers of Chinese tea—a change of *who*), or production of some similar traditional luxury good in China (silk—a change of *what*), or the larger setting (Chinese village agriculture in general—a change of *where*), or tea production in some other society (Japan—a big change of *where*), or production in some different period (a change of *when*), and so on. All of these are straightforward moves, but ones that students find surprisingly hard, in my experience. Usually when students think I have given them particularly insightful advice about their projects, I've just listed to myself all the actors or settings involved in their empirical situation and have noticed that they have ignored one or two. Going back to your conceptualization will provide you with lots of suggestions for areas that you have overlooked.

Having defined a general area for browsing, you must next create and fine-tune the particular selection of things that you are going to browse and the filter you will employ in browsing. There are three key issues: (1) the search string or strategy that generates the selection of material to browse, (2) the size of the database and the range selected for browsing, and (3) the quality of the material. The reasons behind these issues are obvious. There are a lot of potential database ranges to browse. My library has about ninety miles of stack shelves. JSTOR has about a million articles. And so on. You can be perfectly prepared, and yet browsing still won't work unless you have selected a reasonable range of material to browse.

The first issue is the search string (in the keyword environment) or the controlled vocabulary term (in the true-subject-index environment). The second of these is the easier case. Most often, if you cannot find useful material in a controlled vocabulary environment, you haven't yet found the right search terms for those sources. The best move is to find the thesaurus itself and follow the "see also" and "used for" links to find the proper search term. But it is often faster to simply try other terms. Thus one of my students was working on the intellectual reception of the work of the Frankfurt school of social theorists. Browsing in our catalog (that is, within LC cataloging terms), there wasn't much to be found. So I told her to switch from "intellectual reputation" as a subject term to "intellectual influence." Bingo. How did I know that *influence* would work? Well, I didn't know that *influence* would work. But I did know that (a) *reputation* wasn't working, and (b) there had to be more material than she was finding. It's also true that once you have worked with controlled vocabularies, you develop a sense of what kinds of substantives they use. For some reason I just knew that *influence* was the right word, not *reputation*.

But most browsing lists are keyword-generated. In that case, switching search strings generally just moves you from one long, flabby list to another long, flabby list. The solution is to limit list size by using restrictions other than an overly specific search string. Thus, another student was working on the history of osteopathic medicine. We were worried that the word *osteopathic* plus *osteopathy* would produce too long a list from JSTOR. So we restricted the journals searched to history, psychology, and sociology, and restricted the types of items to articles, in order to make sure the list was relatively short and strong. (The restriction to articles misses book reviews, which can be a disadvantage, but doing book reviews separately is easier because there are often five or six of them for a particular title, so they respond well to rapid scanning.) Note that in many databases you can also restrict by date and language, which also allows you to shorten the results list without narrowing the subject string unduly.

The overall aim in creating a list for browsing is to create a list in which about one quarter of the items will be useful. You want a list that is relatively rich (at least 15 percent worthwhile items), but not too long (under 250 items).

Identifying a good search string is made vastly easier by finding one or two high-quality pieces. As I noted earlier, you do that by using citation rankings in WoS to identify the most highly cited material. The titles and abstracts of these particular articles will contain the conventionally important keywords in a literature, which allows you to maximize returns from a pure keyword tool. By contrast, if you are working in a controlled vocabulary index like LC or *Sociological Abstracts* or one of the old Wilson tools, you need to identify the right search string for the indexers, not for the writers. Again, however, this is most easily accomplished by inspecting the list of index headings associated with a couple of articles that are dead center in your project. Then you search those subjects, using various other restrictions (discipline, type of material, currency) to keep the list down to a reasonable size.

The "reasonable-size" criterion is one reason for paying attention to the overall size of the various tools you are using. But knowing overall size is important also because size is related to quality. All other things equal, the bigger tools have lower average quality, and so the bigger the overall size, the harder to define a reasonable list.

That is, quality is the third basic variable in creating a list to browse, and ascertaining quality can be very difficult. For example, sometimes you may want to browse dissertations, both as a source of bibliography and for their substantive interest. After all, there is much bibliographical work concentrated in dissertations, and by now about one hundred thousand American dissertations are online. That's a nice, small dataset from which to select a couple of hundred items to browse (not to browse the whole dissertations of course: only the abstracts, in order to determine whether to look at the bibliographies). And PhD dissertations are fairly easily ranked in quality. Although there's plenty of variability within institutions, in general, dissertations from more prestigious universities are better than those from less prestigious ones, so you can focus your browsing by choosing dissertations from elite places. But as always, there's a tradeoff. A dissertation directly on topic from a lower-prestige institution will be far more useful than a vaguely related dissertation from a high-prestige institution.

By contrast, JSTOR contains about a million articles, which is an order of magnitude bigger than the dissertation pool. So it requires more restrictions to get a reasonably browsable subset, as well as more specific attention to quality. Luckily, one can use subject area, type of material, and dates to restrict JSTOR search results. Unfortunately, as I noted earlier, there is no direct quality criterion in JSTOR other than to focus on particular journals, whose quality you have to decide on the basis of another source (typically WoS Journal Citation Reports).

WoS is yet another order of magnitude bigger, probably including (in the social sciences and humanities indexes) about 1.5 million items per decade, close to ten times what is in JSTOR. Of course this means that average quality is far lower and that you have to use much more dramatic restrictions to achieve browsable lists. Here you will absolutely need to use particular journals to enact your quality restrictions. For example, sociology has about one hundred thousand citations a year in WoS, spread over 3,581 articles in 114 journals, the last time I checked. But almost a quarter of those citations are to the two top journals, which publish only 80 articles a year between them.

Browsing has its highest payoffs in areas where you are presently low on sources. This is something you should assess for yourself by looking at your currently located sources. Once you have your bibliography and materials well classified, it will be pretty obvious where you need to find more sources. As a rule, you need at least six good sources on any topic you want to pursue in depth. Once a topic breaks into subtopics, you need six sources on each of the subtopics you want to pursue in depth. And so on.

In summary, you identify areas to browse by choosing topics near to your own but not exactly the same. If you have been finding little, then if you are in a controlled vocabulary environment, you try some synonyms for your search string. If you are in a keyword environment, you try something more general, but restrict the list using quality indicators, dates, language, or other such restrictions. In that environment, the best way to prepare a list for browsing is often to begin with two or three excellent items that you have already identified. Use their vocabulary and their subject headings and move outward.

Keep the list of items you browse to a reasonable size—a couple of hundred items on a list, a couple of shelf bays in the stacks. Online, limit your lists by using language, date, and format restrictions rather than making your search string too elaborate or exacting. Boolean operators can be useful, but don't get overelaborate with them in creating lists for browsing. In browsing you aim to create a rich pool to troll in, not to identify sources directly. The most useful Boolean restriction is *not*. Often, your own specialized interest is buried under some general subject; the *not* operator can exclude that general overlay. If you are researching the poet Alexander Pope, for example, you can use "not Vatican" or "not Rome" to get rid of a lot of irrelevant material, which may be better than requiring *poet* or *Alexander* in the search string. But again, do your limitation using language, date, format, quality, and other such things rather than by trying to create a perfect search string. The latter strategy is self-defeating when you are creating browsing lists.

Once you have your browsing list prepared, it's best to browse in the library itself, where you can follow the trail immediately to physical sources if that need arises. Work at browsing in many short bursts, interspersed with immediately chasing after a few of the best finds. This keeps you attentive and interested. Doing any library task continuously for too long will make you bored and ineffectual. Above all, don't try to be efficient. Browsing isn't efficient work. It's letting randomness happen and collecting the wonderful results.

3. The Theory and Types of Browsing

Once a range of material with a certain level of potential payoff is identified, you must browse it. It is helpful to reflect in detail on how this browsing actually works.

As I have said, browsing is the intersection of two things: your mind and a database. The database can be anything: an electronic list, a shelf of books, a single book, an article, a bibliography—anything. Typically, the database has a good deal of order and/or selection built into it. This could be because you yourself have selected it, via a keyword or a search string or a controlled vocabulary term. But it also may have its own prior order. The shelves are ordered by their LC or Dewey call numbers; an encyclopedia has its headings. That order may also be purely arbitrary. Dictionaries and encyclopedias have alphabetical order, and many statistical compendia and substantive handbooks have an author-imposed subject order.

All of these orders create arbitrarily "noticeable" points in the database: page breaks, headwords, subject headings. In the electronic search context, most of this "alternative order" is suppressed. Lists retrieved by keywords and key strings are just consecutively ordered by relevance. So keyword-retrieved lists have the worst of both worlds. They are ordered by a "relevance" that is determined by a general-purpose popularity contest, not by your specific interest. But they also strip out the arbitrary break points and peripheral information that are necessary for real browsing.

By contrast, in physical contexts and in deliberately created online browsing lists, the order properties of the underlying database guarantee that you will see much information that is quite close to what you want, but not exactly what you want. Sometimes this is automatically associated information about items that interest you. Books on a shelf show their size and age. Terms in a handbook show their importance (via the length of space given to them), and so on. There is also information that you run into "on the way" to where your search is focused: shelves of books you pass in the stacks corridor, or terms glimpsed at the top of pages as you flip through an encyclopedia. This information is produced by the order internal to the data and the "arbitrarily noticeable points" that that order creates in it. In summary, the database has its own order and its own set of "nearby-ness" information, some of it nearby-ness for substantive or theoretical reasons, some of it purely arbitrary. All of this is one side of the browsing equation.

The other side of browsing is the browser him- or herself. To benefit from browsing, that browser must have a good deal of knowledge of the things contained in the database but ordered differently than they are in the database. As I noted in the case of bibliography, it is not the case that items in the database "have" importance ex ante. They are important because your questions make them important. They have significance and utility for browsing because there are things in your mind that identify them as significant and useful to you in particular: things that make you think "I've seen that name before; wasn't he the guy who invented the focal infection theory of insanity?" or "I've seen that organization's name somewhere else; now why was it important?" or "Aha, that term *devolution* again; I had better figure out what it really means." Browsing succeeds because the name, the organization, and the word were already in your mind, although not in any particularly well-ordered way.

Thus, as I have said several times before, successful browsing is completely dependent on prior work that loads your mind up with these attractors. If you look back at the chapter on the preliminary phase, you will see where these attractors come from. In the first place, they come from doing the work of bibliography. By reading the names and titles and locations of dozens of articles (of which only a few enter your bibliography, of course), you will have begun passively to learn the big names and the important concepts. In the second place, they will have come from your background reading. (I cover background reading in more detail in the next chapter.) Here too there are names and dates and organizations and concepts that keep coming up again and again. Some of them will quickly be assembled into your preliminary view of the whole area, but others—far more, in fact—will remain as isolated memories.

In formal terms, browsing works because the two bodies of knowledge—one in your head and one in the database—come together. And it is most productive when the order in your head is not the same as the order in the database. In your head, topic A may be related to your narrower topics (YNT1, YNT2, YNT3, etc.) and to your broader topics (YBT1, YBT2, YBT3, etc.) and to some related topics (YRT1, YRT2, YRT3, etc.). But in the database, topic A may be related to different narrower topics (DNT1, etc.), to different broader topics (DBT1, etc.), and to different related topics (DRT1, etc.). So instead of duplicating things you already know, the process of browsing offers to lead you in many new directions. The best databases for browsing, thus, are not ordered "from nowhere," but have a point of view that is somewhere near yours but not exactly the same. That raises the chance that browsing in them will take you somewhere useful.

Beyond these browsing successes induced by the encounter of the two different orders lie the browsing long shots produced by arbitrary break points. You may notice an "attractor" word on the top of a page as you flip through an encyclopedia. You may notice an attractor name as you scroll through a subject index. You may notice a very useful table because you had difficulty finding the one you wanted in the *Statistical Abstract*. These long-shot browsing successes are the physical analogy of what is produced when you browse the typical keyword relevance order. Even such orders can be useful, because they are arbitrary with respect to what you want. But they lack the strong order and plenteous peripheral information that make real browsing so effective.

In short, browsing success happens when you are looking through a database's narrower, broader, and related topics and even its somewhat arbitrary adjacent topics (annoying because they are "getting in the way of finding exactly what I want"). Suddenly the database's adjacent topic 5 sets off the alarm of your narrower topic 3. An attractor has found its object. And as a result you may change the way you are thinking about the relation of your narrower topic 3 to your main topic. Or perhaps the connection suggests a new related topic that you hadn't thought related. Or perhaps it suggests a way of rearranging your narrower topics.

This kind of experience is continuous during browsing. Many library researchers love to tell of the one magic moment when they randomly found the crucial book when they looked at the wrong shelf. They call it serendipity and act as if it happened only once or twice in their lives. But the fact is that such serendipitous discovery takes place quite steadily in library research. It is in fact a (or the) central constituent of the process through which your project gets focused and completed. (Recall my story about pensions in chapter 5.) Yet this randomness is precisely what is taken out by excessively efficient searching—by "seeing exactly and only what you want." That's why efficiency is not useful in library research.

That browsing requires an informed browser as well as an ordered object of browsing has some obvious implications for research. As I noted in chapter 4, you shouldn't browse much at the beginning of your project. Browsing is generally a midproject exercise, best done once you have learned the attractors that are necessary for browsing to work. Second, because browsing depends on delicate connections between a database and what is in your head, concentrated, long sessions of browsing are good. But they should consist of bursts of browsing work alternating with chasing the results. In a long session, your working short-term memory will have more little details in it to serve as attractors for browsing insights, while the occasional chasing of results will keep you attentive.

It is useful also to distinguish two different kinds of browsing, explicit and implicit. In explicit browsing we are reading a database with the explicit intent of finding some relevant material, even though we aren't exactly sure what it may be. In implicit browsing, we are doing something else in a database, browsing in the background while we do so. In each type, we should reflect about the database involved, the ordering principles in it, the typical searcher, the typical result, and the advantages and disadvantages. And, although we have already covered these things to some extent, it is also helpful to go over the particular forms that browsing commonly takes.

A. EXPLICIT BROWSING

For my generation, the most familiar kind of explicit browsing is browsing in the stacks. Here the database is the stacks themselves, and the order principle is the LC classification. As I have noted, a lot of information is visible at a glance in the stacks that would take more time to get from a digital record because you have to read it; this is a place where skills honed on video games will be most helpful. You literally see the size of a book. After a bit of experience you equally "see" the age of a book—at least within about twenty years—by the cover design, spine printing, and binding materials. You can see the use of the book. (In scholarly libraries, books with broken bindings are important books.) You can see the publisher and therefore the rough quality. All of those things are evident in a fraction of a second, far faster than you could get them from a digital record, which—even worse—contains no use information. Better yet, an interesting book can be pulled off the shelf and itself browsed at once. (As in all forms of research, the stack browser must be a prepared reader: you must know the big names, the important concepts, and so on. You have to be able to *see* that something might be important.)

Stack browsing enables you to locate important books very quickly. You find them and retrieve them at the same time. But you will also be reminded of important issues for further investigation, because the varying aspects of your topic and the varying attitudes toward it will leap out at you from the jumble of titles on the shelves. They don't jump out that way from the computer screen, because on screen all books look exactly the same; they lack the individuality that makes the physical artifacts so informative so quickly.

The advantages of stack browsing are that it is very fast, that it takes in multiple variables at once, and that it leads immediately into a physical book browse because the book is there to be taken down. The disadvantages are, first, that important books may be checked out, and second, that if the collection is immense it can be unbrowsable. (For the early, unfocused parts of undergraduate research papers, our main library is too big to browse. Even on a fairly specific topic, we have hundreds and hundreds of books.) If you are at a great university with a huge library, you may want to find a much smaller university library that has a shelf-list function in its online catalog and browse there. It's not as good as physical browsing, but nothing will be out on loan, and you will be able to consider finite quantities of items. A third disadvantage to stack browsing is that there is, in the stacks, no equivalent of hyperlinking. If you want to move to a new area, you have to go to the online catalog, find a new location in the library, and go there to browse.

Obviously related to stack browsing is physical book browsing, which I have already mentioned. Here the database browsed is a book, and the ordering principle is the chapter and section order of the book. There is usually a good subject index. Immediately available is information about style of writing, level of scholarly machinery (footnotes), personal qualities of author (preface), as well as logical structure (table of contents), major terms (index), and so on. In about five minutes you can know a great deal about a book, things that would take you half an hour with an online book.

Typical results from a book browse might include ideas, issues, people, and of course references and citations. The advantages of physically browsing a book are that it is far faster and more comprehensive than anything you can do with a book online. You can scan deeply in one area, but lightly in another. You can nest it within stack browsing for a fast scan of a large amount of subject material. The disadvantages are that it can be hard to take notes (that is much easier online), and that you have to stand while doing it (if you're doing it within a stack browse), which gets very tiring. (In the research reported in chapter 2, I found ethnographic accounts from the 1950s of scholars standing in the stacks reading whole chapters of books.)

Another useful place to browse is in an online library catalog, typically in its (LC) subject index. In addition to the information you seek, you get a feeling for the structure of headings, particularly if, as in a good catalog, you can see many lines of subjects at a glance. Of course you can click through to the book lists under the headings and get the usual MARC record information on any book, which gives you the bases for your quality and relevance decision. Catalog subject browsing is a very useful thing but demands a lot of skill. LC is a world of its own and needs to be mastered to be browsed effectively. But do remember that keyword browsing in online catalogs is pointless; it's like eating hamburgers when you could get filet mignon (browsing the LC subject headings) for the same price.

There is usually not much side payoff in catalog browsing. The aim is to find directly relevant material for in-depth investigation, and catalogs are more or less optimized for that purpose. But there are some conspicuous advantages. One of them is that you can catalog-browse libraries that are not your own. Although it may seem surprising, even giant collections like Harvard, Michigan, and Illinois each contain hundreds of thousands of items not owned by the others. If you are seeking really esoteric materials, it pays well to troll a couple of catalogs besides your own local one. And I have already noted the utility of browsing a smaller collection, particularly early in the research process when you are seeking background works. Important background works will be much more evident in a small teaching catalog than in an immense research-driven one. Another crucial advantage is that in an electronic catalog, hyperlinkage allows you to change course very quickly in midstream and direct your attention elsewhere. This can sometimes be problematic—you lose track of what you have done or how you have gotten to where you are. But it does enable very rapid brachiation through complex structures of material.

The disadvantages of catalog browsing are those of many such mass tools. One can find large lists of marginally relevant material. (Here again you should rely on whatever other restrictions are available to you: date, language, and so on.) There is also the difficulty that LC cataloging places books as specifically as possible, and so it is often necessary to check not only certain main categories, but also all subcategories under them in order to cover an area fully.

Tools that supposedly browse for you—like AquaBrowser (it's called Lens at our library)—are useless. They have the usual silly relevance rankings. They put too much information on each page, reducing the number of items you see quickly and thus slowing your browsing to a plod. They contain large amounts of nonscholarly material, and hence reduce the average quality of items found. Worst of all, they "assist the user to find what he wants" which means, in practice, that they do a lot of selecting and arranging of which you the user are unaware. That selecting and arranging is based on the erroneous theories of library research held by the programs' designers, who are not themselves serious library researchers and have no idea how such research is done. Never use such tools. Also, never use a one-size-fits-all "portal," unless (as with ArchiveGrid) there is no advanced search tool. Portals are optimized for novices, because they surrender all actual control to the machine. (That's as true in JSTOR as in catalogs. Never use JSTOR's basic search; always use advanced search, which you yourself control.) Always use a traditional catalog for subject browsing, with its tight logic, its controlled vocabulary, and its transparency.

A fourth place to browse is reference works. Hundreds of reference works, both online and print, are listed in the ALA *Guide*. They aim to be authoritative works on specific topics. Most of them are produced by consortia of authors, who typically divide up the various areas of expertise. Some are handbooks, some are statistical compendia, some are miniencyclopedias, some are lists or catalogs. There are thousands of them, of varying quality and provenance. (I noted in chapter 4 some techniques for judging which of these are the best.) Since your topic most often does not lie exactly within the ambit of some particular chapter of some particular reference book, you will often be browsing these books for information, rather than reading them in detail. Such browsing in reference works can be extremely rewarding. They are already highly concentrated in terms of their subjects. They tend to have very strong internal organization, usually by subject or other substantive classification (place, organization, etc.). Because they have very concentrated focus, they will have a large amount of adjacent, immediately related information that you wouldn't necessarily think of looking for, but that may well be very relevant to your project. Most important, unlike most forms of browsing, browsing in reference works really does help novice users or people starting in new fields. It does so by suggesting one or more of the standard ways to arrange and see things in the field. It can thus be done at a project's beginning for orientation. It can also be useful late in a project, to remind you of things you should have studied but have not. It enables you to see the minor holes in your research.

The great advantage of reference works is their strong subject organization, which means they provide reasonable overviews at the beginning of a project and reasonable checklists for the end. Their disadvantage is that when you are in the thick of a topic you will know most of what you see in them but find it slightly out of focus or slightly backward, because you will be reacting to the inevitable theoretical slant all such books must have. It is also true that they can flatten topics out (as does the computer screen), and so make it difficult to identify which are the genuinely important parts of a topic and which are peripheral. But the risk is well worth running. Such books can be very useful.

I have already discussed browsing in databases, which was the basic model for browsing discussed earlier. So I shall not cover that further here. But there does remain one other important form of browsing, browsing in the reference lists of monographs and articles. Here the "database" is simply a previous scholar's work on a topic. Reading through the bibliography of a well-selected article of high quality is probably the first move of most senior researchers on entering a new area. It's the only sensible thing to do. Note that in many libraries' systems, you can click directly through to the articles cited. This can be distracting, however. Do one thing at a time until you have your project well structured. Otherwise, you will end up with the world's largest bibliography and no way to shorten it.

B. IMPLICIT BROWSING

In contrast to these various types of explicit browsing we have also implicit browsing. By this I mean the browsing that is continuously ongoing when any serious scholar is at work. Library researchers are always browsing in the background, peripherally noticing odd things in whatever sources are in front of them—articles, books, data, minianalyses, reference works, indexes, anything. Much of this browsing is forced on them by the fact that search tools are "inefficient." Because of this, you have to look at a lot of "irrelevant" things on the way to "what you wanted." The scare quotes identify the problem with this argument. Good scholars *want* to see closely related but slightly irrelevant material. That's where 90 percent of their ideas come from. They do not want efficiency.

Examples of implicit browsers might be a person paging through a monograph looking for something in particular, or a person paging through an indexed item looking for something in particular, or a person searching a bibliography, or an encyclopedia, or a dictionary, a gazetteer or statistical data source, looking for something in particular. Or even a person walking through the stacks and idly watching the books on the ends of the rows he is passing. All of these items have in them some kind of alphabetized or other "headings" that you must see as you pass through: start and stop words in dictionaries, table titles in statistical sources, LC numbers and subjects on the ends of stacks. If your implicit browsing checker is on, you will retrieve four or five things a day from random hits between these things and one of your browsing attractors.

And indeed implicit browsing happens when you are working with the primary materials you have gathered for your project. Serious scholars are always browsing in the background any time they are working in their materials. These materials can be primary materials or even one's own project files. They are usually full of extraneous information of all kinds, and suddenly some piece of it will strike you as more relevant than you thought. A whole new line of investigation may open up. These insights may even happen when you are coding data—extracting it from some bunch of extraneous material. The extraneous material—which disappears in a perfect-retrieval world—suddenly tells you something important.

While implicit browsing reveals all sorts of peripheral ideas and hypotheses, and provides a sense of the great depth of your subject, it has some disadvantages as well. Sometimes it reveals material so important that you have to go back and rethink a major part of your project. Sometimes it becomes distracting. To avoid that distraction, as we shall see in a couple of chapters, is one reason you should refile your data often. Indeed, an overload of implicit connections in your own files is one sign that you need to rethink and reimagine your project, either by reorganizing the files or by changing the design itself.

4. Scanning and Brute Force

At the beginning of this chapter I noted that scanning is the proper search strategy when the payoff rate is below 10 percent and brute force is the proper strategy when the payoff rate is over 50 percent. In each case the techniques are a little different from those of browsing.

With scanning, there are two general strategies. One of them, which I shall discuss more in the next chapter, is to fix a very specific template in your mind and rush through a long list of material—two, three, four hundred items—looking for just that one thing. Of course, if the one thing is a keyword and the list is electronic, the machine will do this for you. But most often, you are not looking for just one keyword, and much of the time the list won't be electronic. Suppose your project is to understand the assimilation of Chinese Americans in Chicago in the first half of the twentieth century. Your scanning template is "anything related enough to Chinese Americans in Chicago to be possibly worthwhile in my project." So no one subject heading will work; no one geographical heading will work (assimilation of Chinese-Americans in California would be relevant); no one journal will work, and so on. You may be forced simply to blast your way through long lists with this single if somewhat flexible template, grabbing everything that looks relevant. You might need to go through several huge LC headings: "Chinese-Americans" (778 items in my library), "Acculturation" (321 items), and "Assimilation—Sociology" (199 items). But you can't afford to browse these, because it would take forever and most of the items are not of interest. So you establish some general idea as a template and scan, rather than browse.

The other basic scanning strategy is to trust your instincts and, not choosing any template, simply glance through a long list very quickly and note anything that looks interesting. Late in a project, your instincts will be tuned enough to the particular project to make this a viable strategy. By that time, the vast majority of what you see in almost any long list will be either obviously familiar or obviously irrelevant. What you are seeking are those rare items that you can't quite classify. You pause over each of them for thirty seconds and make a quick decision, then move on. If you find yourself slowing down, then either you aren't ready for this kind of scanning or the list calls for a slower procedure. Nonetheless, this is a useful form of scanning under certain conditions, when you are making sure that you haven't missed anything, toward the end of a project.

The main danger in scanning is disattention. Scanning is highly disciplined, concentrated work. You are moving very fast and looking for very particular things. If part of your mind drifts off to think about last night's date for a few minutes, you can easily think you are scanning material when you are actually just passing it under your eyes. If you find this happening, take a break. Drink a cup of coffee and relive all the details of the date. Then go back to work.

By contrast with scanning, brute force means looking through everything with reasonable care. You use brute force at a number of moments in a project: in analyzing certain kinds of data, in reviewing certain kinds of bibliography, sometimes even in refiling your own materials. The first criterion calling for brute force is that more than half of the items you look at will need action: whether they are data that has to be coded, potentially important bibliographical items to be retrieved, or potentially movable filed materials to be refiled. When 50 percent of the entries in a bibliography are relevant; when you've located and isolated primary sources that are completely relevant to your project; when you have created a numerical dataset that must be analyzed in its entirety to justify quantitative judgments: under these conditions, working through every single item is the only strategy.

A second occasion for brute force is when the potential loss caused by missing a relevant item is very large: that is, when any other procedure may sacrifice too much of what you need. Often this will happen when there is no reliable index and no guaranteed scanning strategy.

Third, you sometimes do brute force when you are specifically interested in gaining a comprehensive sense of the phenomenon you are studying, of its interconnections and peculiarities. That is, you do brute force sometimes as a statement to yourself that you are committing yourself to the research, surrendering to the phenomenon. This comes back to the remark that you can't do real library research purely by surface methods. You must actually enter into the world of the phenomenon at some point, just as the ethnographer has to "go native" even while maintaining distance. Brute-forcing your way through some materials will accomplish that.

These criteria explain my brute-force search of the University of Chicago Graduate Library School materials in chapter 2. I was desperate for anything I could find that (a) took a rigorously social-scientific approach to library use by scholars and (b) dated from before 1970. Since the University of Chicago Library School had been the center of such rigorous work for the middle decades of the twentieth century, I felt obliged to look at every single MLS or PhD thesis from the school. So as I said, I printed out the entire list (of about 600 items) and spent a whole afternoon brute-forcing it. That got me down to 100 potential items, and I checked every single one of them out of the library and eventually looked through all of them. About thirty were so important that I would have been devastated to have lost them. There was certainly no faster way to have found these things by subject search, and any subject search would have missed quite a number of them. So the task met criterion 2 for brute force: avoidance of catastrophic loss. There were, of course, other library theses at other institutions. But I found the gems at other universities by going through the bibliographies of the Chicago theses. By brute-forcing a dataset well below my 50 percent threshold (my actual hit rate for gems was around 6 percent), I made a clean sweep of the relevant materials, both at Chicago and probably elsewhere. I couldn't afford not to.

We all know the danger in brute force: boredom. If you find yourself going to sleep, take a break. If you find yourself missing things, take a break. Indeed, if things get too bad, take up another task, something that's more exciting and immediately rewarding. There's no point in sentencing yourself to brute force if you're going to fail at the one thing it is good for: making sure that you've looked at everything.

SCANNING, BROWSING, AND BRUTE FORCE ARE THUS THREE CRUCIAL modes of operating in library work. They apply to bibiliography, of course, but also to the intensive trolling for primary materials that is at the heart of many library projects. As with my library-use project, the primary materials of our projects today are often analyses that were the secondary analyses of their time. At times, huge ranges of primary materials will need to be browsed—as in my library-use project I checked out and scanned the ninety scholarly autobiographies, then browsed about thirty more carefully, ultimately finding fifteen that had centrally important material and needed to be read in detail.

And that brings us to our next subject: as one might expect, the heart of a library research project is reading.

7 | *Reading*

Library research involves a lot of reading. Yet in the current environment, reading seems less central than it was, even in the research practice of experts. Our slightest intellectual whim can be instantly indulged, so we all spend more time surfing and less time reading. We need to carefully study this tradeoff between searching and reading, because it shapes modern research practice decisively.

In economic terms, there is an obvious tradeoff between searching and reading. If a researcher finds only a very few sources and reads them very, very well, then while his work may be superb in its limited area, it may also be misconceived because that specific area is highly unusual or because those particular sources were biased in important ways or because contextual information would have revealed obviously preferable interpretations of the sources. By contrast, if a researcher spends all his time searching for things, but then reads them only cursorily, he is likely to be misled by surface appearances, by biases that would have been obvious on deeper reading, by the happenstance logic of the hyperlinks he has traced.

The economists represent such a logic by the curves shown in figure 2. In this graph, reading (R) is on the x-axis and searching (S) is on the y-axis. Each unlabeled curve represents a single level of the overall quality of the research project, produced by various combinations of the two factors—searching and reading. As we move to the left along any given curve, we substitute searching for reading. But as you know well, at a certain point searching becomes counterproductive. You find things that are too disparate to pull together. You find so many things that you have no way to decide which are important. That is, in this section of the curve, additional searching is actually getting in the way of the scholarship. In fact you could have searched less and written a better paper with the same amount of reading. This is symbolized in the figure by the curve's starting to bend back to the right as it rises. You could drop

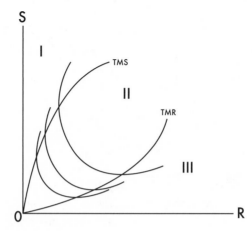

FIGURE 2. Tradeoff between searching and reading

straight down (same amount of reading) and combine it with less searching, and be on a curve further out from the origin—a better paper. On the figure, reaching out from the origin is curve TMS, which joins the points—one on each different quality curve—where this transition to too much searching takes place.

Of course a similar argument holds at the other end, when we move to the right, substituting reading for searching. Eventually, you are reading so much that the project is undermined. Perhaps you have been captured by an idiosyncratic point of view in the sources you are reading, or perhaps you are buried under unnecessary details. Perhaps you have become trapped in a backwater, a black hole in the research area. Excess reading is so confusing your scholarship that you must undertake further searching to offset that problem. (The curve has begun to bend up, away from the x-axis.) In fact, you could write a better paper reading less, for the same amount of search (moving left parallel to the x-axis would put you on a quality curve further out from the origin. The curve from the origin to TMR joins the points on the different quality curves where this transition to too much reading takes place.

In between the TMS and TMR curves, on any given curve of quality, lies the zone in which the tradeoff between searching and reading is positive. More searching can produce an equivalent output with less reading, and vice versa. This is the range of sensible factor substitution. On the diagram it is zone II, as TMS is zone I and TMR is zone III.

What about cost? A given cost line is represented by a diagonal line sloping downward to the right. It represents the units of searching or reading that can be "purchased" with time, since time is the principal cost constraint in library research. The diagonal cost curves all have the same slope because the relative cost of searching versus reading does not depend on how much work the researcher has already done. (Let's forget about boredom, sleepiness, and screen jitters for the moment.) In figure 3, I have inserted some particular cost lines. They happen to be those tangent to the production curves. That's because for any given amount of time spent on a combination of reading and searching (any given cost line), the best (furthest from the origin) product curve will be the one to which this cost line is exactly tangent. All this is elementary economics. There is, for any given project, and for any given cost tradeoff between search and reading, a particular combination of search and reading that will produce the best possible paper.

Now suppose the technology of search changes, such that search becomes less and less costly. (Obviously, this is what has happened over the last twenty years.) The cost lines become more and more steep—a given amount of reading (a given point on the x-axis) costs as much time as a much, much larger amount of searching. Some examples (the dashed lines) are shown in figure 4. The tangents are at new points. Indeed, for the first curve from the origin, we are now very close to dysfunctional amounts of search. Note that if search is completely costless, the cost line is vertical; reading becomes

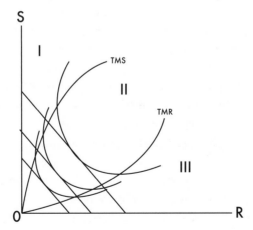

FIGURE 3. Optimizing searching and reading for a given relative cost of searching and reading

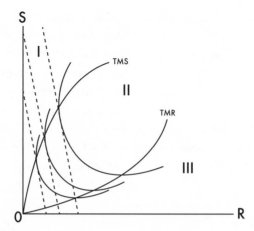

FIGURE 4. Substitution of search for reading as searching becomes cheaper

the sole determinant of the cost and therefore the quality of the project. But more generally, as the time cost of searching falls, the researcher gradually does more and more searching, in the sense that more and more of the final product is the product of "search work" than of "reading work." As the economists say, searching substitutes for reading.

Now there is a crucial assumption built into these graphs, one that is implicit in the width of the three zones of each curve. I have drawn these graphs so that the sections are roughly symmetrical. But they aren't. As I have no need to tell you, diminishing returns for search arrive very quickly. You find too much material; you have no way to order or prune it; you are quickly overwhelmed. To deal effectively with such huge searches, one needs considerable intellectual capital in terms of accepted terminologies, prior knowledge of research areas, and so on. Only experienced researchers have those tools, which enable them to handle the overload that comes so quickly. That's why many faculty are enthused about the new digital universe. They have the wherewithal to use it effectively. Not surprisingly, they are bewildered when students seem to get lost in what is for faculty a paradise.

FOR STUDENTS, THE GRAPHS PROBABLY LOOK MORE LIKE FIGURE 5. IN these graphs diminishing returns for search set in very quickly. By contrast, diminishing returns for reading take a long time to arrive. That's because the need for attractors in browsing means that reading very directly facilitates search, while search does almost nothing to facilitate reading. Both of these things mean in turn that the actual quality of a project is largely determined by the productivity of your reading, not your searching. Anything that could reduce the time cost of reading—making it more productive—would be extremely useful.

So there is a very strong purely economic logic that points us toward the importance of reading in research. Ironically, the easier search becomes, the more research productivity depends mainly on reading. Luckily, it turns out there are different kinds of reading. Choosing the proper reading strategy for any particular material will make your total reading time much more productive. Reflecting about reading is of course important for other reasons as well, for it is while reading that we focus on a single argument, a single topic, a single set of data, a single universe of meanings, a single author. So for both instrumental and normative reasons, it is crucially important to have a separate chapter on reading.

Reading is in some ways continuous with browsing and scanning. On a first approximation, reading simply means going slower, paying more attention. But actually there is a deep difference between scanning, browsing, and brute force on the one hand and reading on the other. Scanning, browsing, and brute force are *associative* techniques. In them, we analyze a text with a template or templates—what I have called attractors. We are hoping to find a few ideas or facts or examples or citations that stick to our attractors. But

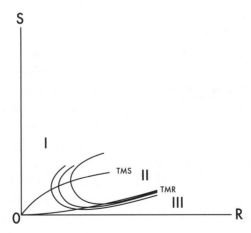

FIGURE 5. Actual tradeoffs of searching and reading for today's students

in reading we aim to find not items, but arguments, descriptions, and other extended intellectual structures. We are seeking things that require thought, not simple recognition. We find them not by associating them with attractors, but by mastering their syntax or pattern. Reading is a *discursive* technique. That requires a different type of attention.

1. Modes of Reading

Like scanning/browsing/brute force, reading can be done at many levels. But in this case the level is not determined by the density of the text in terms of expected return, as it is with browsing and scanning. Rather it is determined by the particular kinds of things we want from reading. Sometimes we want simply to follow a story. Sometimes we want to be stimulated intellectually. Sometimes we want to master the bare bones of argument. Each of these has its own strategy.

A. NARRATIVE READING

Narrative is the most familiar type of reading. We read to get the story. Thus, narrative fiction is written on the assumption that you will read every word, as if the story were being told out loud. Especially in nineteenth-century fiction, this structure was exacerbated by the use of sentences so complex that they are impossible to understand without subvocalization. One must hear such a text in order to parse it.

Reading of this kind is seldom necessary in any social science research materials, primary or secondary. Few of them are written with self-conscious elegance, and most of them are conceived not as narrative but as exposition, not as story, but as analysis. As we shall see below, expository texts are amenable to various forms of accelerated reading, which take advantage of their topic sentences and section summaries to skim much of the intervening text. In many expository books, there is even a complete summary of the book's argument in the final chapter. For harried researchers, this is a useful thing indeed.

But in library research there are some occasions for narrative reading. In the humanities, of course, narrative reading is often the first method for reading primary materials. (Later readings will be not narrative but analytic.) But more generally, a library researcher reads narratively when reading "in the background." In background reading you are orienting yourself to an area, getting used to the important names and concepts, and immersing yourself in debates and problems. You aim thereby to fill your medium-term memory with browsing attractors and to start building a general sense of your research area. To be sure, you may want to take some notes on background reading. A timeline might be helpful, if the background material is a history. Or a sketch biography, or a listing of some major arguments. But the purpose of background reading is not to master things. It is to orient yourself to the research area and to prime your browsing eyes with attractors. Narrative reading is the proper mode for this. It is a familiar technique, so I won't discuss it further.

B. MEDITATIVE READING

In most library research, only very occasionally do you want to read more slowly than everyday narrative reading. But sometimes you may want to do such "meditative reading." You read meditatively when you are looking for new general ideas: ideas about how to attack your basic project or about new theories or interpretations. So you choose a rich text, often one that is not immediately related to your specific research questions, but rather related to the general set of theoretical issues that concern you. You read every word, slowly, and allow your mind to resonate freely with the text. You attend to possible allusions, to interesting themes, sometimes even to the sounds of the words. You read a paragraph or two, then look at the wall and reflect. Then perhaps you jot a few notes in a theory folder as ideas drift into your head: "What if I simply disregarded my second theoretical question and refocused the project?" "Is institutionalist theory really helping me here?" "What about a functionalist way of organizing the subsections?"

Then you read some more. You are going to spend three or four minutes per page. Perhaps even more. You are not aiming to get through something; your aim is simply to stimulate your own thinking. You therefore let the text come apart into shreds of insight and allusion. Obviously, such a strategy works only with very rich texts. Hence meditative reading is used for important works of theory or central passages within larger texts.

In library research, you should choose for meditative reading a major theoretical work in your own project area. One of my course students was studying the rise of environmental politics in Ecuador. So I suggested reading R. G. Collingwood's *Idea of Nature*. It's a general philosophical work about the concept of nature itself. There was no need to understand Collingwood's arguments in detail; the idea was rather to let them stimulate her thinking, to point her in new directions.

Above all, meditative reading reminds us of the importance of thinking. Even a careful researcher can get caught up in the excitement of detection, the bravura of brachiation, the thrill of the chase. All the more reason to remember that research is not ultimately about discovering something. Our project does not have an answer waiting somewhere for us to arrive. Rather, we aim to assemble a new and exciting collection of found things in order to resolve an empirical puzzle and reflect theoretically about social life. The heart of research is a creative act in the researcher, not a clever detective routine. Research cannot be done without hard thinking, and meditative reading guarantees that we do that hard thinking.

One should always therefore remember that the authors we read during a research project had ideas; they didn't simply recite facts. They struggled to put those ideas into words to be printed. They said their ideas a dozen different ways because no particular way sounded quite right. They wrote long books because they thought they could tie down the ideas by specifying more about them. But all that extra writing simply made the rich ambiguity of the ideas even more evident. The ideas of an author don't become more specific as you read more of him or her. They become more generative. You become more able to anticipate, to channel an author. Only then are you able to use an author's ideas in your own thinking. To achieve this, you read meditatively.

C. SCAN READING

At the other end of the scale is scan reading. Scanning is done very quickly, in a text where most of the material is irrelevant, but some small portion is something you need and can quickly identify. You first use the index, table of contents, or headings to find the likely parts to scan. Then you rush as fast as possible through the pages selected, employing a template or search term. It helps, of course, if the latter has easily distinguishable features: capital letters, an extended pattern of several words, etc. (Thus in chapter 2, I scanned the ninety scholarly autobiographies looking for discussions of scholarly practices and within them for the word "library.") Your scanning speed is a function of various things. The less organized the text, the slower you must scan. The less obvious the template or search term, the slower you must scan. The more it matters if you miss something, the slower you must scan. The quality of the index, the detail of the headings within chapters, and—particularly—the length of the paragraphs and even of the sentences may make a big difference.

Scanning always involves a particular search term or terms. In scan reading, this template will come from the current minianalysis or data source. Because it is template-dependent, scan reading is sometimes easier with digital texts (if there is an obvious keyword). But if the template isn't specific (e.g., if you're looking for "anything about environmental issues in Ecuador"), string search won't work well. More problematic, while you can scan articles in JSTOR, you can at present scan books only through Google Books, which is prevented by copyright law from allowing full access. So you should learn how to scan-read physical books.

In scan reading you are likely to be distracted by browsing opportunities. Background reading and controlled vocabulary building will have put attractors in your head, and you will constantly be tempted to slow down to browsing speed as you see those attractors in the text. But force yourself to move on. Scan reading is a brute-force exercise: straight through, no skips, absolute focus. It will be quite tiring.

D. READING FOR MASTERY OF ARGUMENT

Mastery reading is the standard mode of full-text reading in social science. We mastery-read when we must know a text's core argument but can ignore peripheral details like examples, asides, and minor corollaries. Several variables affect the ease of mastery reading. Texts vary in length. They vary in density. Third and most important, they may or may not follow the standard rules for high-quality expository prose, which make texts easy to ransack for main points and overarching ideas. At the level of prose style, these rules include mostly short sentences mixed with occasional long ones, very clear use of referents and logical markers, short paragraphs with obvious topic sentences (usually as opening sentences), and clear logical linkage. At the book level, these rules call for clear and helpful chapter structure, strong (and possibly multilevel) subdivisions within chapters, paragraphs of sane length (two or three per page), and, above all, clear summaries at the ends of subsections, sections, chapters, and possibly even at the end of the book.

All these make a text easier to master. But even if a text is not particularly well written, you still want to apply as many of the well-written-text strategies as you can. Fall back on bad-text strategies (discussed below) only when absolutely necessary.

To mastery-read a well-written book, you first master the table of contents. Read it four or five times. Memorize it. Then scan the index to find the dozen or so most-cited abstractions. These will be the core terms of the author's argument. Memorize these so that you will recognize them immediately as you scan pages. Your main task is to understand how these words are logically connected by the author's argument.

Third, check the last chapter to see if there is a summary of the argument. Also check the ends of each chapter for summaries. (Some writers write uninformative summaries, by the way—perorations rather than recapitulations.) If you find summaries, read them carefully; note how they combine the major terms from the index. Try to recite the book's main argument to yourself, as if you were explaining it to someone else. Remember, you are not reading narratively. You are reading "from the top down." You should always be flipping pages, always moving back and forth, always forcing yourself to summarize your knowledge so far. If you catch yourself reading steadily for five minutes, stop. You are out of mastery mode.

Once you have mastered the layout, terms, and basic argument (this will have taken about half an hour and feel like lot of work), scan the book for about fifteen minutes, looking for anything else to absorb or to add to your understanding of the argument. Then and only then, allow yourself ten or fifteen minutes to write summary notes of the argument. Refer back to the table of contents, index, summaries, and text as necessary.

This entire process should take about an hour for a well-written 300-page book. By this process, you can, for example, probably master my own first book's six theoretical chapters in about an hour. Of this hour, you will have spent as little as a quarter to a half actually "reading" sentences. The rest is all mastering the organization and finding what to read. You can be very sure that after an hour spent this way, you will know ten times as much about the book as you would if you started at the beginning and read narratively. (A really good mastery reader, for example, will have found that the first three theoretical chapters are summarized almost completely on pages 111–113.)

It is because you spend so much of this time flipping back and forth, by the way, that mastery reading is virtually impossible online. You can't flip pages fast enough or scan large blocks of text as fast. Curiously, the online environment favors narrative reading, which is useful only in a narrow range of research activities. That's why e-books—which allow paging—are becoming more common. But they're still slower than physical books.

At the article level, too, good writing is relatively easily to mastery-read. This is particularly true because there is a limited number of logical templates for articles: compare-and-contrast, case-analysis, quantitative-causal-analysis, adjudication-of-two-theories, tell-the-story, and so on. You know these templates well, and how to read them. Unfortunately, writing at the sentence and paragraph level is often pretty bad in articles, usually because of slavish imitation: sometimes imitation of scientific style, sometimes imitation of obscure philosophy or theory. Also, in an article there is no table of contents or index. So you must rely on the abstract, the headings, and the conclusion to produce your initial impression of an article.

The mastery reading of a well-written article follows the same algorithm as the reading of the well-written book. It will take about twenty minutes. First, master the abstract. Get the whole thing into your mind. Become familiar with all parts of it. Notice what aspects of it are unclear, and mark them in your mind for further investigation. You will need to read the abstract five or six times to do this. It will take five to ten minutes. Next, comparing the abstract to your own concept of an ideal version of this particular article, figure out the necessary parts of that ideal that aren't evident from the abstract.

In an empirical article, these nonevident things may be details about methods, the data description, and the major qualifications or limitations. Make a list of them in your mind as questions you need answered in your remaining time. Note that the theory and the main results of an empirical article should appear in a well-written abstract. If they aren't there, then you apply techniques given below for articles not well written. (Authors do sometimes write bad abstracts, by the way, but copyeditors generally fix them in production.)

In a theoretical article, by contrast, the entire argument will usually be outside the abstract, which will be purely formulaic. You should notice this immediately and at once scan the article for a basic summary of the main argument. There will be one somewhere. Treat this summary as if it were the abstract (read it five or six times and master it). Often, this summary will be at the end of the next-to-last section, just before the author begins to discuss "further directions." (Ignore all further directions. They are meaningless filler.) This second phase will take another five to eight minutes.

Finally, scan the text quickly for the necessary things that are missing from the abstract (or the summary or the equivalent passage in text). Then read (narratively) enough text (found by this scan) to fill the holes you have found. Then set the article aside. You are done. You should be able to process a well-written article, at least well enough to get its main points, in about twenty minutes. Write a set of short notes in summary, in a text file, just as for a book.

E. PARTIAL MASTERY READING

Most often in research, you will not need to completely master a book or article. Rather, you need to extract and master some part of it. This is partial mastery reading—in practice, the most common mode of reading in the social sciences and humanities. When we read a book or article we usually want to know only some part of it. We want to know not "what Laumann et al. said about sex" but "what Laumann et al. said about sexual identity among homosexuals"; not "what West and Zimmerman said" but "how West and Zimmerman's concept of 'doing gender' differs from Mertonian 'role performance.'" In each case we want something very specific, and we need understand only what is necessary to answer our particular questions.

Thus the central requisite for partial mastery reading is a very well specified question. As always, being a good library researcher is not about finding things but about knowing what to look for. Reading without questions always reverts to narrative reading, and narrative reading always fails for anything but the first reading of a novel. (Or sometimes of a history. In practice, however, narrative reading fails even for history most of the time.) Like mastery reading, partial mastery reading is very hard work. If you do not have to rest every half hour because of sheer reading exhaustion, you are not working hard enough.

In partial mastery, you begin by specifying the things you must retrieve from the text: Results? Theory? Steps of an argument? Data? Data elicitation methods? Statistical procedures? Attitude to this or that concept? Text? Scholar? Finding? Usually it will just be one or two of these things. Then tell yourself "This means that I do not need to know. . . ." and recite to yourself the things you can and must ignore. (If you are a good browser, the temptation to slow down is always great.) Then read the text rapidly and mercilessly, insistently asking yourself, "Is what I am looking for on this page?" If it is not, then immediately go on. Do not look at this clever paragraph or that interesting citation. Just go on. You should be able to "partially master" any article in about ten minutes. (Not ten seconds, by the way; take the time to find what you really need.) Again, this will be very hard work. Do not underline or select-and-paste. That takes extra time and is postponing mastery of the text. Rather, extract what you want the first time and write your own note about it in a text file with the citation. You must aim to think the ideas of the text, not simply to find them.

You will note that my recommendations for mastery reading always involve two stages: (a) figure out what you want to discover, and (b) search for that and that alone. The most common mistake in research reading (also in scholarly reading more generally) is to read narratively when you should be reading for mastery. Never read a text without having specified ahead of time what you want get from it. Any other approach degenerates into narrative reading. Save that for Tolstoy.

TECHNIQUES FOR WORK THAT IS NOT WELL WRITTEN VARY, FOR THERE are different types of hard-to-read material, and different reading strategies are appropriate for each. First, there is material that follows a prose aesthetic different from that of modern English exposition. In the current research environment, one encounters such materials mainly in two places: in foreign language theory and in parts of the humanities. Translated foreign language theory (Foucault, Bourdieu, Habermas, et al.) will be read mostly for theoretical stimulation (in meditative mode). It is fine for that purpose. Modern French theoretical prose is best read very quickly, without any attention to logic and argument, of which there is often very little. But it is usually beautiful and always stimulating. German theoretical prose has the somewhat different problem that it usually employs specialized terminology from the German idealist heritage and makes little sense unless you already know some Kant, Hegel, Heidegger, and so on. If your research project requires reading German theory, find a good trot.

As for humanistic writing, it too can be very useful for meditative use in library research. Occasionally it is useful for partial mastery, particularly the older material that is often highly focused and articulate. In more recent years, however, many articles in literary studies affect a deliberately obscure prose. Often, their aim is to be art or culture as much as it is to discuss art or culture. Such articles self-consciously demand narrative reading. Occasionally, they are worth it.

As for badly written social science, of which there is a very great deal, you will have trouble reading it as efficiently as you can read well-written material. (Do not let this make you think it more important.) Since the article or book itself is not well organized, you yourself have to hypothesize and complete the necessary organization. You begin by deciding on the closest template to what you are reading: Is it a story? (Perhaps put better, is it trying to be a story?) Is it a case study? An adjudication of theories? Once you have decided on which of these it is, imagine the ingredients that are necessary for a good version of that template. Scan the article or book to find as many of them as you can, then build in your mind a version of the article/book as it should have been written. Do not allow yourself any more time than for a well-written work; an hour for a book, twenty minutes for an article. Most likely, the weak writing is a sign of careless thinking and there isn't anything wonderful to find, no matter how long you work with the text.

THE VARIOUS MODES OF READING PROVIDE A DIVERSIFIED REPERTOIRE for dealing with the various secondary materials you confront in a library research project. You will use narrative reading on the background materials that you read to orient yourself at the outset. You will also use it when new areas and subareas emerge during the research. You will read meditatively when you need to see the project from the outside: when you need to rethink, perhaps redesign. You will scan-read throughout the project, because most secondary sources will be useful only in part; you need to extract what they say and move on. You will also find yourself scan-reading some of your primary sources as you try to uncover which of them are the most worthwhile, the most productive in terms of your research questions.

Mastery reading is necessary for the theoretical and empirical works central to your project. Even here, however, you do not need to master every sentence, every subargument. You need rather to have a firm command of the major arguments, the major ideas, the major empirical analyses. Remember, the center of your project is your work, not someone else's. Partial mastery will suffice for most of the dozens of peripheral secondary sources that may bear on your project. Get what you need and move on at once.

All of these, however, are modes of reading mainly for secondary materials. That is, they are ways of reading work that is itself self-consciously outside the subject of your research itself. As for primary materials, they require a quite different approach.

2. Primary Materials

A. NOTE-TAKING

First of all, primary materials require disciplined note-taking. Sometimes this is physically necessary: you may be reading primary materials in an archive that does not permit you to photograph them with a digital camera or to otherwise copy them. But you also will take notes as part of analytic reading. You must abstract the themes and issues from primary materials so they are available to you instantly once you start analysis. Note-taking is as much an analytic strategy as it is an occasional necessity.

Some rules, then, about note-taking. Do not keep notes on primary materials in continuous text. Keep them in bits so they can later be indexed and possibly put in different places. These bits should be relatively short. If you keep notes in thirty-line paragraphs, you may have to distribute copies of a given paragraph to four or five different analysis folders (physical or virtual). Then you have to underline, or otherwise demarcate, those parts of the paragraph relevant to that folder, and you will have unnecessary, peripheral materials (the nonunderlined bits) associated with them.

It is better to take your primary-material notes in shorter, codable units. The note-taking unit should be small enough to have only one or two analytic uses. Typically, this will be two to ten lines of text. Then make a line break (in straight text notes) or start a new indexable unit (if you are working in a codable database). In the database approach, this level of detail seems to me cumbersome, as you will end up with long units with several tags, rather than putting the vast majority of units in unique locations. (I myself take notes on primary material in the form of straight text with blank-line breaks to mark new units.)

Whatever the size of unit you choose, it must carry with it complete citation information. Get into the habit of typing some identifier at the beginning of each note-unit. An example from my archival notes: "2.19, Ltr EOL to CEB, 24 Feb 72 says that he has doubts about the managing editor." This telegraphic note means that the content comes from box 2, folder 19. It is a letter from Edward O. Laumann to Charles E. Bidwell, dated 24 February 1972, complaining about the managing editor of the journal in whose records this letter appears (the *American Journal of Sociology*). Since the entire string of notes comes from the *AJS* archival files, I don't bother to include that information here.

This telegraphic form of citation explains why you must build a detailed list of people (or organizations, or whatever are your main units of analysis) in your data folders. It will contain the abbreviations of names (of people, institutions, organizations, etc.) that figure in these short identification headers for primary material.

B. DOUBT

Reading of primary materials is not like reading of secondary materials. Secondary materials are part of a scholarly literature. They have been vetted, edited, challenged. By contrast, primary materials stand alone. You may be their only reader. So your responsibility is greater. You must constantly ask critical questions of any text: Who wrote or produced it? For what purpose did they (he, she) write it? Under what circumstances did they (he, she) write it? You must ask such questions because your reader must trust you to have read carefully, subtly, even suspiciously. When you read primary material, you are the reader's agent, and you must be worthy of that trust.

Thus, you never read primary material in narrative mode, like a novel. There is nothing simple about a primary document. Do not be lulled into passively letting its story roll over you. If you find yourself doing this, take a break. Most of the time you spend reading primary materials should be spent puzzling over what you are reading: Why this? Why now? What did she think she was doing? Who was the audience? Why? Try to think of alternative readings, especially of important documents, and of what kinds of evidence you need in order to choose between those readings.

You need to do this questioning at the time of reading, rather than later. Why? Because the results of this questioning may change which facts you think are important to record, which texts are important to read, which leads are important to pursue. Unless you are doing an utterly mechanical, brute-force minianalysis of primary documents, you must think critically about them all the time. Even if you are simply photographing a large number of documents for later reading, you have to pay enough attention to them to let them guide your future filming.

Of course, you will also ask all these contextualizing questions later, during analysis. But they must be at the front of your consciousness while you are gathering primary materials as well. Indeed, throughout a library research project, you must critically evaluate all your materials as you get them: bibliography, primary, and secondary materials. I have already talked at length about the critical evaluation of bibliography—of tools, of secondary works. But here we consider the critical evaluation of a given primary source. These dimensions of doubt are relevant to all forms of primary sources: government records, manuscripts, published work, old numerical data, and so on.

To operationalize doubt, I follow a five-step approach rooted in the work of the literary critic Kenneth Burke. Burke discussed five basic terms in dramatic analysis: action, scene, act, agency, and purpose. When we apply these to primary documents, we have: author, provenance, production, mechanics, and aims. For any document, we must ask about these five things.

The first questions concern the author of a document. Suppose you are reading a congressional report: Who actually wrote it? What is known about that person? What sources did the author use, besides the ones listed in the document, if any? Did this author write other things—legal opinions?

popular articles? memoirs?—and if so, how does the present document re-late to those other works? Was the author alone, or did he or she work as an agent for others—a senator? a party official? a political think tank? If so what was the agency relationship? On whose behalf was the author really writing? These questions go well beyond the usual "He was a Republican so he thought X" kind of analysis. We need to see an author in a place, dynamically situated, subject to a variety of forces. We need him or her to come alive for us.

The second question involves provenance. To take an example from a re-cent project in my course, suppose you are reading a pamphlet on the impor-tance of getting Papanicolaou smears. You would ask, first, of course, about the author: who wrote it, with what evidence. But we should ask second where it was produced: in what country? what place? by what social class of person or organization? in what kind of a physical setting? Such pam-phlets produced in the US will look different from those from Ivory Coast, and knowing whether the pamphlet is good or bad, learned or foolish, ideo-logical or scientific, always requires knowing the place of production and the universe of comparable documents in which it takes its place. A pamphlet that might be a poor effort for a well-funded international nongovernmen-tal organization (NGO) might be a superb achievement for a local clinic. As that example suggests, provenance also refers to the issuing organization, which may well have solicited the author; such pamphlets might be issued by national governments, school systems, health departments, cancer-related NGOs, individual hospitals. There is a history behind each. All of that must inform how we read the document.

Another part of provenance is the context of surrounding events. What else was going on in the life of the author, in the history of the issuing organi-zation, in the situation and setting into which the document was issued? An American pamphlet on Pap smears meant one thing in an age when relatively few women got them, but quite a different thing when smears had become a standard annual practice. The country had changed in terms of audience knowledge, average levels of morbidity, and so on.

Third, consider the production of a document, most often the act of writ-ing. Take for example a work like Lady Mary Wortley Montagu's *Turkish Em-bassy Letters*. These were originally produced by the twenty-seven-year-old Lady Mary during a trip with her husband to take up his new position as British ambassador at the Ottoman court in the early eighteenth century. The letters are somewhat informal, addressed to Lady Mary's friends and relatives in England. They present themselves as written on the road, often in haste, filled with circumstantial detail. Yet they were ultimately published, and it is hard to imagine that Lady Mary did not envision publication from the start. Over many years, she carefully edited the letters from her own diary copies and gave a complete copy to a Rotterdam clergyman on her way home to England from self-imposed exile near the end of her life. They were thus published many decades after writing, and after years of editing that had transformed the originals of a young woman into the matured and stylish final drafts of a lady in her seventies. One cannot read these texts without always recalling these conditions of production.

A fourth question concerns the mechanics that brought the text into your hands. Lady Mary's letters survived their intended destruction by her son-in-law (then prime minister and somewhat scandalized by his wife's mother) because Lady Mary made sure that a surreptitious copy had been made. At other times, inheritors have violated express commands to *destroy* manuscript material. The accidents of survival and distribution radically affect the representativity of what you are reading. It may or may not be a good representation of its author, much less of its author's class or gender or race or other social group. Survival and distribution can be highly biased—often toward elites and toward things that sound proper for elites, but sometimes in other ways as well. Moreover, many manuscripts are saved precisely because they are unusual. This makes them problematic if you yourself are interested in the everyday rather than the unusual.

Finally, you must always ask the aims of the writer. Was the document produced to accomplish something? Was it designed to persuade someone, and if so, of what? If you are reading a series of data on mental hospital care in the nineteenth century, for example, you can be pretty sure that the statistics are inflated because of the need to acquire more state funds. The question is simply one of how much they were inflated. Or suppose that you are reading a festschrift volume in honor of some old scholar. Obviously the writers will be emphasizing the importance of their relation to their teacher, and obviously those who did not have a good relation with him will have been omitted from the collection altogether. How then should you steer your reading to recognize these kinds of biases?

If you always remember these questions of author, provenance, production, mechanics, and aims, you will come to a much sounder reading of your primary sources. But the bias is not all in the sources. You must also continuously ask questions about yourself. The aim of careful reading of primary sources is to understand an old or different world as it was for itself, not as it is for you. To decide whether Lady Mary was a "true feminist" or a "dangerous Orientalist" is to apply the terms of a contemporaneous political debate to a woman dead for two centuries. You can do that if you like. Every generation rewrites history, and every social group rewrites social science in terms of its own agenda.

But you should aspire to something better than the mere political use of the past or of the Other. Humane scholarship aims to understand another world on its own terms and by that understanding to improve its own world. The famous English historian E. P. Thompson put it well in speaking of historical research: we must, he said, "rescue [the past] from the enormous condescension of posterity." Indeed, one can say the same with respect to library research about our contemporary as well as our past worlds: we must rescue them from the enormous condescension of elitism, or universalism, or politicization, or whatever our current shibboleth happens to be. We should see the subject of our research as a particular example of its own way of being human—good or bad, sightly or unsightly, politically correct or devastatingly evil.

So from time to time, you must ask the same five basic questions about yourself, the reader, that you ask about the sources. They are a ritual you should perform at the beginning of a day in the archives, before sitting down to do an important analysis. First, who are you, the reader? In what ways are you like the person or group you are studying, and in what ways different?—in age? gender? politics? race? religion? temperament? Would the writer have seen these similarities and differences the way you see them? Have you prepared to read carefully or are you simply reading lazily or contemptuously or accusingly?

Second, provenance. Are you reading seriously? Is something in the rest of your life directly shaping how you are reading? My own reading of sources for the latter half of my published history of the *American Journal of Sociology* was obviously influenced by the fact that the *Journal* itself had refused to publish the first half!

Third, what about the production, the doing of the reading? Are you in quiet surroundings? Do you have enough time for the mode of reading you are employing? Are there difficult conditions? For example, I hate to read things on the computer screen and am always more likely to dislike something I've had to read onscreen, whether it's a student paper or a brilliant monograph. And certainly reading things on microfilm, where you are forced to read very slowly and often with excessive care, makes it very difficult to form an estimate of a text that is comparable with the estimate that would come from reading in another medium.

Fourth, what about agency? Is your reading of primary materials strongly influenced by somebody else's earlier reading? Are you reading with a genuinely open mind, or do you already have a view that comes from elsewhere—advisors, friends, scholars? Indeed, has the material you are reading been modified from its original primary condition, by an editor, say, or a bowdlerizer?

There is a crucial but unsolvable problem here. To read primary documents without having read some background is foolish. You are likely to make elementary mistakes because words have changed their meanings, because you do not understand old or foreign institutions, and so on. But on the other hand, the more you know about the context—which in practice means knowing more about other people's interpretations of that context—the less you are going to be able to read against the grain, to see new possibilities. It is a difficult line to walk, and you must always be aware of error on the one side as well as on the other.

Finally, you must think about your own purposes in reading. Are you truly prepared to be surprised? Are you just looking for a perfect illustration of something you have already decided is true? Why exactly are you reading?

All these questions need to be addressed. Not always, not every five minutes, perhaps not even every day. But it is essential to be honest with yourself. Those who read what you ultimately write will rely on your judgment. You need to have disciplined that judgment and defended it.

Reading primary documents is both a delight and a privilege. You must desire to understand, but to understand without judging. You must confront the difficulties of translating someone else's world into yours, yet recognize that ultimately no perfect translation is possible. Remember always that the person you are reading was living a life that may be completely foreign to you, and that discovering something about that person's origins and biases does not authorize you to read with smugness, contempt, or irony. If you bring such attitudes to your reading, your own readers will read you the same way, for your want of magnanimity and charity will be plain in what you write. Read as you would like to be read, and you cannot go far wrong.

8

Midphase Files and Organization

In the midphase, you will continuously create notes, copies, references, records, and other material. So you must elaborate the file structure sketched in chapter 4. Out of this mundane file work come two crucial results. The first is your own controlled vocabulary of theoretical terms and essential issues. The second is a "cross-walk" linking your actual files to your general research questions and your empirical and theoretical puzzles. Together, these will be the binding that ties your various minianalyses and arguments into a cohesive text. Yet they grow out of the everyday task of managing your project. This chapter first covers the mechanics of files, then turns to the more important matter of the conceptual organization of both files and project, embodied in the controlled vocabulary and the crosswalk.

1. Files

The need for careful filing may seem puzzling. After all, the information age lives on hyperlinks and the networks they create. URLs provide arbitrary addresses for items, but the real location of something is the ensemble of its links with other things. Nothing could be simpler.

In fact, hierarchy is considerably simpler. In a linkage network, everything is potentially related to everything, just as most people in the United States are linked to every other person by six or seven personal connections. That kind of connectivity is what produces the long lists of irrelevant material from Google. The dozens of different versions of the same thing at the top of the list are the "small world" of material immediately surrounding your search, and the strange junk that starts not far below comes from single connections that bridge out of that small world to everywhere and nowhere. To be sure, sometimes we want sudden links leading elsewhere. That's the essence of brachiation. But brachiation isn't random swinging through hyperlinks. It relies heavily on prior information, quality rankings, and highly educated guessing. It takes advantage of hyperlinkage without getting lost in it.

As a researcher, you need more control than a network-derived relevance list provides, because you aim to create a cohesive and ultimately linear argument. Moreover, once you start analysis, you need instant, painless recall of materials. You need not only organization, but *fast* organization. It turns out that hierarchy is the easiest organization system for instant recall, even though hierarchy sacrifices some hyperlinks. That's because a hierarchical classification requires less mental work.

To understand why this is true, let's consider an abstract example, where we have N objects of some kind and we want to know which objects are tied to which others. The objects could be items in a bibliography, students in a high school, or companies in an industry, for example. The ties could be ties of meaning, friendship, or investment, respectively. Full knowledge of the network of ties between these N objects requires $N \times (N-1)/2$ pieces of information—one for each possible pairing; we have to know whether there is or is not a link between each possible pair, and this formula gives the number of possible pairs. But we could simplify a bit by arranging the N objects into a hierarchy, placing "close" items in little groups, then tying those little groups to other little groups to make bigger groups, and so on, until we have the whole set of objects together. (Thus we might list bibliography items in tiny subcategories, which we then link into broader subcategories, and then into broad categories and finally into the whole bibliography. We could do the same for friendship groups and companies.)

Now if we do decide to represent the ties between objects by such a hierarchy, it will take many fewer pieces of information than it takes to represent the full network exactly. With L levels and N objects, it takes only $L \times N$ pieces of information, one for each level for each item. Thus to specify all the ties between 64 things precisely via full linkage takes 2,016 ($= 64 \times 63/2$) pieces of information. But to place 64 items in a hierarchy with two subitems under each heading will take six levels, which means six pieces of information per item. That totals 384 pieces of information, about one-fifth the amount necessary under the full linkage or network approach. If we're willing to have four-item groups at the bottom of such a hierarchy, we can throw away two levels and need only 256 pieces of information, about one tenth of the total under the alternative approach.

You actually know this already. Think about friendship groups in your school or college. You could try to know about friendships in your school by knowing, for every single student, exactly what that student's relation was to every other student. But of course you don't do that. You think about this clique and that clique, and how cliques A and B tend to hang out together and cliques C, D, and E hang out together, while cliques F, G, and H may just look like a big blob to you. And you know that there is a lot less information to remember if you let each clique be four or five people, not just two.

Note too that a linkage-network model requires virtually complete data because network structures change quite suddenly if a crucial bridge between groups happens to be deleted (if the student who linked A and B with F and G leaves school, for example). Since we don't know ahead of time which links are crucial bridges, then if we didn't already have the loosely hierarchical clique groupings, we would need to know nearly all the links to specify the total network of friendships. By contrast, in a hierarchical classification, we already know which links are less structurally important, because we identify those substantively at the outset and place them at the bottom of the hierarchy. They are the links inside the cliques, and we know already that the details within the cliques probably don't matter; what matters are the crucial students linking the cliques. Hierarchy focuses our attention on those students.

In short, hierarchy takes much less mental effort. Of course it accomplishes this by simplifying assumptions (assuming that everybody in A hates everybody in G, for example), so in practice we augment it with cross-references (that is, particular hyperlinks—the two people who actually do talk across that barrier). This causes little increase in cognitive load. To continue the previous example, 64 items in four levels with four-item groups at the lowest level requires 256 pieces of information. If we add two cross-references per item, we are still only back to requiring 384 pieces of information, one fifth of the amount required for full linkage. Already in this book, we have seen such a marriage of hierarchy with cross-references, for this is the strategy of the LC classification. The main subject heading provides the call number and the physical location, while the extra subject headings provide a few very important cross-references. This is a very powerful halfway system, combining most of the advantages of both locational strategies at a fraction of the cognitive demands of a linkage approach to cataloging.

In your own filing work, you can use cross-references if you need them, but my experience is that I very seldom need them. The hierarchy of my files carries so much of the cognitive load that I find I am easily able to remember the necessary cross-reference information in my head. I can always find everything very quickly.

Hierarchy thus enables you easily to maintain a large and comprehensive file system. Let me give a couple of examples. The files for my 600-page dissertation occupy 2.7 drawers in a file cabinet—about eight linear feet of folders and paper. Research and data folders themselves fill two of these drawers, while the third drawer contains writing folders (early drafts, etc.). At a smaller level, the files for a typical research article of mine (about forty to fifty manuscript pages with footnotes and tables) typically occupy about one linear foot. In digital terms, at 1,500 pieces of paper per linear foot of material and roughly 2K per sheet for typical ASCII text, that's roughly 3MB for a typical article and 24MB for the dissertation. (It would be several times that much as Word documents or PDFs, because of the formatting overhead.) These files consist mostly of my handwritten and typed notes, filled-out data forms, pages of quantitative analysis, and so on. There are a few copies of other scholars' work, but not many. But overall, it's a lot of material. When I bring the files for a couple of articles to class, my students are invariably amazed. But I tell them—it's the simple truth—that my files are what makes my work easy.

A professional academic of course needs such elaborate files. You do not. But your filing should be detailed enough to allow you to locate any project item within one minute maximum, whether online or on paper. So if you don't have a lot of items, you don't need a lot of files. But at the same time, fundamentally different kinds of things should go in different folders, so they can be quickly found. With files, as with bibliography, you should follow the six-item rule; when you get more than six items in a category, you should break it up. That's not an absolute rule, of course. If you have a long set of very similar items, they can go in a single folder or subfolder, as long as you can keep them in some kind of sorted order. But in the main, follow the six-item rule.

At the same time, don't overdo it. Files exist to enable you to find things fast, not to be wonderful in themselves. Your filing system should grow only by subdivision. As you get larger and larger amounts of material, you keep the low-level files at a constant size, by subdividing them as necessary. In the following pages, I will describe all kinds of detailed files, but most readers won't need most of them. For a term paper, you will need only the most basic folders: four or five different folders total. You need only skim the next section of the chapter. For a seminar or master's paper, you will generate much more material, and probably need a couple of dozen folders. For a dissertation or major project, you will produce many dozens of folders and subfolders. You will need most of the file structure I discuss.

In chapter 4, I outlined a basic structure for any file system. All projects need a master folder, a design folder, a log of activity, and substantive folders. Substantive folders can be of varying types: published material, primary data, analysis, writing, and final text. In what follows, I will consider all of these types of folders. But remember: you want enough folders and organization to provide quick access, but no more than that.

A. THE MASTER FOLDER AND ITS PROGENY

Typically this will be the original folder from which everything else gradually differentiates. Early on, it will contain the original ideas and bibliography; notes of conversations about the project; correspondence and any business records; contact information for people related to the project; a to-do list. As time passes, many of these subfolders may become separate folders. Bibliography and ideas will certainly split out, and to-do will probably do so. But you should always keep the formalities together as the project evolves. You need a single master folder that governs the business end of the research.

To-do and ideas folders can be started for subparts of the project as they grow large. As I noted in chapter 6, however, in my experience it is not a good idea to proliferate bibliography folders. Keeping bibliography for the project in one place, whether in hard copy or electronically, avoids needless duplication. Bibliographies for minianalyses are the one exception, as we shall see.

Here are some suggestions for master folder subfolders:

Business. Keep here all business notes, bills, travel documents, formal permission documents (except access documents for particular archival collections; keep them with the data). If there is only a small amount of relevant correspondence, keep it here. Otherwise have a separate subfolder for correspondence. For most readers, all correspondence will be electronic, so you need a project-relevant mailbox in which you put all relevant e-mail. Back it up regularly.

Contacts. Keep a list here of everybody you have talked to about the project. These could be archivists, librarians, co-researchers, conference session chairs, journal editors, classmates, or people who have commented on your work. Keep what contact information you need: name, phone, e-mail. If you have done project-relevant interviewing, however, you should keep contact information with the interviews, in data folders. If there are confidentiality issues, be sure to handle them carefully.

Bibliography. This will become a separate folder quickly. Once bibliography becomes a separate folder, you will need a to-do subfolder in it. In midphase, however, you start doing bibliography minianalysis by minianalysis. It is more effective to keep those minianalysis bibliographies in the files for the mini-analyses themselves. For me, the main project bibliography recedes from my consciousness as I get into the details of minianalyses. I have to rediscover it when I start to write the final text. Note that you will finish the project with dozens of bibliographical questions left unsolved. This is normal.

To do. This should be an ongoing list. You may think you will remember what you need to do. You won't. Even a medium-sized library project gets very complicated very quickly. Give your memory a rest and just write all the action items in a to-do folder. To-do items come from everywhere: from continued reading and rereading of the design folder, from odd thoughts jotted down in the middle of the night, from unfinished research sessions. Keep the to-do folder up to date. You'll enjoy crossing things off the list. In fact, that's one of the main purposes of having such a list.

Ideas. This is the folder of substantive ideas about the project. They are the germs of what you will analyze and write. "Maybe the real reason the American Sociological Association was founded was some members' anger at the American Economic Association" and that sort of thing. Eventually this sub-folder may need to be subdivided, but once minianalyses start, you will find that your ideas pile up within them. In any case, wherever and whenever you have ideas, always write them down. You'll never remember them all.

To be filed. Throw everything in here—ideas, to-dos, data, notes, and so on. Then burst it often and put everything where it belongs. Bursting not only maintains organization but also will remind you of many important things that have been overwritten by more recent ideas and discoveries. And it keeps your attention on the work of organization. Filing things will often give you new ideas, precisely because your filing categories will always seem a little wrong. Thinking about and resolving that wrongness are what advances your theory.

Acknowledgments. A really extensive project involves asking a lot of people a lot of things. Keep a general list of people who helped you out. You won't remember all of them at the end of the project. So make a note now, when you incur the obligation. Giving acknowledgments in the final text is as costless as it is gracious.

B. RESEARCH DESIGN FOLDER

After the master folder and its progeny, the research design folder is the most important; it provides the guide to the project—the reasoning that guarantees that if you do the proposed research you will answer your basic puzzles and questions.

Proposal: keep the current version of the design document (defined in chapter 4) at the top of the file. Until you are a full-blown professional, you should always do a formal design document, and it is helpful to keep doing them even then. Above all, you must always have a list here of the basic puzzles and questions that are animating the research. In fact, you should know the current versions of these puzzles and questions by heart.

Do keep copies of the old versions of the project design. They will show how much has changed. This is easy electronically, although you must remember to give every new version a version number. And, by the way, since you will be sharing this document with other people, do not call it "library research paper. doc" or "dissertation plan.doc." Your advisor's hard disk already has dozens of files with that name, and she doesn't know which is whose. Use your full name in the file name: then your friends and advisor can identify it.

Plan of research (including schedule). This should be a short subfolder with a list of (a) the tasks to be done with primary materials, (b) the order in which you plan to do them, and (c) a rough schedule for how long they should take. Examples of primary material tasks are "Go through the Thai administrative documents to find all reports on brothels" or "Look for materials in the W. I. Thomas papers" or "Copy and analyze all Sunday crosswords in the *New York Times* from 1951 to 1983." That is, these are tasks organized by source. You might also include in here plans that are organized not by task (i.e., by source) but rather by subquestions in the design document. As you think about each separate research question in your design document, it is probably best to put together a short plan of research for it. Thus, for an organization study, you might sketch a plan of research on "the founding of the organization," specifying what information you need to cover that topic.

As my focus on sources suggests, you are likely to do your primary research not by research question, but by source (particular database, library, or archive) and source type (book, manuscript, archive, government documents, etc.). But it is wise to organize your research plans both ways. The question-based plan will help you know when you are done with certain questions. The source-based plan will make you work efficiently. But you have to see how the two approaches are related. It is therefore best to organize one single matrix plan—sources across questions. I will discuss this matrix in more detail in the later section on "crosswalk."

It is also useful to keep throwing into this planning subfolder proposals for new minianalyses—whether primary data-gathering or analysis. Examples are "Measure the duration of all the organization's projects and compare them" or "Do a matrix showing all the coauthorships of people who worked for the organization."

C. LOGS

A library research project is complicated. Moreover, it is only one part of your already complicated life. You will quickly forget what you have and have not done. Therefore, you should maintain a continuous log of what research tasks you have done. This does not have to tell what exact search string you used with which database (although that can be wise in the early stages). But at the least, maintain a simple log of each research session, telling what you did in fairly specific terms: for instance, which indexes you cruised, or which finding aids you inspected. In a big project—one that has minianalyses that may be taking a week or more apiece—you may want to keep logs within the minianalyses.

As with everything organizational, you should maintain in your logs the level of detail that is necessary and no more. The aim is not to preserve a perfect record. It is to avoid duplicating searches and analyses you may already have done and to keep track of your progress on the main schedule of research. If you find yourself wondering whether you've done some task or not, then it's time for more careful record keeping. If you can keep the whole thing in your head, then that's fine. As a rule of thumb, you can probably keep fairly sketchy logs for a term paper, but a seminar paper or MA paper will need more detail, since the research will take many weeks or even months. A major research paper or dissertation will take months or years to complete and requires serious logs.

D. PUBLISHED MATERIAL FOLDERS

Keep separate folders for the two kinds of published material: primary and secondary.

Primary material. Actual publications of the organization or person or event or whatever you are researching, copied for your research purposes. Even if these are electronic, keep an electronic copy of the actual file in the folder, so you can see at a glance—without clicking and without having to look around—what materials you have on hand. Don't put a hyperlink in your folder. Get a PDF or other actual copy. When you need to glance at the thing quickly during the write-up phase, you want it available instantly. Don't be misled by the concept of permanent address, typically a DOI. A DOI is simply a permanent alias, supplied by a third party. It enables the holder of the document to change internal names for the document without having to maintain a translation dictionary from old names to new names. But the holder is still responsible to inform the firm providing the DOI when internal addresses change. (That is, there's still a translation dictionary, but it is centrally held and holders of documents continuously update their records in it.) If it fails to do so, the DOI doesn't work. So put a copy of the actual document in your files, not the DOI or (even worse) the current address.

Secondary material. Publications about the organization or person or event or whatever you are researching. These are articles, notes on books, and so on. Again, get real copies, not an address.

Published material folders are inevitably dynamic. You will need to refile and subdivide them from time to time, to keep the folders at a reasonable size. It's the same task whether you do it physically or electronically. To some extent, however, doing it physically is more intellectually rewarding, since you must actually handle articles to refile them physically. You will inevitably read a bit, and that reading may give you new ideas that wouldn't occur if you were just dragging and dropping. Remember, much of the reason for being organized is that doing organization catalyzes your thinking, just as doing bibliography (rather than simply having bibliography) catalyzes your thinking.

E. PRIMARY DATA FOLDERS

Primary data folders should be kept by the source structure. If need be, you can later recopy everything and reorganize it in your analysis folders. It is very easy to lose track of where things came from, particularly if you found them online. Be sure to get sources and locations for electronic documents as well as physical ones. And especially if primary material is extensive, keep one full set of originals organized by source.

Indeed, you may want to have a separate primary data folder for each basic type of information you get from a source. For example, if you use three different collections at one archive, you should keep them separate. If you collect three different bodies of census data from one census, you should keep them separate. And of course keep separate files for every general data source (archive, database, etc.), since that keeps the access records straight. The problem with getting away from source-based data files is that you may lose provenance information. Of course, you could just keep addresses and re-find the material online. But often it can't be found, because the source pages have changed.

Why am I so obsessed with provenance? Because scholarship requires replicability. The dense citations and obsessional research practices evident in scholarly articles and books are the reason that real scholarship is better than the so-called "knowledge" of the Internet. Research practices enable public scrutiny of one's work by other experts. And that commitment to precision and public scrutiny is what makes academic knowledge—sterile as it can sometimes be—solid and believable in a way that no generically crowd-sourced expertise can ever be. Crowd sourcing has many virtues, but producing truly excellent knowledge is not one of them, unless the crowd is itself made up of experts. But in that case, there is a name for such "crowds." We call them academic disciplines, and of course they aren't really crowds at all, but disciplined groups of trained peers.

To return to primary data folders—part of your data files will be your own reading notes, which I have already discussed in chapter 7. But remember: even your reading notes must include all the necessary citing information: enough data to identify the source exactly.

Be sure to write down—somewhere—any conventions you have adopted in making notes. (For example, I always type "ltr" for letter. You need a list of such abbreviations.) Ditto for other shortcuts you have used in your notes—people's initials, organizational acronyms, and so forth. You may think you will remember all such things, but you won't. It is even worth reading through your notes occasionally and making sure you can still understand them. At that time, you can write down any abbreviations you are starting to forget. In these days of electronic materials, this labeling may be less important than in older times. But particularly if you do a research trip to an archive or other setting that will not let you take photographs, you will need to work very hard at making sure you can work fast but at the same time produce notes that you can later decode.

In a really extensive project, you may want to keep a separate folder containing any personal conversations you have bearing on primary data. These could be primary data themselves (oral history interviews), conversations about data availability, interpretations. My own experience is that it is best to keep the originals of your notes on these conversations in one place, rather than scattered around in the primary data folders. Be sure to keep people's names associated with their ideas or suggestions. Crediting others is one of the duties—and pleasures—of scholarship.

Some possible subfolders within primary data folders:

Business. Since primary data folders are kept by source, they may need separate business subfolders. Keep here all the access information and your copies of any forms you had to fill out, both for access to material and (if you did so) for making any copies of it. The access information should be precise and detailed. So also should any specific copyright information, for copyright can be important.

The general rules about copyright are easily stated. For the United States (copyright varies by country, of course), nearly all printed or manuscript material of any kind produced after 1923 (except US Government material) automatically enjoys copyright protection. There is no need for anyone to file any forms: copyright is the presumption, as the lawyers say. Because of this, in your final text, you must obey certain rules with respect to such materials, whether published or manuscript. Short quotes will be OK under the "fair use" provision (they may also be regulated by the rules of a particular archive or collection, of course), but longer quotes and any quotes with potential for harm will require formal permission from the holder of copyright, who is typically *not* the archive, but the heirs of the writer. By "short quote" is meant a few lines (or perhaps a paragraph) necessary to the argument of a paper, review, or other secondary work. The central issue in copyright is of course harm or damage—diverse and complicated legal concepts. If you are in doubt about whether you have copyright issues, consult your advisor. The issue is more important than you may think, for while a course paper is considered to be educational and hence not subject to any of the copyright limitations consequent on publication, putting your finished paper on a website or your blog is in effect publication and does raise copyright issues.

Copies. Keep here copies you have made from archival, government, organizational, or other sources. At most archives and organizations, the official copy request form will usually identify materials by box, folder, and so on, but you should record in your actual notes that you got a copy of this or that document, for extra surety. Reconciling your handwritten notes and the copies can be difficult sometimes. I find it best to write the provenance on the photocopy itself. It's only worse for digital photographs, which are rapidly becoming the standard tool for archival research. Store copies of pictures in a single folder, with clear identification in terms of date, archive (or other source), and formal citation information. Be sure to record when you have switched to filming a new box or folder of the physical materials, because you will have to provide that information to guide your readers to the exact location of the material you have filmed.

Keeping provenance information on digitally gathered data is particularly difficult. It is very easy to just drag-and-drop a PDF of some document. But if you're working above the undergraduate level, you must be able to identify whence any document came. There is little sign that serious scholarship will start recognizing websites as definitive citations. That's because the information on sites can and does change, and it does nobody any good to know that you accessed a now-changed site "on 3 January 2009," because readers would have to go to a web archive to check your references or retrieve the information.

F. ANALYSIS FOLDERS

Your analysis folders will be rearrangements, prunings, and examinations of primary material. Ideally, you make second copies of everything primary and cut them up to assemble in an analysis folder that you build for a particular minianalysis. That's easy with computer-based files—your notes, most importantly. Just reprint them and cut them up into bits if necessary (now you see why every separate note has to have citation data on it—otherwise you lose its identity when you cut the sheets up.) You can then allocate the bits to the relevant electronic or physical folders.

Thus, for example, in my project on the history of the *American Journal of Sociology*, I had folders with names like "editorial," "subscriptions," "book review," "authors," and so on. When I worked through the papers of the successive editors, I typed continuous notes on each letter as I read through the folders of the manuscript collection for that editor. When I was done, I printed the whole thing, and then quite literally cut up the paper copy (each letter note was its own paragraph with its own provenance information) and distributed the pieces to the analysis folders, where I stapled them onto pieces of blank paper. You can do the same with copied documents.

In the electronic filing environment, cut-and-paste (you see why it got the name) is the equivalent. I could now do the same thing I did before full digitization by just pasting the letter notes into separate word documents for each "folder." (Again, I would make very sure that the provenance information goes with the material.) This has the added advantage that I could put copies of a given letter note in different folders.

But at the same time, multiplying copies of things is the fast road to perdition. It is tempting to see four or five possible points of interest—and hence four or five possible filings—for each item. But making five copies of every note and distributing them to five different folders gradually defeats the purpose of having folders. You move toward simply having five copies of everything, all in a mush; it's just like having too many tags on an item or too many subject headings on an LC card. To be frank, I almost never have copies of primary material in more than one analysis folder. Since I am very unlikely to use a given item twice in my final text, I might as well accept the most important classification as the only classification, and be done with it. Again, as with all hierarchical classification, it's easier to remember a few extra cross-references than to think about your data as a continuous network where every piece of data bears to some extent on every topic.

The names or types of your analysis folders will be determined by what you are studying. You might want to have folders on individuals, on organizations, on particular events, on offices, on forms of work, on important episodes, on all sorts of things. You will figure out what is needed as you go along.

Some special types of analysis folders:

Biographical. Not all biographical information will come from primary materials or the web. Remember that biographical sources are legion. Between *Who's Who*, various area indexes, manuscript censuses, and the like, you can find a lot of detail on nearly anyone. The ALA *Guide* has good lists of where to go. Googling might be useful too, but web information can be unreliable. *World Biographical Information System*, if it covers your person, is truly excellent, and should be your first recourse; it has PDFs of published biographical information on over six million people. In any case, most of your biographical information will come from general sources, not manuscript materials (unless your topic is basically the person him- or herself). Make subfolders within biographical folders if you need them; as usual, don't let any single folder get too cluttered.

Organizational. For national-level organizations there is "biography-like" coverage in the *Encyclopedia of Associations* and similar but more specialized sources. The *Encyclopedia*'s information—as I noted earlier—can be erratic, particularly because of the routine migration of past information to later editions. For local organizations, international organizations, and subdivisions of nationals, secondary information may be more difficult, although in recent years the *Encyclopedia* has expanded to include them. Remember that there is no conceivable business plan for making this information painstakingly accurate, any more than there's a conceivable business plan for making World-Cat painstakingly accurate. So you need to corroborate whatever you find in the *Encyclopedia*. If necessary, build up subfolders on major figures involved in an organization, membership lists if relevant, publications, subdivisions, tasks, routines, events, and so on.

Database analysis: Some of your folders will be files of data and/or analysis for particular collections of primary facts. These might be case statistics, attendance records, publication patterns, network data, statistics on juries, or whatever. Sometimes this data comes direct from primary sources, sometimes it is calculated or abstracted from it. For such self-contained minianalyses, keep the data and analysis material together unless it is too much. As chapter 9 will show, you may need separate subfolders on things like coding conventions and decisions, rules of abstracting or otherwise constructing the data, notes on types of analyses, copies of database or computer programs if you wrote any to do the work (or records of the analytic algorithms you yourself followed in analyzing the data) and—of course—results. Basically, database analysis folders should look like folders for a generic quantitative project. Your records for any complicated analytic work, up to and including formal quantitative analyses, must be as excellent as your archival records. They should be good enough that you can go back after several weeks or months and replicate any formal analysis without hesitation.

G. WRITING FOLDERS

Writing folders are straightforward. Keep them by section or chapter. Although I write on a computer, I still keep working physical copies of my writing once I get to a second or third draft. Onscreen editing does not compare in speed and depth with paper editing. (Moreover, onscreen editing produces texts that are chatty rather than concise.) For example, the last five editing passes on this book manuscript were done with physical copies.

IN CLOSING THIS SECTION LET ME REMIND YOU THAT ORGANIZATION is meant to help you, not overburden you. Maintain a file structure that is sufficient to help you locate everything quickly and to provide a solid base for analysis. But do not go beyond what is necessary.

Finally, no matter what file system you use, it eventually will get out of control. I'm an extremely organized researcher, but even so, I nearly always lose control after a while. I gradually drop everything in late midphase to focus on writing. I maintain the filing necessary for my last minianalyses, but I neglect the main files. As a result, all of my projects finish with unfiled materials, unfollowed leads, fat and ignored to-do files, and so on. Filing is not its own purpose; it exists to help you think and write.

2. Organization

Maintaining the organization of your project means maintaining your files and keeping a close watch on where you are in the schedule. But in the process of doing these things you are doing important intellectual work on the project by developing your controlled vocabulary and your crosswalk. It's not just a matter of pigeonholes.

A. CONTROLLED VOCABULARY

Once your project gets going, primary and secondary material, along with notes, references, and other things, come in like a flood. So you must channel all this material into your files. As you develop your filing system, you need to associate your own personal keywords with each item you put in the files. On paper, you just write them across the top of the sheet. If you are virtual, you can attach them as tags, or as headers in text files. For example, in my *AJS* history project I started with "editorial" as a file and a keyword early in the project, because the initial editor did everything himself. Later I had to subdivide this into "editorial policy," "editorial work," and "editorial relations," because later editors behaved quite differently. For another example, let's return to the project on the rights of nature in Ecuador. In such a project you may start out with headings for a word like *rights*, but gradually realize that you also need to discuss whether documents involve *preservation*, *protection*, *symbiosis* or other such concepts. That is, new ideas become important as the project evolves. As a result, you may have to go back and write some new keywords on documents. You may even want to start some new files. By continuously rereading the materials in your files and reflecting about what they say, what they ignore, and how they articulate, you will create a solid, rigorous vocabulary.

That personal controlled vocabulary will become the foundation of your analysis. The concept of controlled vocabulary has come up before, in chapter 3. But that earlier discussion of indexing took the point of view of the user, the person seeking references and bibliography. Here we take the point of view of the indexer, for you as analyst must be the indexer of your own materials. In part, this is just a cognitive convenience, as we have seen: you can't remember the location of each piece of material, and, in any case, doing so is a waste of valuable intellectual energy. But in fact the index you design for yourself will not only be embodied in your set of files, but will also become the foundation of your analysis. This solid and rigorous vocabulary comprises a set of concepts that for you accurately characterizes all the material you have found. It emerges from reflection on your files, from random ideas that occur while you work with primary material, from a thousand little places. It is not an exaggeration to say that my own first book was essentially the writing down in words of a controlled vocabulary that I had developed in the process of reading dozens of studies of professions over four or more years.

Your controlled vocabulary will to some extent grow out of your idea files. In the beginning of a project, these idea files just contain random thoughts: "Could it be that the establishment of the Red Cross played a crucial role in consolidating the civil society?" "Creating an organization is more about creating a boundary than about creating an organization chart." "Maybe Fanon is better understood as a psychiatrist whose mind was blown by his Algerian experience than as social theorist pure and simple." After a whole bunch of these things pile up, they can be classified into subtypes, and you will begin to see important words that cut across them: *theorists, boundaries, organization, establishment*. You may end up redefining *establishment* as two separate keywords: *founding* and *institutionalization*. You are creating your theory by worrying about how to characterize and categorize your data.

Your idea files will grow steadily. So you need to reclassify them from time to time. You may eventually separate some particular concepts as themselves subjects of data files. More often, however, the ideas that coalesce into the keywords of your project will be abstractions. From time to time, you will need to sit and think about all these ideas and try to put them into a more formal and rigorous relation to each other. (Time for some meditative reading, perhaps?)

Of course this emerging and shifting vocabulary should be used as necessary to index articles and data that go into your files so that items are easily identified as relevant to this or that abstraction. Remember that many of your files will be kept by source ("all the material from journal X," "all the material gleaned from Treasury Department documents," and so on). So a quick scrawl (physical or electronic) of a keyword on a page or file will remind you that a particular document is going to be important for a particular topic. (That way you can sometimes avoid creating the full-blown analysis folders I discussed earlier in the chapter.) By doing this indexing and commenting work as you go along, you force yourself to classify your materials; you continuously improve the thinking in the project; and you strategize how to direct your next efforts. All these things are building the intellectual machinery that makes writing the ultimate text quite straightforward.

If you work on more than one project or on a dissertation with several parts, you probably keep idea notebooks. If you don't, you should. Personally, I use written notebooks to keep a subject-indexed record of ideas that go across my various projects, for like most working academics I have gradually built a quite general controlled vocabulary of my own. I write in my notebooks by hand, because I find that the task of physically writing an idea makes me more serious about it, makes me reflect more about it, and makes it reach deeper into my pool of further associations. But you can of course maintain a notebook-type file in virtual form.

Whether you are digital or physical, the key to a notebook is the indexing, and the key to indexing is doing it as you go along. Each new page or other unit of reflections should get a few controlled vocabulary (CV) terms at the top. If your new reflection or idea doesn't come under one of the CV terms on the active page, then start a new page with the new CV terms appropriate to that new idea. You will find that you have several active pages at once.

When you have a new idea, you look through your notebook to find the first page possessing (a) the main CV term for your current idea and (b) enough space to write that idea. (Space is not a problem if you're electronic, of course; but even my most technologized students seem to be keeping notebooks by hand.) Then you write the idea down and at the same time you enter any new CV terms appropriate for this idea in the list at the top of the page. But most important, *you also add the page number to an ongoing alphabetized CV term index at the back of the book.* The result is a continuously subject-indexed notebook in which ideas are clustered by CV term but not absolutely separated into independent pages. At any time, if you want your ideas on topic X, you just go to the back of the book and look up the pages for that topic. Then you go read the indexed pages, which will have not only those indexed ideas, but also some nearby thoughts to browse.

If you keep a notebook on computer, the convenient procedure is simply to add any new idea to the "page" (the portion of a notebook document) that is governed by the dominant CV term for the idea entered. This won't have quite the random browsing density of the written notebook, but it is quite sufficient. The crucial matter is constant, ongoing indexing both on the page and in an ongoing back-of-the-book-type index. Then you have all your ideas on a topic, available immediately, at any time. Not by simple word search, but by your own conscious reflection and indexing.

B. CROSSWALK

The keys to organization are thus the controlled vocabulary that grows from your ideas and the file system that develops for the materials themselves. But although you build the controlled vocabulary in part by working with the file system, these two forms of organization will not be exactly the same. Most of the controlled vocabulary terms will be abstractions. They will relate closely to your theoretical puzzles and your general research questions. (Indeed, they may suggest important ways in which you can rephrase and improve your theoretical puzzles and your general research questions.) But they won't be the organizing principles of your data files (mostly organized by type of source) or of your analytic files (which will be organized by the type of analysis, as we will see in the next chapter). There is thus the issue of the crosswalk between them.

Crosswalk is a term from database management. It refers to the set of connections that allows one database to be recoded automatically into the categories of another database. When the Bureau of the Census changes the occupational classification for a new census, it has to create a crosswalk between the old and new classifications to enable scholars to compare the two different censuses: "accountants and bookkeepers" in the old classification might be split into "accountants" and "bookkeepers" in the new, or into "public accountants," "corporate accountants," and "bookkeepers and clerical personnel." So two people coded together in one census might be coded differently in the next and vice versa.

In a library research project, you have two basic "databases." One of them is the set of specific research questions that issue from the empirical and theoretical puzzles and the general research questions they create. The other is the set of sources (and later analyses) that you have sought (or created through your analyses) as the research proceeds. At the start of the project, your crosswalk is simply an array of all the specific research questions (as rows) across all the proposed data sources (as columns.) Obviously, you need to have at least one data source for each row, and preferably more than one. Conversely, you won't have any columns that aren't useful for at least one row. (If you think you do have such a column, then it suggests that you have forgotten to include an important question and need to state it explicitly.) But in a well-organized project, most data sources will bear on more than one question.

This initial crosswalk is purely speculative. It predicts which sources will answer which questions, but it doesn't actually know that for sure. And as the project unfolds, you will find that your data—and more important the analyses you undertake of that data—gradually resist the structure you have tried to impose with your questions. They won't quite fit. They don't answer the question you want, but the next one over. They suggest that it was the wrong question. They may put together three questions you separated and then transform the way the result is posed. At the same time, your new controlled vocabulary will be suggesting ways to restate and reframe the questions themselves.

Put another way, you will predict one connection between your puzzles and the real world, but to a considerable extent you will discover another. Attention to the crosswalk resolves that misfit. You must continuously recast your specific research questions into terms closer to your emerging controlled vocabulary, and you may also need to recast the specific research questions themselves, lumping some together, dividing others, relating them to new general research questions. You will also need to restate and reframe them in the terms of your controlled vocabulary. Indeed, analyses may have uncovered some completely new specific research questions that need to be added to your design. Developing a more sophisticated crosswalk between your idea-terms and your materials thus means a gradual focusing, specification, and in many cases revision of the design document's original prediction of which particular research questions would—if answered—allow you to resolve the proposed puzzles.

In the original, purely speculative crosswalk, as I noted above, each row-question has at least one column-source that provides information that can answer that row-question. Each of these filled cells in the matrix is, in principle, a minianalysis, a specific and limited body of data-gathering and analysis, rooted in a specific source and bearing on a specific question. In the next chapter, we shall take up in detail some types of minianalyses, but here I want to underscore that by developing this matrix of questions across sources, you have broken the large research project up into smaller, more feasible pieces— the minianalyses.

Doing these minianalyses gradually modifies the crosswalk itself. If you're an experienced researcher working in a familiar area, you can deal with this change on the fly. You're likely to have a fairly settled controlled vocabulary and have probably developed the habit of making sure that you have (or can get) the evidence you need at all times. I myself tend to make up my crosswalk as I go along, rather than putting effort into an initial crosswalk based on pure guesswork that I know will turn out to be wrong. But even dissertation students invariably get lost if they haven't started from a clear specification of the possible data sources for their various questions.

So you should probably create at least a sketch version of an actual initial crosswalk document showing which sources you expect to answer which parts of which questions. From time to time throughout the project, you should revise this document, as your reflection reshapes the rows—the various research questions—and even the idea terms in which those research questions are posed. You will revise the columns also because the sources themselves have inevitably done different things than you expected. But gradually, through the project, the connection between questions and sources gets stronger and stronger, as they modify each other and gradually shape each other into complementary patterns that fit together better than you could have possibly imagined at first.

That connection depends most strongly on the intersection of a particular row-question and a particular column-source. These are the minianalyses that make up the analytic heart of library research.

9 | *Midphase Analysis*

Analysis means the assembly, examination, and interpretation of the materials you have gathered to answer your research questions. It begins early in the midphase and continues through to the end of a project. Like all other aspects of library work, analysis is nonlinear.

In specific terms, analysis means preprocessing your various kinds of data so they can be synthesized into the written text that speaks to your empirical and theoretical puzzles. The more you preprocess your materials, the more easily you begin to see how they relate to one another. Eventually it will become clear how these related materials can be articulated together to become coherent interpretations of the situation you are researching. This synthesis will take place gradually, late in midphase.

This gradual articulation has three sources. First, it comes from the kind of synthetic vision we saw in action in chapter 2. This vision is rooted in art and heuristics. It's the skill of seeing old things in new ways. I have written about it at length elsewhere, in the book *Methods of Discovery* (New York: Norton, 2004). So I shall not discuss it here.

Second, the gradual articulation of your material comes from the writing itself. There is a logic to prose that begins to shape your arguments on its own. Indeed, many students think that they can find their arguments only through writing. We shall examine the writing process in chapter 10.

But third, and most important, the articulation of your materials into larger interpretations and arguments happens through what I have been calling minianalyses, preprocessing exercises that answer specific research questions or that systematically prepare data so that it can more easily inform reflection about larger questions. In this chapter I examine those stepping stones in some detail. (The term *minianalysis* was coined by one of my students, Diana Kim.)

A minianalysis addresses a specific research question with a finite set of research acts done in a limited time. Thus, in chapter 2, my census of twentieth-century American academics was a minianalysis, as was my assembly of research library statistics. Each was a specific, limited research endeavor addressing a very simple and particular question: respectively, how many scholars were there, and how big were the libraries in which they worked? By doing such delimited exercises as you go along, you not only slice your analytic problem into feasible bits, you also discover further leads for other parts of the project. Moreover, a completed minianalysis will support text; the first paragraphs you write, after hammering out your design document, will be write-ups of minianalyses.

The present chapter covers four broad types of minianalyses: (1) timeline and biography, (2) categorization and colligation, (3) numerical analyses, and (4) content analysis. Put less formally, you can put data in order, you can put data in groups, and you can analyze data quantitatively, whether it is numerical or verbal. I use many extended examples, because such analyses are impossible to understand in the abstract. The examples may seem overly detailed, but they aim to show the complexity of the analytic process.

1. Timeline, Biography, Narrative

Timeline and biography, simple and composite, are the first basic types of minianalysis. They tell a systematic story: spare in the case of timeline, more detailed in that of biography. Timeline is the simplest form of story, a listing of items by date. For any person particularly important in your inquiry, having a timeline of that person's life or career is always useful. Preparing them is a good task for early in the midphase, when you haven't gotten into real details.

By contrast, timelines for a group of people can be much more complex. You can stack the individual timelines vertically on a page, one above the other, with time flowing to the right and with the individuals ordered by the starting dates of their timelines. This gives you an instant reference tool showing your characters' relative age and experience at any given moment. An example would be the list of professors who ever worked in a particular academic department.

Figure 6 provides the demography of my own department from 1966 to 1976, leaving off the names (irrelevant, although they do tell you that only two of these were women.) Rank is shown by number—1 for professor, 2 for associate professor, 3 for assistant professor, and 4 for instructor. Individual careers span the rows, and department membership by year is thus shown in the columns. The demography of the department is instantly clear. The rows

School of PhD	Year of PhD	1966-67	1967-68	1968-69	1969-70	1970-71	1971-72	1972-73	1973-74	1974-75	1975-76
U of Minnesota	1932	1	1	1	1	1	1				
U of Chicago	1939	1	1	1	1	1	1	1	1	1	1
U of Pennsylvania	1940	1	1	1	1	1	1	1	1	1	1
U of Chicago	1948	1	1	1	1	1	1	1	1	1	1
U of Michigan	1949	1	1	1	1	1	1	1	1	1	1
Princeton	1950	1	1	1	1	1	1	1	1		
Harvard	1950	1	1	1	1	1					
Columbia	1952	1	1	1	1						
U of Chicago	1952	1	1	1							
Harvard	1950	2	1	1	1	1	1	1	1	1	1
U of Chicago	1958	2	2	2	2	2	2	1	1	1	1
Columbia	1956	2	2	2							
Harvard	1955	2	2	2	2		1	1	1	1	
U of Chicago	1961	3	2	2	2	2					
U of Michigan	1962	3	2	2	2						
U of Michigan	1963	3	3	3							
Columbia	1967	3	3	3	3	3	2	2	2	2	2
UCLA	1967	3	3	3							
Purdue	1955	3	3	3							
U of Chicago	1965	3	3	3							
U of Chicago	1964	3	3								
Harvard	1969	3	3								
Yale	1957		2	2							
U of Chicago	1966	3	3	3							
U of I Urbana–Champaign	1966	3	3	3							

FIGURE 6. Department demography, 1966 to 1976. Based on an original chart prepared by Gerald Marwell on data provided by Erin York.

School of PhD	Year of PhD	1966-67	1967-68	1968-69	1969-70	1970-71	1971-72	1972-73	1973-74	1974-75	1975-76
Johns Hopkins	1970			3	3	3	3	3	3	3	
Cornell	1970		3	3	3	3	3	3	3	3	3
U of Chicago	1971		3	3	3	3					
Harvard	1976		4	4	4	4	4				
Harvard	1966				3	3	3	3	3	3	2
U of Chicago	1952					1	1	1	1	1	1
U of Pennsylvania	1970					3	3	3	3	3	3
U of Chicago	1981					4	4				
U of Chicago	1953						1	1	1	1	
U of Chicago	1956						1	1	1	1	1
U of Chicago	1960						1	1	1	1	
U of Chicago	1962						1	1	1	1	1
UNC Chapel Hill	1971						3	3	3	3	
U of Michigan	1971					4	3	3	3	3	3
Washington State U	1966							3	3	2	1
Harvard	1972							3	3	3	3
Harvard	1965							1	1	1	1
Columbia	1955							1	1	1	1
Berkeley	1960										1

FIGURE 6. (*continued*)

tell you that Chicago treated its assistant professors harshly; we see denials of reappointment (three- or four-year runs of 3s) and denials of tenure (six-year runs of 3s). Several important departures of young senior faculty are evident in the truncated runs of 1s for relatively recent PhDs. (Truncation of a run of 1s after an earlier PhD means retirement.) On the inflow side, we see the hiring of eminent outsiders as full professors over the heads of the assistant professors. We also see that hirings come in bursts and that the department liked to hire its own. Such a display makes a whole world of facts instantly self-evident, as a single whole.

Obviously you can create similarly dense timelines and combined timelines for important organizations relevant to your project: nonprofits, legislatures, denominations, industrial firms. To be sure, organizations, unlike persons, can amalgamate and divide. But these are contingencies you can address by placing merging or dividing organizations adjacent in your vertical array.

You can also do timelines of events, breaking them up into subevents and stages. And you can combine those timelines across events or types of events. Thus a student interested in studying the dynamics of social policies in Argentina arrayed events in different policy areas (housing, exports, labor force, etc.) above one another in a time-flow diagram, just like the careers of the individual sociologists above. That gave both a comparative overview of the unfolding of events in any given policy area (left to right) as well as the simultaneous mix of events (vertically) in any given period.

There are some basic rules for combining much information into composite timelines. First, try to keep the pulse of time visually regular; it should always take the same space. (Most spreadsheets won't do this unless you enforce it; they take whatever space is necessary to contain the text.) Second, separate thematic areas. For example, on a timeline for the project on environmental rights in Ecuador, oil-related events might be divided into legal changes, changes related to indigenous rights, and changes related to the international context, shown as three broad bands in a horizontal set of stacked timelines.

Third, within those bands you should separate things that are more or less instantaneous from things that endure over time. Events are usually instantaneous and can be so marked on a single left-to-right timeline. But an organization endures after its foundation, and you may want to represent that endurance by an ongoing band, not by a single date. Hardest to represent are what we might call "pervasions": background realities that have no real date but that capture trends or background facts of importance. Suppose you are writing about medicine and want to represent the gradual replacement of one preventive medical practice by another. (This was needed in the Pap smear project mentioned earlier.) You might use a shrinking band to represent the vanishing practice and an expanding band to represent the emerging one.

As with any aspect of a library project, you choose for your timelines the options that offer the most utility for your particular puzzles. You want to concentrate the most relevant information in one place, not simply the most information. In one project, you might want to put organizations together rather than theme areas. In another you might concentrate a group of individual people. (With spreadsheet programs, you can rearrange the displays several ways at will.)

Answers to your underlying questions may well be made obvious by a thoughtfully designed composite timeline. But timelines are only the bare bones versions of minihistories. When we start to add substance to them, we call them biographies. We are all familiar with the idea of the individual biography, and a short, careful biography of a particularly important individual or individuals in your project is an obvious choice for an early minianalysis. But systematic comparison of such biographies across many individuals is much more powerful. It is called prosopography. Historians of groups often proceed by prosopography, developing short biographical studies of many individuals and then melding them into a single comprehensive analysis.

I did this myself in two chapters of my dissertation, studying the four professional positions that psychiatrists could hold in my period: mental hospital superintendent, assistant hospital physician, sanitarium director, and outpatient psychiatrist. The analysis of each position was sustained by the abstracted lives of many individuals, which I had retrieved from a variety of sources using a one-page form with the names, durations, and nature of a doctor's education, employment, publications, unusual experiences, and so on. I spent several months creating such abstracted lives for about a thousand physicians from old *Who's Who*s, obituaries, and other sources. While doing this, I noted down and categorized dozens of career contingencies, giving me an intuitive sense of the most common job transitions and of the typical career. I also realized that I needed (and could easily do) a simple network analysis of the links created by individual people moving between a number of important institutions (the same employing organizations kept coming up again and again). And, in fact, the writing of those two chapters—a hundred pages—was quite easy, given the dozens of insights I got from coding the data into my forms. Often in library work, the gathering and coding of the data is the discipline through which you do the analysis. To be sure, I could have quantified the whole dataset with some further effort, but that would have added very little to the interpretive command I had already acquired merely by recording the data by brute force from the various biographical sources.

Such biographies of course can be done for organizations and groups of organizations as well. And for communities, for that matter. Another chapter of my dissertation comprised minianalyses of the psychiatric and neurological specialty communities in Boston, New York, Philadelphia, and Baltimore, each such community "biography" developed from a combination of published, archival, and personal biographical data. Pulling apart a large project into several such smaller tasks helps you get started on analysis.

It is harder, however, to write a minibiography of a physical or social area. One could undertake a study of labor relations in Kansas City, for example, and approach this through "biographies" of separate areas like the building trades, the manufacturing trades, the service sector, and the government sector. But what are "the building trades"? What about membership drives or collective bargaining contests that cross these lines? How much information is necessary about the organization of these employment sectors themselves? One of the virtues of a minianalysis is that it is bounded, and "area biographies" have a particularly unbounded quality. That is probably why so many of our great monographs concern organizations; they have sharp edges. (In this case, for example, one could much more easily organize the study not around areas of work and employment but around particular unions.)

Yet while such "area biography" may be difficult, it is nonetheless uniquely powerful if you can do it. As you may recall, the paper whose writing is discussed in chapter 2 created "biographies" of "areas of reference works" based on the tools listed in successive editions of the ALA *Guide to Reference Books*. For hundreds of reference works, I listed date of publication (at the left to facilitate sorting) then a space, then a short title and author if necessary. A sample of the raw data is given in figure 7, without editing or spellchecking, so you don't get the idea that my notes are typed without errors. The "areas" (in this example, the headings "Encyclopedias," "Dictionaries," "Societies") come from the original documents and thus from the librarians. But I would later completely reclassify reference tools into serial bibliography, book bibliography, dissertations, archives, government documents, and so on. A new definition of my "areas" of interest arose from my attempts to understand the gradual shift of the librarians' own categories.

From this raw data file I produced time-sorted versions of the data as well as a version sorted into my new categories. On these processed listings were

ENCYCLOPEDIAS:

1818-   allgeneime encylopaedie der Wissenschaften und Kunste 170 vols
1866–90   Grand dicionnaire universel larousse 1866–90 17 vols
1875–88   Britannica 9 24 vols
1874–99   universal cyclopedia 12 v. (seems gone in 1923)
1885–1902 la grande encyclopedie 30 vols later (1923) sold by larousse , Winchell still
          loves it.
1892–5   Brockhaus encycl 17 vols. retited 1923 konversations lexikon this was the 14th
          edition, the first is 1796–1808
1903–4   first edition of americana (not mentioned till winchell)
1911   Encyclopedia Britannica 11th ed.
1914–1916 new international encyclopedia competitor with americana
1913–20   Encyclopedia Americana
1928–35   15th edition of Brockhaus, first since 1890s.
1929   Encyclopedia Britannica 14th (winchell recommends 9,11,14 ALL be kept.
1929–37   E. Italiana, fabulous for its illustrations 35 vols.
1949–50   Colliers—a junior college encyc.—note that winchell is starting to make these
          diffs.

note that english lan encyclopedia world changes greatly in 1923 period
larousse is differentiating into several different sizes.

note that winchell gives long edition histories of the major Encyc.
she also discussses annuals to encyclopedias—which continued or were in the
"events of the year" "ideal chronicler" approach. I have put these under
history.

DICTIONARIES (mostly English only. The basic Fr d is petit larousse,):

1854–1940 Grimm brothers, D. woreterbuch, 16 vols, still incomplete
          in mid 20th. like OED, but not as detailed on
          pronunciation, less systematic use of quotes and
          work on etymology.
1873–78   Littre, Emile. Dict de la langue Franc. 4 vols, some etymol
1888 ff   OED (up to K by 1902)
          (to TH by 1923)
          (finished in 1928, with suppl vols or dicts covering
          1. middle English, 2. american, scots, 4. new words
1889–91   century dictionary and cyclopedia (put in 1902) 12 vols
          incl cycopedia of names and atlas
          winchell thinks this the best encyc form of dictionary
          latest ed as of winchell = 1911 in 12 vols
1891   Webster's latest (from 1828) (dictionary with biographies,
          gazetteer etc.
1891   Worcester's dictionary newed. (gone by 1923)
1893   Funk and Wagnalls first ed (from winchell)
1909   Websters new international first ed.
1911   first ed of fowler
1913   Funk and Wagnalls standard dictionary—
          current, spelling reformed to some extent
          not revised by 1951, w says OK one vol work.
1928   completion of the OED

1934   websters New int. second ed, divided page, useful.
      oldest and most useful of one vol dictionaries.

FIGURE 7. Reference book data notes

there is now (1923) a long section on foreigh language dictionaries.
in winchell, this whole thing becomes a free-floating section on language
dictionaries. note also that end of the 19th saw a lot of combination
dictionary ency. of the larousse forms. The sharp separation comes later

It seems, after looking at Winchell, that the dictionary world is pretty
stable by mid 20th. the OED has set the standard, the french have no
equivalent, Grimm is not yet finished and is weaker.

SOCIETIES:

Directories:

1883	die Wissen. Vereine und Gesell. deutschalnds 1883–7
	later editoin 1917 thus, two vols.
1884 ff	yearbook of the scientific and learned societyes of GB
	and Ireland
1891 ff	Minerva (in german, yearbook of higher ed, museums, societies)
	finally ceases in 1938.
1899	cyclopedia of fraternities (stevens, albert clark)
1907	Griffin, APC. bib of am historical societies, 2d ed (1=1905)
	guide to soc AND index of contents of pubs. AHA
1908	Carnegie institution, handbook of lnd socs and Insts.
	never revised,
1908–12	Union des assocs. Internat. Annuaire de la vie internationale
	2 vols, never reissued to 1951
1919–39	index generalis (french) annual univs, societies, museums,etc
1947	world of learning, annual, london. continues Minerva,
	but without the personnel index.

Publications:

1867–1902	Royal Society catalogue of scientific papers, addenda to 1900
1888–1916	Lasteyrie du saillant, RC: bib. generale des travaux historiques..
	6 vols—ALL historical societys and pubs in france.

society pubs has disappeared as a heading in 1951. Even in kroeger, this is a
thin section. The preference was to put major society stuff unde rhte special
topics to whichit was relevant. It should be noted, then, that these general
sections of the work gradually get overshadowed, through the century by the
special subjects.

FIGURE 7. (continued)

marked (by hand) the periods I was describing in the paper. The final text file that I used when writing the reference-book sections of the paper was twenty-one single-spaced pages. It covered the reference situation up through midcentury in great detail. The various forms of "analysis" (sorting, reclassification, and so on) took about two weeks total, once the raw listing had been produced by brute force, done part-time over several weeks. The fully analyzed data produced a comprehensive set of "area biographies" of reference tools that sustained my discussion of the research experience in each period.

The various timelines, biographies, and narratives that you produce as minianalyses will not necessarily themselves appear in the final text, although they did in the case just discussed. Sometimes you may write a short narrative passage directly based on a timeline or a biography. Once in a while you might use a display like figure 6 to make a point about a particular organization's demography. But most of the time you use a timeline as guidance while you are writing. It is a visual reminder of a whole set of important and related facts. It brings disparate things together, suggesting new connections. That is what I mean by speaking of minianalyses as "preprocessing." They provide an intermediate step between raw data and written analysis.

2. Categorization and Colligation

As this example suggests, much analytic work in library research involves categorization. I said in chapter 8 that by enforcing the six-item rule on your files you would develop new categories and subcategories for analysis. Here we can see how that happens, how categorizing and recategorizing are actually part of analysis.

Consider my project on psychiatrists. At the very beginning of my research, I had only one file containing data on individual psychiatrists. Soon this divided into two: a file for particular people and a file for career contingencies. With the former, I quickly realized that I would encounter so much information that I needed for each individual a form with space for name, birthplace, education, employment history, publications, clubs, and miscellaneous social class indicators. (And at the bottom, a place to note all sources for this information.) As I noted, this form became the basis of the prosopographical dataset mentioned in the preceding section.

But the contingencies folder also soon split up. As I worked through the biographical sources, I got information on all kinds of career contingencies: political appointment and removal, salary changes, trips abroad, career-changing marriage, opening a sanitarium, taking a demotion to stay employed, moving to another state system, being sued by a patient's family, being killed by a patient, and so on. Each time I ran into something unusual, I wrote the contingency and the doctor affected by it on a scrap of paper and threw it into the contingencies folder. Soon that folder needed to be broken up into separate subfolders on political contingencies, on salaries and their evolution, on career management, on geographic mobility, and "other."

In this simple example are shown many of the basics of categorical analysis of library materials. I was brute-forcing my way through biographical sources. Out of that effort were coming not only the abstracted lives of my psychiatrists, but also dozens of intriguing little events and possibilities that shaped their lives. Notes of these were going into a substantive folder, which eventually needed breaking up into subfolders. I was also maintaining by hand the "key" tables (as they are called in relational database theory) that could now be done automatically online: lists by sanitarium of all the psychiatrists who had ever worked in that sanitarium (there were about 200 sanitariums in my data), lists by medical school of all the psychiatrists who had ever served at that school (there were close to 400 schools), and so on. That is, I produced all the subtables of a large relational database by hand. In the process I not only noticed all the events, contingencies, trends, and issues that I just mentioned, but also began to know at firsthand the staffs of sanitariums and the members of medical schools, and indeed the policies and histories of those sanitariums and schools. I learned, for example, that sanitarium names changed arbitrarily and often, something that was otherwise invisible. (New owners always renamed them.) Thus, from this biographical brute-force work, categories of analysis were emerging not only for the biographical data, but for organizations, schools, and sanitariums as well.

In many cases, these categories came simply from piling up large numbers of examples which were then sorted on substantive grounds into groups. It is a very simple procedure, but from this continuing exercise came the types of psychiatrists (superintendents, assistant physicians, sanitarium owners, outpatient practitioners), of medical faculties (university-based, substantial private, fly-by-night private), of journals (neurological, psychiatric, both, general medicine). These may seem obvious after the fact. But they were not so before my data work, nor were the essential qualities of each type knowable without that work.

Such categorization is inductive. The data tell you what is happening, not vice versa. That's why you can't have a database program do the work for you.

In my library infrastructure paper, for example, I did not at first even separate my files by period. Only after I was well into the project did I decide one day that I would have to organize the paper around periods because otherwise it would be unwritable. I then had to reread all of my data files and choose a best set of possible periods. As this example shows, categorization can be by time and place as well as by substantive difference. Sometimes one way of breaking up the data is much better than another. An essential part of library research is reflecting about which subcategories are preferable and why. It may look like simply deciding how to maintain your files or how to organize your text. But in fact it is always a major intellectual choice, and should be made with an eye on your theoretical puzzles.

But one does not merely create categories. One also assembles categorized information into composite pictures: of typical psychiatric careers, of typical research practice in libraries, of typical types of environmental organizations, and so on. And types are not the only possible form for such composites. Even an analytic biography of a single individual or organization is ultimately a composite. Such assembly of disparate parts into a composite thing is called colligation. (The term is from the British philosopher William Whewell.) A traditional ethnography is thus a colligation. A study of an organization is a colligation. So also is a study of an elite or of the members of a profession or of the neighborhoods of a city.

Much analysis in library research takes the form of colligation; one creates a composite picture of something using multiple disparate pieces. Thus, in the chapter 2 project, I had to create pictures of library practices out of bits and pieces, partial views of various aspects of scholarly life, from which I had to infer the overall nature of the scholarly world I sought. One of those pieces was the list of reference works whose development I just discussed. But there were many others. Here, for example, is a list of what was actually in my folder on library research practice in the postwar period. (These are all in separate subfolders, shown here by sequential numbers.)

1. Copies of the relevant portions of two Columbia University library school theses—one from 1948 on strategies for cataloging in English literature and their relation to faculty interests and one from 1961 on a survey of libraries about faculty use of the LC classification.
2. A nineteen-page text file of my own notes on a total of thirty-six items, thirty of them MLS or PhD theses from the Chicago library school. This file—which was my basic "notes" file—also included my reflections on

and interpretations of that data, along with tables that I either copied from these texts or made up on the basis of numerical information available in them. Also in this text file were notes on period-relevant essays or papers that were in various books on libraries (by other scholars) that I had charged out.

3. Copies of eight papers of varying provenance on social science indexing and bibliography in the postwar period.

4. A subfolder called "library use in the 1950s and 1960s" containing
   a. detailed notes on one ethnographic MLS thesis on that topic,
   b. a printout of a bibliography from Web of Science,
   c. the photocopied tables from the mid-1950s ALA catalog-use study,
   d. the tables (and the results recalculated by a computer program I wrote to select out portions of the data) of the Johns Hopkins catalog-use study of 1962,
   e. figures on browsing from another ethnographic MLS thesis,
   f. all the tables from Mahmoud El-Sheniti's 1960 PhD thesis, which has data on all books charged out to University of Chicago faculty on one day in May 1956, classifying them by department across LC numbers, and
   g. the current data (from the university library) on the languages of books checked out to faculty, showing that exactly the same level of faculty checkouts are not in English in 2009 as in 1956 (30 percent).

5. Copies and notes of a 1950s University of Illinois library school thesis on dates and library-provenance of all material checked out to a random sample of U of I dissertation students.

6. The data tables from the 1950s thesis just mentioned, classifying books checked out by type of book and by individual surveyed (so one can calculate medians, better than the averages that were actually published—I had gotten the actual thesis via interlibrary loan in order to do this recalculation).

7. The bibliography from an MLS thesis on scientists' use of periodicals.

8. Copies of ten articles on postwar bibliography in humanities and/or social sciences (e.g., the UNESCO mimeographed report on this subject—which must be from our library, as I have no other note on its provenance. I should follow my own advice and keep better records!).

9. A subfolder called "postwar minor"—which has some data on catalogs published in book form in the postwar, notes on a thesis about circulation of books in various call number ranges that circulated within five

years of acquisition, a list of cities ordered by the number of libraries in them that appear in the *Union List* 1943 edition (hand counted by me from the book itself), data retrieved from JSTOR on the numbers of articles in various years with the word *dissertation* in full text (to show the decline of dissertations as important scholarly documents), plus some random notes on bibliography in this area.

10. Xeroxes and tables from a 1946 Columbia MLS thesis on users of the Columbia University depository catalog.

11. A folder of various data on numbers of journals in the various disciplines, from diverse sources.

12. The copied introductions to the *NUC* pre-1956 catalog (volume 1 of 754) and to its 1942 predecessor, the *Catalog of Books Represented by Library of Congress Printed Cards*.

As you can see, these materials comprise numbers, surveys, and quantitative analyses by me and by others as well as primary materials and materials that were secondary at the time but are quasi-primary now. My notes and interpretations are sometimes hand-scrawled on the data sheets, sometimes collected neatly into text files, sometimes written out on independent sheets of paper. (These files are filled with leads still to be followed, open-ended reflections, and data and material unused in the final paper.) Many of these subfolders contained little minianalyses of their own: recalculations of data, interpretations of texts, or assembled tables.

Out of all this mess came what reads like a seamless account of the habitus or feel of scholarship in that period. That colligation required three things. First, that I bring all this material together in one place. Second, that I do as much preprocessing as I could: by creating tables, making quantitative comparisons, taking notes, and so on. Third, that I put all this data into the framework provided by my own abstract description of "library work," my version of the "conceptualization" I discussed in chapter 4's section 1.B. Those three preparatory activities created the situation where reflection and insight could produce the interpretation that I eventually wrote out.

By the way, the data reduction involved here is very large. The twelve subfolders just mentioned contain 264 pages of published and unpublished material and notes. That sustains a section of text that has a little over 1,500 words and occupies about four pages of print.

Colligation is like cooking. There's a loose recipe, and there are some things that have to be done exactly, while other things cannot and indeed should not be done exactly. But once you become a practiced cook, and learn how to choose the right range of ingredients and do the right forms of preparatory work, you will have a delicious meal at the end.

3. Quantitative Minianalyses

A. INTRODUCTORY

Most traditional library research eschews formal quantitative analysis. There are to be sure some important exceptions. From the 1960s through the 1980s a generation of "social science historians" applied quantitative social science techniques to various kinds of old numerical data. They were historians first and foremost, and treated their numerical data with care as well as a great deal of doubt. More recently, sociologists and others are ransacking libraries for old numerical data which they then analyze in a fashion that is—for any historian—fatally naive. Unfortunately, the social science historians were right. Library researchers need to be very cautious about numbers, for good quantitative reasons.

This is not to say that we do not often make quantity assessments in library research projects. We may not use elaborate inferential statistics, but we use index or citation data to study the trends in the diffusion or reception of some word or work. We use census data to measure the population characteristics of some place or time. We compile data on organizational memberships or labor turnover or Farm Belt depopulation.

The degree to which you can do or need to do quantitative analysis is a function of your project and question. At the least, nearly all projects face the issue of "how important was phenomenon X?" (where "phenomenon X" is your puzzle or central subject). More generally, there are quantity questions about all the dimensions of conceptualization discussed in chapter 4:

- Dramatis personae: How many? Of which types? How many kinds of relations between them?
- Routine activities: What are they? Who does which ones how often? How much conflict is there?
- History and events: How many events? Of which kinds? How often in a given period?
- Environment—How many surrounding actors are there? Of which kinds? How often are they important?

- Symbols and Images—Which symbols are how important? Does this balance change? Which actors use which symbols how often or how much?

In fact we very often conceal answers to these quantity questions in the texts we write. We may write "The dominant feeling of the Southern states in 1864 was exhaustion." But who says the feeling was dominant? What is the quantitative evidence for this statement, which has no doubt appeared in dozens of histories of the American Civil War? In reality, any library-research-based text is filled with quantity judgments, many of them unsupported.

Paradoxically, if one does provide real data on such matters, doubting critics can then apply all the standards appropriate to contemporary, purpose-gathered numerical data. Yet the "found data" of library research seldom meets such high standards; it often has bad measures and dubious sampling. Because of these problems, many library researchers don't justify their quantity judgments at all. But I believe that some justification is better than none. You should do quantitative analysis, although only to the extent it is defensible.

There are three possible kinds of quantitative minianalyses. The first of these are simply counts and numbers: of persons, of behaviors, of groups, of organizations, of events. The second are more elaborate quantitative procedures: relative distributions of various individual or group qualities; counts of demographic events like marriage, turnover, and migration; spatial patterns and their changes. The third are formal statistical techniques: network analysis, sequence analysis, inferential statistics, data mining, and so on.

Obviously these various analyses could command an entire book of their own. So I can merely sketch here the issues that they raise. But they are an important part of library research, and you should be prepared to undertake them when they are needed.

B. THE PROBLEMS OF FOUND QUANTITATIVE DATA

A word first, then, about the central problems with "found data." When we formally create social-survey or census-type data we handle the known impediments to quantitative analysis ahead of time. Universe and units of analysis are specified, sampling is careful, questions are pretested, coding ambiguities are minimized. All these problems command large literatures which have reached scholarly consensus. But library data is simply found by the analyst in the physical library or online. It is there to be found because of a complex and highly biased process of production, survival, and acquisition. This bias results from past judgments about the data's importance as well as from the differential resources available to different data-gatherers, and also from the various biases they brought to their tasks. Unlike contemporaneous data-gatherers, we latter-day analysts cannot foresee and control these earlier biases. We cannot retroactively design cleanliness into data any more than we can retrospectively discover the universe of which they are a true sample.

There is, to be sure, a considerable amount of data in libraries that has been gathered under formal conditions. There are censuses, for example. But outside the developed countries even censuses are often politically motivated. Moreover, even formally deposited social science data can be governed by sampling and coding decisions that enforce particular views of the situation surveyed. For example, the well-known and excellent IPUMS datasets from the US Census employ occupational codes that are constant from 1880 onward. But any historical sociologist of occupations knows that occupations grow, die, merge, and divide in ways that make a mockery of such constant codes. As a result, these datasets are useful for only the grossest of occupational calculations. Wonderful and important as they are, they encode into themselves the perverse idea that all occupational mobility is by individuals of varying qualities between occupations that are eternally constant.

Thus, even some of the best formal data that we find in physical libraries and online has its difficulties. And most library-based quantity data is not like censuses and deposited survey data. Most of it is collected by the researcher him- or herself in minianalyses counting this or that occurrence in primary sources. Typical examples include counts of journals published in a certain year; data series of associations' memberships over many decades; numbers of articles on certain subjects appearing in certain newspapers; numbers of patients in mental hospitals over many states and long periods. For many reasons, such counts and administrative numbers have quite obscure sampling properties. Indexes and directories vary in their coverage of journals. Associations merge or split or dissolve, not to mention deliberately overestimating their memberships. Newspapers select articles not by some universal or theoretical criterion but by their newsworthiness or political utility. States may count mental patients by episodes of admission (which permits duplicate and triplicate entries by single individuals) or by resident population on a given day (which varies by season and by the availability and policies of other kinds of institutions like prisons, almshouses, and sanitariums).

As a result, we usually have little idea of the sampling basis or sometimes even the underlying meaning of found quantitative data, nor do we know whether it was consistently gathered across time and space, or what were the various preprocessings it may have received before being recorded. It looks very enticing, but in reality the most elaborate quantitative analysis that it will sustain is usually a simple cross-tabulation.

The retrieval of historical data automatically, by digital tools, does not avoid these problems. For example, the advent of online indexes for historical newspapers has produced a bonanza of quantitative work on newspaper data, despite the overwhelming problem of what gets into the newspaper to be coded and the minor problems created by the vagaries of the OCR process. That a machine is searching via keywords does not change the fact that on sampling grounds alone, such data do not meet the stringent assumptions required by the statistical techniques typically applied to them. Nor can you avoid these problems by coding the data yourself. Coding your own data from library materials simply adds further problems, induced by your own decisions about data interpretation and coding, to the problems already discussed.

Taken together, all these problems mean that retrieving and coding detailed quantitative data from library sources is usually a lot of work for a very tenuous result. When you write up or present the results, the sampling and selection issues will bother a quantitative audience, while the coding simplifications will bother the qualitative area experts. By trying to steer a middle course, you will be condemned by both sides. You should therefore think long and hard before undertaking formal quantitative analysis of found data and even longer before coding and quantifying found data that is not already explicitly quantified.

To decide whether that quantitative analysis is worth pursuing in a given case, you need to evaluate the found data explicitly. You must pose the same doubt questions asked in chapter 7, but recast them as questions about explicit numerical data instead of questions about generic sources. (I will use the word "numbers" here to mean found numbers and also any found data that you intend to code and then analyze quantitatively; the same questions apply to both.)

- Author
  - Who produced the numbers?
  - What sources did that producer use?

- On whose behalf were the statistics produced?
- Detailed provenance
  - Where were the numbers produced?
  - What was the social and historical context?
  - What was the sample and how was it defined and located?
- Production
  - On whose behalf were the statistics produced?
  - What kinds of controls existed over the gathering of the numbers?
  - What happened about missing information?
  - How long did the process actually take?
  - How was it brought "to market," and for what audiences?
  - Where and how was it printed?
- Mechanics
  - What are the mechanics through which these numbers survived?
  - Were they arbitrary or selective?
  - Are others besides the writer or gatherer involved in preservation or production? How? For what reasons?
- Purposes
  - Why were the numbers gathered?
  - What was intended for them? (E.g., police like high crime rates because they produce new resources for police)
  - Whom did the author think he was addressing and why?

Answers to these questions will tell you whether the numbers are worth the effort to clean up and possibly recode. In general, their verdict will recommend extreme caution.

With respect to the more specifically statistical properties of found numbers, there are some quite particular questions to ask about the data itself. First, what were the units of analysis, and would the data look different if other units were used? A classic example is crime rates. Is three fights in a household three fights or one episode of "domestic abuse?" That is, is the unit of analysis the fight, or the longer episode, or the individual (the fighter/abuser)? Second, what were the codes chosen for the data and why? Again, these will contain all sorts of assumptions: existence, for example. Just because something is a counted category doesn't mean that it counts anything meaningful. The US Census collected detailed data on African Americans of varying degrees of racial mix for many years, but the actual coding rules were clearly unreplicable. So the "data" is simply nonsense. Also, many historical data series have either a large residual category or an imponderable denominator. Either one of these means that the data cannot be used in any statistical analysis.

Third, be sure to reflect about the definitions of the edges of the universe from which the numbers drawn. Can you tell anything about sampling? Even the simplest count data is always a sample; "medical school foundings" is just a sample of "attempted medical school foundings." What was a medical school anyway? A bunch of doctors calling themselves one? A substantial organization with interpersonal continuity? On the former definition, there have been over five hundred medical schools in history of the US. (Five hundred such names appear in the various medical directories of various periods.) But since many of these "medical schools" were simply associations of two or three physicians who came together for two or three years and gave themselves some common name, that number is in fact preposterous as an estimate of medical schools in any institutional sense.

C. APPROPRIATE QUANTITATIVE ANALYSES WITH FOUND DATA

There are thus many difficulties with quantitative data based on library materials. But despite all these doubts, we still have to defend our quantity judgments. So here are some ground rules for quantitative minianalyses.

The simplest case of implicit quantification is simply counting numbers of occurrences of various kinds. Such data will support modest conclusions perfectly well. Allow yourself a fairly simple coding scheme and a few cross-classification tables, but don't do much more. Of the three kinds of quantitative minianalyses given above, stick to the first two: counts, cross-classifications, distributions, simple demographic patterns, and so on. Such data will not support inferential statistics.

You can be a little more adventurous with explicit quantity information—information already formally put in quantitative format in your sources. An enormous amount of such information is available. You can find out the total number of any type of handgun ever made, the circulation of all the newspapers in the US in 1922, the number of pharmacies open after 6:00 p.m. in the state of New Jersey, the wages of every musician who worked in the Hapsburg *Hofkapelle* in Vienna from the fifteenth century to the nineteenth. Even for things like attitudes there are surprising amounts of data over time and across space. Indeed, you can start from the assumption that somebody has probably gathered numbers on nearly anything that interests you.

With such numbers the first difficulty is finding data series that are truly continuous over long periods. A continuous series may be invisible because of change in (1) the name of the series or publication in which it is located, (2) the name of the publisher, and/or (3) the identity of the publisher or surveyor. If the series appeared in periodicals, then it can be traced through the usual bibliographical means. If it was located in a reference work, you can trace its history through the various editions of the ALA *Guide*. But assembling long-running series from disparate sources is a task to be done with great care. With US government statistics, you can be guided by the magnificent introductory chapters in the *Millennial Edition* of the *Historical Statistics*. These are essential reading for anyone attempting to create historical series on the US, as they go into great detail on the issues involved. In most other areas, you are on your own. You have to look very carefully at the sources, weigh and evaluate, then combine very cautiously. As you will see in the *Historical Statistics*, it is quite common to offer broken or overlapping series in cases where provenance or coding has changed in unaccountable ways. Do not despair if you have only partial data. It can be used to estimate larger things. Such estimates will involve assumptions, but by having made the effort to make a serious quantity judgment, you will at least know what those assumptions are.

Example 1. Using found data for careful description. Even when you have found explicitly pregathered quantitative data, you will need to be cautious about using inferential statistics looking for causal relations. You are on much safer ground using such data for careful descriptive analysis. As an example of such a careful but descriptive analysis let me discuss a calculation I have several times mentioned: my attempt to estimate the numbers of American scholars in the humanities and social sciences over the twentieth century. This is the first major minianalysis mentioned in chapter 2, seeking figures in two ways: from numbers of PhDs and from numbers of members of learned societies. It illustrates many of the problems here discussed.

Scholar numbers are not easy to discover. Continuous, consistent PhD data by field over time simply do not exist for the US. There is supposedly consistent historical data on PhDs overall (in the *Historical Statistics*), but it turns out that definitions changed (early PhDs sometimes took only one year!), so even those listings are not really consistent over time. Moreover, the figures are lumped into units like "Letters," "Foreign Languages," "Other Social Science," and so on. (This happens in part because definitions of fields and disciplines changed steadily over time.) The alternative approach to counting the scholars—through figures on membership in various scholarly societies—is even more problematic, especially after 1960, because what appear to be solid figures in major reference works are most often simply repetitions of the preceding edition's numbers. Prior to 1960, the figures in the annuals of the American Council of Learned Societies (ACLS) seem pretty accurate, because they change all the time and do not involve round numbers. (By contrast, the standard published source on associations thought the American Anthropological Association had exactly 10,000 members in 1970, 1980, 1990, and 2000. This number cannot possibly be exact, and it is very likely that it conceals a simple forward migration of the 1970 data.)

As a result of these confusions, my subfolder on PhD and society numbers has several different kinds of data in it. The first is exact figures on PhDs in certain disciplines for varying periods from 1926 to 1970 from various editions of *American Universities and Colleges* (an American Council on Education publication). The second is a continuation of those figures after 1970, so far as it is possible, by rough equivalents from the *Digest of Education Statistics*. (These tables were pieced together from various editions of the *Digest*, which, taken together, produced field-specific trend data that could then be analyzed for detailed fluctuations.) The third item is the downloaded PhD data from the *Historical Statistics* (in the lumped categories given above), which start only in 1920 (and of which I had to add together various subcolumns, since I wanted to count only humanists and social scientists).

The fourth item is a computer program that does certain types of estimation. I wanted to be able to talk about PhD population as of a certain point in time, as well as about the numbers of degrees up to that point in time. So I had to estimate the number of PhDs granted between 1890 (arbitrary start of system) and 1920, when the actual data began. I did this by a linear interpolation from 0 PhDs in 1890 to 140 (the actual number) in 1920. I also had to assume a fixed career length and a starting population of German-trained academics in 1890 (the original American graduate supervisors got their own training abroad), together with an assumed age distribution. Since death would remove people from the pool of PhDs, I also had to take account of death rates. These came from the period death-rate tables on the Social Security website, but had to be adjusted a bit to approximate academia's race and gender composition.

My computer program produced the fifth item in the folder, an estimated total number of humanities and social sciences PhDs alive and able to serve in academia as of each year from 1890 to the present. The next subfolder, a collection of analyses of the scholarly society data, ended up with a table for the society figures for 1908 and for every five years from 1920 to 1975, then for

1984, 1991, and 2001. It was based on data even more complex than the PhD data, but at least involved no computer estimation. (It mixed Office of Education data, ACLS data, and *World of Learning* data.) In short, "minianalysis" here means everything from finding the data, to recopying it and noting its provenance, to doubting it and worrying about its stability, to checking it against other data, to manipulating it numerically, to setting it up for presentation.

The most important result of this minianalysis, as I said in chapter 2, came because these two different approaches to the problem of "how many scholars there were" produced wildly different results. They were obviously counting different things, so of course I calculated the quotient of the two. (There's no need to call that a minianalysis; it took five minutes to recognize that it ought to be done and then do it.) It turned out that the quotients decline gradually with time, showing that non-PhDs had remained strong in the learned societies much later than anyone had thought. This was a completely unexpected but extremely important result, and although I would not guarantee accuracy for any particular number, the trend was so clear as to completely justify the conclusion. That is why careful descriptive analysis is often better than inferential statistics based on dubious assumptions. My identified trend would remain even if I radically changed most of the assumptions I had made. Note too that the only other research strategy that would have justified this conclusion would have been the direct analysis of titles and addresses of society members across time, an immensely detailed task, and one for which the data do not in fact exist.

Thus, you can have an entire quantitative project embedded as a minor piece of a much larger library project (and indeed, with little subprojects within itself!). This entire effort—society and PhD numbers—was in the final paper squeezed down to less than four pages. But those three pages, and the three tables produced from them, give unique insights into the dynamics of academia in this period. It was a crucial conclusion, and that made this not-so-mini analysis worth all of the weeks of full-time work that it required.

Example 2. Using found data for corroboration. Another legitimate use for found quantitative data is to corroborate a point already made on the basis of other kinds of evidence. Let me discuss an example from my work on American psychiatrists. I had found a 1916 source on all the mental hospitals in the US. For about half of those hospitals, it provided lists of physicians who had served there, most often with dates of tenure. It was clear from these lists that turnover among hospital doctors was astronomically high. Many physicians spent only one year at a given hospital. I wondered if this meant that a lot of American towns had a doctor in them who had worked at some point in a mental institution: such people might be a kind of proto-profession of outpatient psychiatrists. Needless to say, there was no cross-sectional dataset locating doctors by town and containing enough associated biographical data to allow me to evaluate this hunch. But I could estimate the situation by making some assumptions and using the data I did have.

First, I used my partial data to estimate the exact number of mental hospital physicians who left the hospitals in the year 1890 and in the year 1920. (That is, for those two years I calculated the departure rate on the half of the hospitals I did have and then assumed the same rate for the rest.) I then used a little calculus to interpolate rates for the years in between those dates. I then combined those interpolated rates with known death rates (from life tables) to estimate the number of former mental hospital physicians who would have left the hospitals at some point after 1890 but would still be alive and presumably in practice in 1920. The result (which I checked by using an alternative interpolation) was about 3,000 physicians, roughly 2 percent of the American medical profession in 1920. On the assumption that these doctors were more or less randomly distributed by county, 78 percent of American county medical societies would have had one or more such "former hospital doctors" in 1920.

So these people probably were the front line of referral to the mental institutions, the "proto-professionals" in the outpatient setting. I did have some anecdotal manuscript data demonstrating their importance. But without the ability to guesstimate their numbers and distribution, I didn't really have much to rely on. By making some assumptions, I could get a ballpark estimate that supported my anecdotal data.

Some of those assumptions were quite unlikely: the notion that the distribution of doctors into county medical societies was random (Poisson-distributed, for the quantitative reader) was almost certainly wrong. So I couldn't trust the second significant digit, or maybe even the first, in the number "78 percent." There's probably a 90 percent chance that the figure was between 66 percent and 90 percent, but there's no real basis on which to form an actual estimate of even that 90 percent confidence interval. But whatever the exact number was, it was almost certainly not below 50 percent, and so the numbers do make it quite probable that over half of American county medical societies had at least one doctor who "used to work over there at the state hospital" and would consequently "know all about people with mental illness." But at the same time, although I could safely say in the text that such a proto-profession probably existed—given the combination of the anecdotal and quantitative evidence, the calculation itself merited only a short footnote in the published article that drew on these data. It was not solid enough to support anything more. Yet it was worth several days of work, even though we can't believe the 78 percent figure precisely.

This example shows what a serious quantitative minianalysis can do in terms of corroboration. It can underscore or extend a point only partly supported by manuscript data. It can suggest or test new possibilities. It can test out a hunch. Those are important things, even if you don't end up with significance levels and t-tests.

D. ADVANCED TECHNIQUES

Under some very special conditions, the library researcher may want to apply advanced statistical techniques to found data. By advanced techniques here I mean multiple regression and anything more: durational methods, network analysis, sequence analysis, factor analysis, scaling/clustering, time series, and so on. Under some conditions, such techniques can be used. But in general, the more powerful the technique, the more stringent the assumptions about the data. Take network analysis. The calculation of network measures and structures like centrality and spanning trees is highly dependent on the completeness of the sample. More than most methods, network analysis is vulnerable to missing data. Thus, as I mentioned earlier, in my psychiatrist project I did do some simple network displays showing the number of links between major psychiatric institutions provided by psychiatrists who had worked at both places at some point during their careers. But I did not dare calculate centrality figures and the like. The sampling frame of the data wouldn't sustain that. In essence, the network discussion simply corroborated facts already clear through the prosoprographical analysis.

You should consult with a faculty expert in any advanced statistical technique before applying it to found data. Have a realistic discussion about assumptions and be conservative.

But that you probably shouldn't do advanced statistics does not mean that you shouldn't code data. On the contrary, as we have seen in the case of the psychiatrists' biographies, working systematically through a large body of data by hand is in fact an excellent analytic technique in itself. It is the gathering of data—even the attempt to code that data—that produces most of your ideas for classification and colligation. To farm such data-gathering out to others—as many a quantitative scholar might do—is like going to a first-class dinner and asking somebody else to eat it for you. You not only lose immediate categorical and colligational information; you also lose the kinds of insights that come from browsing-type contacts between attractors in your head and various facts in the data you are coding.

Thus, it is paradoxically very useful in library research to work very carefully with data, as if you were going to quantify it, even when you do not plan to do so. You thereby force yourself to undertake a kind of brute-force analysis via the coding itself. At some point, you may find yourself tempted to make some extravagant assumptions and code the data carefully enough to sustain quantitative work. When that happens, it's time to stop. If you have kept your eyes open and taken lots of notes, you should by that time have learned all the things you can learn from the coding work. And extravagant assumptions mean meaningless results.

4. Content Analysis

For text materials, the equivalent of quantitative analysis is content analysis. In a content minianalysis, we try to be more formal than we are in a colligation. This makes content analysis not more rigorous, but simply different. Instead of intepreting, we count. Instead of emphasizing the coherence of our interpretation, we emphasize the solidity of its quantity judgments.

Many of the same issues arise as with quantitative analysis proper. They are best seen by considering the most common form of content minianalysis: an analysis using popular media to study attitudes in past time.

A. TEXT DATA AS A SAMPLE

Any study of attitudes must first consider the mechanisms by which people's attitudes come to our attention in past popular media. First, people have attitudes, stances, emotions. That's true enough. That these attitudes are separable things, like responses to questionnaires, may be a little more dubious. People's attitudes are usually all of a mush. Also worrisome is the idea that people's attitudes can be reassembled into paradigms, *Weltanschuungen*, and so on. Actually, attitudes are fluid things, and people can think themselves liberal even though they have many particular attitudes that are quite conservative.

Next, some portion of those attitudes gets into popular media. Of course the assumption in a content analysis is that the portion that has made it into the popular media is either representative or specifiably biased. But this is a quite radical assumption. Popular media are found data. We cannot "purify" them ahead of time, by design. We have to purify them after the fact with careful doubt and criticism, and if we have no basis for those, we are in trouble. So we make assumptions. We assume first that more important attitudes are more likely to find their way into print. We assume second that what is printed is a reasonable sample of the important attitudes, even though some groups have more media-relevant resources than others—financial, or educational, or even linguistic—and these advantages make such groups (and their views of the world) overrepresented in popular media. We assume third that the media themselves have no biasing interests, even though the people who run the media of course have interests in profit, visibility, and triumph over rivals. In short, there is no news that is "simply found." It's all produced by a complicated and biased collaboration between the newsmakers (the objects discussed) and the news breakers (the journalists).

Beyond these biases in the origination of the data, a popular report must have survived to be found by us. Yet there are many reasons why survival and access are uneven. In particular the same groups who are more likely to be noticed in the first place are more likely to have their media presence survive. Survival is extraordinarily arbitrary, particularly for newspapers, little magazines, pamphlets, and such. And the popular sources most easy to locate and access are often the media most strongly driven by news-breaker interests.

As a result, it is quite unclear what exactly is the thing of which "attitudes"—in the sense of words or concepts or ideas commonly observed in popular media—are a sample. And as you can imagine, this means that it is not worth coding such past newspaper "attitudes" in some elaborate way and undertaking quantitative analysis. You do this only if you have clear answers to the issues just raised and if the payoff is very high.

B. SIMPLE CONTENT ANALYSIS

But there are still many questions that can legitimately be addressed by a content minianalysis. Some of these will be quality questions and others quantity questions. On the quality side, you can address various questions:

1. What are the general types of views in existing media?
   a. What are the principal parts of each?
   b. What pieces go strongly together, within this or that view?
   c. What kinds of people seem to hold which kinds of views?
   d. How do they put those views together?

2. What are the lineages of attitudes and systems of attitudes over time?
   a. Do the systems of attitudes change over time?
   b. Are those systems combined in different ways at different times.

The first set of questions are all "existence" questions: they concern not the number holding particular views, but the content, internal diversity, and social roots of particular views. You can use such an analysis to develop a "cast of (attitude) characters." The second question involves creating lines of descent, showing the relations of different views over time. You can infer this from lines of group succession, from common authors, from the co-occurrence of certain attitudes and views.

You can also make some quantitative judgments.

1. Which of a set of views was probably the more common?
2. What kinds of attitudes and views were totally absent?
3. Which views dominated (and how much) the particular media in which they appear?

For the majority of library research projects, these simple quantitative measures will suffice. Such projects base their conclusions on a broad set of minianalyses, which cohere into a general interpretation. The quantitative text arguments are not sustaining the conclusions by themselves, but are corroborating arguments that have other supports.

C. FORMAL CONTENT ANALYSIS

Beyond these relatively simple questions there is a great no-man's-land until you get to truly formal quantitative analysis of texts. There are essentially two strategies for that: keywords and coding. Keywords is easy, replicable, and stupid. Coding is hard, idiosyncratic, and intelligent. In my view, given the sampling issues behind most text collections (not just popular media), neither gives particularly solid results.

If you are willing to base your minianalysis purely on keywords, you have no coding to do, except to the extent that you need to correct for OCR errors in data that was graphic rather than digital. You must, however, make strong assumptions about the connection between words and concepts, a connection discussed in chapter 3. Given those assumptions, you can ask questions like: How often do certain words occur in a text unit? and What words commonly come together in text units? The latter can lead to "distances" between words and thence to cluster analysis and scaling, both of which can provide useful

representations of text spaces, although the general judgment among sophisticated users of clustering and scaling is that both techniques have their
principal use as validations and extensions of things discovered by other
means. You can also write a program to list all the sentences or lines that
contain your word of interest in them. Just reading through such lists may
give you important new ideas. Word counts over time can allow you to make
trend judgments if you standardize with respect to sampling (at least as long as
your sources don't shift their practices underneath you).

If you choose to base a quantitative content analysis on coding rather than
keywords, then again, you have two choices. The truly formal route means
meeting the usual standards: stability of coding over time, intercoder reliability, face and construct validity of your concepts, and so on. These are the
conventions of such analysis and you must address them. Since they are almost insuperable, formal content analysis is almost never worth doing with
found data.

The less formal choice is simply to code some data yourself. Even then,
however, you still must do the following:

1. Use a replicable method for choosing a sample of texts. This can be one
   of a wide variety of strategies, but it needs to produce a sample that is
   as representative as you can make it (something that is not even easy to
   conceptualize, much less do). It also needs to be repeatable by somebody
   else, who will get either the same material (e.g., if you've decided "every fourth article about the family") or who will get a probabilistically
   similar sample.
2. Define a set of mutually exclusive categories for coding. The big issue is
   whether to make them wide (easy to code in the middle but with hard-
   to-make decisions on the edges and doesn't produce fine-grained results) or narrow (hard to code, lots of ambiguity, may be a lot more work
   than the quality of the data makes worthwhile).
3. Test the coding on a sample. This is how you find out how long it takes,
   what doesn't work, etc.
4. Assess reliability. Even if you are coding the material alone, do it twice
   and see how well you replicate yourself. You may be surprised.
5. Revise coding or abstracting rules as necessary.

As you can tell, I am profoundly skeptical about the more formal versions of content analysis as minianalyses for library research. In my view, the
data are unlikely to meet the necessary assumptions of either the traditional

qualitative or quantitative kind. But the simple content analysis methods suggested above can produce important results in minianalyses. If you need something more formal, a more useful strategy is the detailed interpretation of a systematic sample of texts. For example, in my dissertation, I surveyed all the editions (about ten each) of two very prominent nervous and mental disease texts, using a particular sample of illnesses, to see in detail how the texts changed over time. The idea was to standardize on everything but time and thus to see exactly how at least two doctor/authors changed their descriptions, diagnoses, etiologies, and treatments of four crucially important diseases. So there was a combination of a systematic sample of texts with an interpretive reading of the texts. This minianalysis produced an important passage of several pages. Such systematic interpretation is far more useful for your research than is an elaborate but precarious formal content analysis based on words that are in fact perpetually changing their meaning.

5. Concluding Remarks

The order in which you do minianalyses is governed by a number of things. The first is availability. You can do a particular minianalysis only when you have the necessary data. The second, and more important, is payoff in terms of the rest of the project. It is for this reason that among your first minianalyses needs to be one that establishes that the empirical puzzle really exists, that the thing-to-be-explained is there to be explained. Put in quantitative terms, if you have no change in the dependent variable, you are in trouble. (Completing this particular minianalysis is the sign that you are entering midphase II.)

For example, you may recall from chapter 4 that the empirical puzzle of my dissertation was "Even though psychiatry started as the profession of mental hospital superintendents in the nineteenth century, there were almost no psychiatrists working in the mental hospitals by the mid-twentieth: Why?" Now, when I started the project, I knew that this was true, but only loosely speaking. I knew it from my own experience working in a mental hospital, from several background works, and so on. But I did not really know it; I couldn't specify the proportion of the profession in the mental hospitals in either 1880 or 1930 (the arbitrary starting and ending points of my dissertation's coverage), much less at points in between. In part, I didn't know this because when I started the project it wasn't clear who was really in the profession and who was not. Not until I had done many minianalyses and a lot of reconceptualization was I able even to state this distinction and thus to know whom to count. Only then—after at least a year of work—did I actually know that the empirical puzzle of my dissertation was "really real."

In most projects, the empirical puzzle will be easier to establish. But it is nearly always true that a really good puzzle is not fully specifiable during the preliminary phase. So it is obviously one of the first things to establish in midphase.

Once you are sure you have something to explain, your minianalyses should, given feasibility, be done in the order that makes them least likely to be changed by later minianalyses. This might be a chronological order or it might be logical or it might be structural. But there will be an order of some kind. You need to discover it and use it to dictate your research schedule. Indeed, you should try to arrange feasibility so that it can follow this order. You want the upstream minianalyses to have a big payoff in terms of enabling and justifying the downstream ones.

But in practice, raw availability will often drive your minianalyses. Once you get into the midphase, you want to start doing minianalyses as soon as possible. They will be the nucleus of the write-up. So you start with whatever is at hand, given the materials available.

A couple of minor criteria for minianalyses in the midphase are also good if you can realize them. First, it helps if an early minianalysis produces something satisfying and secure. Having a satisfying moment can propel you through long stretches of dull work. Second, it helps if a minianalysis is writable as an independent section. If this is so, you can immediately write it up once it is done, and that feels good.

Watch out for getting sucked into minianalyses. They are meant be mini, to be finite. The whole idea of minianalysis is to avoid facing a huge mountain of unanalyzed material late in the project. All projects can be broken into bits. Just make sure they are bits and not boulders. Even in a major project, no minianalysis should take you more than a full-time week unless it is utterly central to a project. I have described a few two-week minianalyses of my own, but I don't recommend them for those just starting out.

Thus, biographies are a good way to get started on analyses for a project, but you don't need that many of them. The same is true for timelines and other such descriptive exercises. They are a good way to get started, but you need to move along. By about a third of the way through the project, you need to have a pretty complete list of all the minianalyses necessary to finish it. And you need to be well into that list by that time. And always remember to judge feasibility ahead of time. Don't start down analytic roads that are virtually certain to require perfect, complete data. You are very unlikely to find such data.

10 | *Midphase Writing*

Students' belief that they must start writing in order to figure out what they have to say captures something important about the writing that closes a project. Serious writing stops your free thinking about your topic. It takes the many things that you *could* say and reduces them to the one thing that you *do* say. There's something frightening about foregoing all those alternatives. That fear of closure is one source of the writer's block that so often emerges in midphase. But the main source of writer's block is a simpler logic of self-defeat. The longer you wait to start writing, the larger grows the pile of materials to interpret and synthesize. Eventually, you panic.

It is therefore best to ease yourself into the writing steadily, over the course of the project. Start writing early, in bits and pieces. It doesn't matter that your research is incomplete. Research is always incomplete, because the truth of social reality is infinite. You will always be starting to write before you are done, even if you wait till doomsday. Moreover, early bits are little bits, and they don't commit you to much. They may be used in the final text or not. They thus allow you to postpone your major writing decisions.

Ultimately, however, after the transition to endphase, you must make those decisions. In writing, we select and emphasize things about the social world that we think particularly important. And we also make those things more rigid than we actually think they are. What we know in our minds remains in a contingent, dynamic framework quite different from a written text. Like a fantasy, it can be changed without loss or regret, whereas a text cannot be unwritten. Writing is thus the result of a gradual decision to restrain the dynamic possibilities of thinking and to say something particular. It is an arbitrary—even an aesthetic—decision. And through that decision, we will ultimately linearize a research process that has so far been joyously, anarchically nonlinear.

1. The Flow of Writing in a Project

Writing begins in the early midphase. It begins to dominate the project in the late midphase. In the endphase, it becomes your main activity. Indeed, the transition to endphase comes when the emerging text begins to direct your remaining research. In endphase you are no longer carrying out the projected design. You are doing only what is required by the text you are writing. By contrast, writing that comes earlier will come in little bits: a paragraph about data, a note on methods, a short biography, a sketch of an event. Such things are more easily written down when the relevant details are fresh in your mind.

The exact flow of writing is a function of the size of the project. A research paper is a single, unified product. A larger project—a long BA or MA thesis, a dissertation, or a book—will have complete subproducts (chapters, sections) which then have to be articulated into an even larger structure. This presents specific problems that change the overall flow of writing.

A. THE FLOW OF WRITING IN A PAPER OR CHAPTER

In a single, unified, shorter work—a course paper, a master's paper, seminar paper, article, or chapter—you will not have already written any complete subunits when you begin the final writing. You will have some minianalyses of varying shapes and sizes. You may have written text for a few of them. But at some point, you must make a conscious turn to writing. Typically, this will be when you are about three-quarters through the time you have for the project.

This decision means finally settling the details of the theory. It means deciding once and for all what the project is really about. It also very often means, as we shall see, deciding the rhetorical form and structure of the final paper. Indeed, it is this decision that begins to drive the transition to endphase, for it automatically places the text in control of your work.

In detail, the order of writing in a smaller project is as follows:

1. As soon as the empirical puzzle is stable (midphase I/II transition)
   a. write basic description (this is the "conceptualization" of chapter 4, section 1.B);
   b. write first sketch of theory;
   c. write overview of general sources.
2. As they become available (midphase II and III)
   a. write discussions of particular sources;
   b. write up minianalyses.

3. When there are enough minianalyses (midphase III)
    a. redraft and finalize theory;
    b. transform design document into the paper's introduction;
    c. select overall rhetorical structure for paper.
4. When writing the main body (endphase)
    a. put together minianalyses;
    b. do cleanup research as necessary to fill holes;
    c. reconcile discordant subsections;
    d. remove repetition;
    e. assemble final bibliography. (Be sure to put the bibliography into all the minor sections as you write them, then assemble the final bibliography out of them. Cutting will remove some items from the text, so you have to check the reference list for orphans at the end.)
5. Edit, Edit, Edit.

While writing the main body of the text, you will put some previously written material into footnotes in order to keep your argument smooth and your text finite. Any preexisting texts that you use will shrink by at least one-third, as it will turn out that they are full of repetition.

If your piece is for publication—at whatever level—you need to think about venues (journals, edited volumes, conferences) in midphase. Different venues have different desiderata, in terms of substance (level and detail of documentation, preferred theoretical literatures) as well as form (rhetorical structure, length, tone). Thus, you must know where the piece is targeted by the time you are in midphase II, because these requirements influence your text from the start. This may seem excessively professional advice, but ultimately we do write to communicate to others, not simply to think aloud to ourselves. So you might as well face the music and let your planned venue shape your writing a bit. When you're famous, you can write whatever you please.

B. WRITING FLOW IN LARGE PROJECTS (FOR THESIS AND DISSERTATION WRITERS ONLY)

The flow is somewhat different in a large project like a long BA paper or a PhD dissertation. (I will refer to "dissertations" throughout, but this discussion covers any text that will have distinct and complete subsections: BA and MA theses over a certain size, dissertations, books.) Here the first substantive things you write are empirical and central chapters, which should be written as "little papers," since they will usually be addressing a particular one of the several empirical puzzles of the dissertation. To be sure, their introductions and conclusions will ultimately need revision to fit into the larger flow of the whole text. (In that context, they will be quite repetitive.) But it is easiest to begin by thinking of the chapters as separate papers. (Some graduate departments allow them to stay that way in a final dissertation; mine does not.) A large project is therefore most often actually written in the following order:

1. General structural chapters (in no particular order):
   a. literature chapter if freestanding, but not if it is integrated with the theory chapter;
   b. sources chapter (there may also be a methods chapter if specialized methods are used).
2. Substantive chapters (in no particular order). At the graduate level, these are usually driven by the need to produce smaller papers for conferences and interim publications that are necessary for the job market.
3. Theory chapter (usually including prior literature, but sometimes not).
4. Introduction.
5. Conclusion.

In a library-based dissertation, then, the first chapter written is likely to be either the review of past work in the area or the discussion of sources. In most dissertations, the latter will eventually become an appendix, while the former will probably be amalgamated with the theoretical discussion. Both of these transformations can use nearly all existing text without change, so there is no reason to postpone writing these general structural chapters.

Your source discussion might helpfully treat the major, dominant sources after the minor ones. But it will more or less be a simple list, without any strong internal organization. The transition texts (paragraph openings and closings) and the order of the list are the only things that will change later. So the source discussion can easily be assembled from bits that you write as you go along.

A literature discussion evolves differently. Since your theory will probably change through the project, the discussion of previous sources should be arranged into preexisting categories, rather than waiting for your own theory to stabilize and provide new organizing categories. (That way you can start the chapter early in the project.) It is customary to use the literature's own categories (which your new theory will revise in the conclusion). Don't agonize over the transition materials in this section, because you may later need to reorganize them a good deal.

Next, you will write substantive chapters, which we might call "meso-analyses," since they will themselves be full of various minianalyses. Often in library-based dissertations, however, single empirical chapters are actually overgrown minianalyses: a single event narrated and analyzed in great detail, a social network reconstructed from directories and analyzed as a formal pattern, a body of letters analyzed with a systematic set of codes. Even so, they will need internal organization—by substantive themes, or particular actors, or different settings, or whatever. No chapter-length item can be a simple list, except the discussion of prior literature.

In a dissertation, the final writing stage comes when you make a firm decision as to what the dissertation is really about. This will mean writing or rewriting the theory chapter. (Often, students write an earlier draft of the theory chapter as a stand-alone piece for publication. They make a theoretical argument that shows "we need to do X" and then, of course, do X themselves as a dissertation). Then, with the substantive chapters and the theory done, you can write the introduction and conclusion appropriate to the dissertation you have actually written. You must also now rewrite the immensely duplicative introductions and conclusions to the substantive chapters, since the introduction will have set forth, once and for all, both the basic puzzles addressed by the dissertation and the empirical situation you are studying.

So in a dissertation or other large project you are likely to have several chapters done as part of late midphase writing, just as you are likely to have written the methods and data chapters (as well as perhaps the literature chapter) during the early midphase, when your main activity is still research. In such a project, endphase writing is just straightening out the theory and writing the introduction and conclusion. You then need to edit the whole thing; you remove repetitions, smooth transitions, and turn the manuscript into a coherent work. Often, advisors don't insist on comprehensive editing, because a much more draconian revision will be required when you turn the dissertation into a book, which must be both shorter and less technical. (A book will involve a new prose style, as well.) In some cases, advisors will let you write a dissertation in book format. This makes most sense with ethnography, where the integration of writing and theory is different than in library research. In library research, by contrast, advisors need to see, once at least, that you can get all the details right. Then we're willing to take the next book on spec, without a dissertation version.

2. Writing in Bits

Most of the time, our writing is not embedded in large structures. And even when it is, the pieces going into those large structures are first written in the short format. So for the rest of this chapter I assume you are working at the smaller scale: paper, chapter, or article.

Start writing early in the project. Knowing that you have some text on paper will keep you going through the brute-force doldrums of the midphase. When you make exciting discoveries, get them into (short) text quickly. Let your excitement push you over the hump of reluctance and onto the page. You may end up using only a quarter of what you write in early midphase, but you make it much easier for yourself later.

Beyond writing that simply bursts out of you, there are other bits and pieces that can and should be written early. The first concerns the empirical puzzle. As soon as you have the minianalysis that shows that the empirical puzzle is really real and a bibliography that locates the appropriate data to resolve it, you should write two versions of the empirical puzzle: a brief, sharp one for your opening page and a longer, better supported one for the main body of your introduction. In a forty-page paper, the opening version will be a paragraph and the longer one perhaps two or three pages. The first just sketches the problem of the paper, while the second covers the basic conceptualization discussed in chapter 4: who is involved, what they do, how they do it, where and when, and, most important, what is puzzling about that. In effect, it restates the empirical puzzle in greater detail.

If you are fortunate enough to have a clear theoretical puzzle, you should also write a draft of that early in the project. In practice, the theoretical framing of most library projects drifts considerably over time. But it's always good to write a version of the theoretical section early, because writing may itself reveal problems in your theoretical thinking. If you don't have a clear theoretical puzzle, clarify it before trying to write. You won't clarify it by writing about how confusing it is. Rather, ask yourself (again), "To what general question is my study the answer?" or "By resolving this empirical puzzle I will help resolve some larger question. What is that larger question?" Most library research papers investigate things that are inherently interesting, so it is easy to get lazy on the theoretical side. Don't. Your paper is the answer to some larger question or dispute. Always keep that dispute in mind.

A library research paper usually does not have a large section reviewing prior literature. We don't think that you are adding one more brick to a cumulative edifice. Rather, you have found a puzzling empirical situation, and resolving that situation can help us understand some theoretical (or sometimes historical) issue. Other people's work may enter into yours as a context, as a background, as a starting-off place. And discussion of prior major writers can be used to set up your theoretical alternatives. But the literature review per se typically appears in the footnotes of a library-researched article, where a respectful and courteous discussion of prior workers is quite appropriate. But in the main text, you include a section on prior literature only if you feel that your empirical analysis will resolve a quite specific ongoing debate. Otherwise, the literature remains in the footnotes and the main text of the introduction is devoted to theoretical questions, setting forth the issues and alternatives that your paper plans to address. In the ultimate paper, the theory section will be fairly short: perhaps three to five pages of a forty-page text.

Many projects need a section on the provenance and availability of sources. This too can be written early. This section will discuss what sources are desirable, what are available, what have been used in the past, what can't be found, and so on. It will be expanded and revised as new sources arise. Once data search is complete, the source section can be finalized. This section will end up as one or two pages of text or possibly as a data appendix. In historical projects, it often ends up as a very large footnote at the beginning of the substantive discussion (that is, after the introduction and its concluding roadmap).

You should also write up a short description of each major data source as you acquire it. Whether it's some letters in archives or Congressional documents or census data or an old survey—you can describe it, give your reasons for using it, discuss sampling issues, note any peculiarities, and so on. In all probability, this text will ultimately become a footnote, appearing when the source is used for first time in the text. But it's still comforting to have in hand—only a single short paragraph, but that much less to write later on.

If you are using any specialized methods, you can write them up early as well. Whether it's cluster analysis or paleography or systematic keyword searching, you will need a few paragraphs on it eventually. These, too, may become footnotes, but again, they are text in hand. Every little piece you do early in the project is something you won't have to do later. More important, you remember all the details now, whereas later you will have to recall things or—worse yet—go back and dig them out. It can be hard to force yourself to write these little bits, because they will seem to you completely obvious and therefore not worth recording. But take advantage of that obviousness; write the little description now rather than later.

Finally, as soon as they are done, you can start to write up any minianalyses that are going directly into the final document. Thus, you would not write up a timeline, for example; that's mostly for guiding yourself in the sources, providing a reference as you write up, and so on. But you could write up the detailed reading of a particular document (otherwise you'll forget it) or the story of a famous episode or an organizational biography or something like that. That is text that may very well be used.

All of these early midphase texts will be short. They will range from a paragraph to half a page or two pages. But they are text in the bag. They will be longer than necessary, because cramming the whole project into forty to fifty pages will prove difficult. But this is a good thing: you have more than enough and so won't need to return to the sources for more detail.

When you are writing the early snippets, do not worry much about the transition portions of the text. For example, when you are writing up a short couple of paragraphs on a minianalysis, don't worry about the topic sentence at the beginning of the first paragraph. You don't yet know where this minianalysis will be located in the final text. So just use some generic introductory sentence ("An important example of X is G" or something like that). Don't worry: the transitions will change later.

For this early writing, it is useful to test your ideas on a peer. Before you write up a minianalysis, set yourself the task of explaining it quickly to a friend or colleague. "This afternoon I was looking at X and Y, and I found that S nearly always happens. I looked for the alternatives T and U, but they appeared only in certain kinds of situations. It could be that this kind of data is biased, but I don't think so." Get your minianalysis results to this level of clarity. Then sit down and record what you said. Cover the whole of what you have done—quickly, clearly, interestingly. Often when students speak about projects, they focus on their confusions and difficulties. They forget that they actually understand a lot of things. By the time you are into midphase, you already know much of what you will finally write. You should begin encapsulating it for others.

Some general advice: Don't worry about having too little to write. You will have far too much. There will not be one perfect quote on subject X. There will five perfect quotes, and you can use only one. You will not discuss more than a quarter of the actual material you have gathered. You did the other three-quarters of the research in order to have the confidence to write the one quarter with such authority that the reader has confidence in you with respect to the other three.

More generally, let your data talk. The reader doesn't know the data, whereas the reader may know the theoretical or interpretive literature as well or better than you do. On the other hand, don't simply recite your data. It needs to be theoretically organized, as we shall see in the next section.

3. Types of Write-up

At a certain point, you will have written a puzzle description, a first sketch of theory and literature, an overview of sources, some discussions of particular sources, and a few minianalysis summaries. You are now probably half to two-thirds of the way through the time you have allotted to the project. At this point, you need to decide how you are going to organize the final text.

This decision comes in the midphase. Put more specifically, this decision is what dominates midphase III. As you will have realized by now, it is easy and fun to do library research. The world is full of interesting facts to discover, and you will have far more than enough facts and analysis. The real question is which ones to write about and for what purpose. By avoiding this question, you can get yourself very, very lost. You do more and more research, and feel more and more confused.

Start thinking about the design and argument of the final product around the middle of the midphase. This kind of stocktaking (see the next chapter) should direct your later choice of minianalyses. It will be easier if you have been continuously revisiting the design document and keeping it focused and coherent, even as it changes steadily. If you do this carefully, you will be able to write the theory section relatively early, which in turn will facilitate the layout of your argument and its evidence.

Many pieces of your research process contribute to this reflection about the organization of your text. There are the crucial terms in your controlled vocabulary. There are the contents of your specific and general research questions. There are the rows and columns of your crosswalk matrix. You have in fact already been thinking about this problem of organization all along: in filing, in bibliography, in translating the research question/source combinations into particular minianalyses. The elements of it are already in your head. The decision how to assemble them is the crucial decision of the project.

This problem, although very difficult, is quite straightforward. After having worked nonlinearly throughout the project so far, you must now create a linear argument. The crazy bouncing from bibliography to minianalysis to redesign to doubt to scanning and so on has to stop. Now you must squeeze the results of all that work into a linear form that starts with empirical and theoretical puzzles, introduces a situation and data on that situation, then draws the reader through a logically organized sequence of analytic steps that culminate in a reasoned conclusion about the proper interpretation of your empirical situation and the consequent implications for theoretical inquiry. That is, you must now reverse the insight with which this book began. At the outset, I said that the linear organization of library-based articles is a mere appearance; in fact the research is nonlinear. Now, you have done most of the research, and it is time to create that linear appearance.

Luckily, there are quite a number of standard rhetorical structures for the write-ups of library projects. Some are more common than others, but all can be useful at various times.

A. CHRONOLOGY OF RESEARCH.

I begin with the rare forms. A very few scholars write arguments in the order in which they did the research. Most often, this is done as part of popularization. Emmanuel Le Roy Ladurie's brilliant *Montaillou* is to some extent done this way, as is that tour de force of library research, Hugh Trevor-Roper's *Hermit of Peking*. Basically, such works write scholarship as a mystery story. They no doubt to some extent fictionalize the research (at least in terms of what actually happened before what) in order to make that mystery supremely compelling. Trevor-Roper's is the masterpiece of the genre. Read it, and you'll see what I mean.

Chapter 2's ethnographic discussion of library research could have been written in this fashion. Indeed, the first, oral version of it did tell the story in classic detective style: "At first I thought digital tools killed the old reference system, but then I realized that the old reference system was really killed long ago and a different body had been substituted. . . . ," and so forth. That is, in the mystery version, the order of the story is given by the successive unmaskings, not by the actual sequence of stumbling around in the sources.

You are unlikely to write a serious paper in this format, but if you have the chance, go ahead. Oral audiences love such a paper; it's the academic equivalent of Salome and her seven veils. As that comparison suggests, however, such a paper rests entirely on the degree of suspense and the beauty of what you uncover at the end. The end result must surpass all the intervening erroneous possibilities, and you the dancer have to time the unveilings very carefully.

B. EMBLEM

Another rare format is what I shall call emblem. This too is a showman's trick, but here the trick is not dance-of-the-seven-veils but rabbit-out-of-a-hat. The most famous example of this format is Clifford Geertz's celebrated essay about the Balinese cockfight. As those who have read it remember, Geertz tells the story of being at an illegal cockfight, feeling the excitement, and, ultimately, running away with everyone else when the authorities arrive. In the process of telling this story, he pulls out of his magician's hat themes that in his view capture the essence of Balinese culture. The cockfight becomes the emblem of Bali.

Nothing could be more artificial than this form. Geertz had already written five books about Indonesian society by the time he wrote the cockfight essay. (It was written for a semipopular intellectual magazine—*Daedalus*, the quarterly of the American Academy of Arts and Sciences.) But the essay, republished in his collection *The Interpretation of Cultures*, became enormously influential. It was imitated by hundreds of students, who tried the same rhetorical trick: making all their insights about a general topic come out of a deep analysis of one particular event. Needless to say, most of them had not already written five books on those subjects, so their insights lacked the coherence and depth that sustain Geertz's masterpiece.

A current student might do one cockfight-like chapter in a dissertation. Then the chapter's interpretations would be supported by the scholarly power of the rest of the work. But attempting the emblem format for a free-standing short paper is not a good idea. It looks very enticing, but it doesn't work unless you're a mature scholar writing about a topic of which you are a complete master. It may be, however, that this is a disciplinary choice, and that I'm showing here my colors as a sociologist. The emblem form is much more common in the humanities.

C. NARRATIVE

If you are a historian, you can write with a straight narrative organization. But even in history, straight narrative is unusual nowadays. More common is a generally chronological framework with subparts that cover topical areas.

You choose narrative organization when your central questions are of the form "What happened when and why?" You also choose it if all of your cases and topics are shaped by ongoing period effects in their larger social world. For example, a paper on comparative reactions to the Korean and Vietnam wars in various European nations could follow a narrative format. Within each nation, the Korea reactions would be analyzed first, then the Vietnam reactions. The second period (Vietnam) reactions would thus be contextualized by those of the first (Korea), but not vice versa. For nonhistorians, however, the real action might be in terms of country differences within a period. (Such an analysis is not really a narrative one, but a "stages" one.) So a nonhistorian might organize the Korea/Vietnam paper as mainly a cross-country comparison nested within the two war periods, rather than a chronological narrative organized by country, which would emphasize the continuities within given countries over the two periods.

You also choose narrative if your interpretation of the material emphasizes contingency. If you are emphasizing the accidents of history, or the conjunction of several forces, or if you are strongly convinced that things might well have turned out quite differently, you will choose to present your analysis as a narrative. On the other hand, if you are wedded to inevitability, to independent trends, and to multiple routes to the present (or the result), you will probably not choose narrative, although you could choose a kind of "multiple pathways" approach, tracing an independent narrative within each case or for each causal factor.

There is one great danger in narrative. In any project about something happening over time, there arises the temptation to write an atheoretical but supremely beguiling narrative history, especially if you are a good storyteller. Once you know a great deal about something, you are always tempted to tell it as a simple story: one damn thing after another. Don't do this. Refer back to your design folder to rediscover why you began the project. What was the puzzle? What kind of outline can evoke that puzzle most effectively? It may still be the case that you will use much narrative. But that narrative needs to be deployed within a structure that is governed by the puzzle with which you began. The real trick in narrative organization is simultaneously to tell a story and to set forth an analysis. This is by no means as easy as it sounds.

D. CASE STUDY

You choose a case study write-up if you are looking at one single unit of analysis: an event, an organization, a network, an area of competition. It is often difficult to pinpoint causality in a case study. More commonly, one uses case study not to adjudicate between different theories of a particular event or place or organization, but rather to show how those different theories or mechanisms or aspects of social reality interrelate in a particular case. The emphasis on plausibility rather than adjudication means that the theory section of a case study paper will be organized around contrasting interpretations of the case rather than around different theoretical mechanisms or patterns.

Alternatively, however, one can do a case study to provide a counterexample to some general interpretation or causal argument. In this form, you emphasize how your case fits the logical premises of some standard argument but doesn't turn out as the argument predicts.

The internal organization of a case study can take several forms. One of these is narrative. But one can also organize a case study around different aspects of social reality. Thus the paper mentioned earlier about the rights of nature in Ecuador could be organized by the different aspects of nature: water, air, seawater, and so on. Or by different actors—peasants, urban residents, the state. If you used either of these lists, however, you would want to find an underlying rhetorical order for the various items on the list, even if there is, in fact, no real, analytic reason for the order that you choose. Go from simple to complex items, or from earlier to later data, or something like that.

Thus, in this example, simple-to-complex would most likely prescribe the order (1) peasants, (2) urban residents, (3) state. But if you were organizing by aspects of nature, you might want to start with air (simple and pervasive), then treat seawater (which at least stays in one place), and finally fresh water (which involves transportation and relocation). As a third alternative, if you used total size or cost of immediate pollution problems to govern the order, it could turn out that (1) seawater, (2) air, (3) fresh water was the proper order. That is, in writing you should impose linearity and direction even if it is not really there in the data. You do this because you want your reader to go through the text in the order that you create, which should be one that is rhetorically gracious and effective.

This arbitrary linearizing may seem strange, given that in chapter 7 I told you that as a researcher you will very seldom actually read academic work straight through. But now you are on the other side of the fence; you are a writer, not a reader. And by subtly embedding linearity and direction in your text you make it more difficult for readers to skip ahead. You also retain control of them when they do. Sometimes you can make this direction even more compelling by linearizing two aspects at once. Thus, to continue the same example, you could do peasants on water rights, urbanites on air, and the state on seawater. That is, you write about three of the nine possible combinations of three groups across the three types of pollution. But of course you will continually remind the reader that the two lists (people and problems) are actually not interdependent, perhaps exploring the remaining six combinations in short sketches, two each at the end of each major section.

E. COMPARISON

Once you break a case study up into particular aspects, you have already created an implicit comparison. And indeed, comparison is probably the most general form of organization. You can do comparison of cases, comparison of different aspects, mechanisms, or narratives within one case, comparison of different sources' accounts of a single case, and so on. Indeed, comparison is implicit in the very idea of having a theoretical puzzle: two alternative views which imply differing interpretations of the empirical situation you have studied. Those alternative views will require different sets of evidence and comparison between them. Alternatively, demonstrating that a particular theory is viable requires both positive and negative cases—another reason for comparison.

Normally in any library research project, there are several possible dimensions of comparison. The main question of organization is always how to nest those dimensions. Theories, cases, types of evidence, chronology, aspects: which should one use as the outer and which as the inner structure? Again, let me remind you that you have all the elements necessary for this decision in your hands already: your controlled vocabulary of major terms, your crosswalk matrix with its specification of minianalyses, your research questions. It's just a question of arraying the results they have produced into a linearly satisfying structure.

Consider the project earlier mentioned about regulation of sex and drugs in Thailand and Burma. There are two countries, two types of social problems, and a time span of about fifty years. A first organization would be chronology within social problem within country:

- Thailand
  - Drugs
    - Chronology
  - Prostitution
    - Chronology

- Burma
  - Drugs
    - Chronology
  - Prostitution
    - Chronology

This organization produces a strong country comparison. It presumes that the coherence of the regulation regime of a country is greater than the coherence of the regulation regime required by a certain social problem. If we believed that the latter was stronger, we would organize as follows:

- Drugs
  - Thailand
    - Chronology
  - Burma
    - Chronology
- Prostitution
  - Thailand
    - Chronology
  - Burma
    - Chronology

But both of these organizations assume that change over time is not particularly salient. We could by contrast imagine a "historical periods of regulation" organization, as follows:

- Early
  - Drugs
    - Thailand
    - Burma
  - Prostitution
    - Thailand
    - Burma
- Late
  - Drugs
    - Thailand
    - Burma
  - Prostitution
    - Thailand
    - Burma

And so on. There are six possible organizations, each of which ranks the three differences (country, problem, period) in a particular order of importance, discoverability, and interest. All of these organizations are possible for the project write-up, but each focuses on certain dimensions of difference rather than others. Deciding which organization to use will give definitive shape to the eventual analysis. One should always therefore make one's choice of organization in as theoretically grounded a manner as possible.

RETURNING TO CHAPTER 2, YOU CAN NOW SEE WHY I THOUGHT IT so important to talk about the impact of writing decisions on the shape of my paper on library use. I realized early that straight narrative would tell the reader something she already knew: that there were more and more reference tools. So I had to create periods, even if they were arbitrary, in order to dramatize what were in fact fairly gradual changes. This gave me a "successive stages" narrative.

But the sheer mass of material, even within the period, meant that I had to tell each period by characterizing different aspects of it, in this case aspects of the "library situation." I chose three things: scholars' demography, core reference infrastructure, and habitus of scholarship. But with my four periods and three aspects within each, I now automatically had twelve subsections. This in turn determined a new filing structure (everything got moved). It also created three temporal breaks, any one of which could be the location of my "end of the honeymoon between scholars and librarians." That is, in many ways the writing decisions ended up determining much of the final intellectual structure of the paper, and the writing decisions were more or less determined by the problem of telling so many events in an effectively linear way. On a more mundane level, the writing choices also meant that given a sixty-page overall limit and ten pages for introduction and conclusion, I had about four pages apiece for my twelve sections.

4. Writing and the Close of Midphase

The final selection of your overall organization is a decisive moment. It closes the last part of midphase. For as I just argued, this choice puts the writing in control of the project. From this point on, linearity reasserts itself. You may still be doing minianalyses. But they will merely be the minianalyses necessary to fill out what is now becoming a fixed structure. These are "just-in-time" minianalyses, required by the development of the writing.

Most important, it is at this point—in the small-scale project—that you will take the design document in its current form and expand it into the introduction of the final paper. The decision on organization is simply another part of this same change. You make a final commitment to the project as it is now designed.

The expansion of the design document into the paper's introduction will use many things that you have probably already written. It begins with the already completed one-paragraph version of the empirical puzzle: the hook. It then continues with a paragraph summarizing the theoretical payoff of solving this empirical puzzle (that will be new—it's the theoretical hook). You can then start the main introduction with your already existing write-up of the conceptualization: the formal description of the actual situation you are researching. This can then close with the longer, expanded version of the empirical puzzle, restating it now that we have a more formal sense of the situation researched. You can then turn to a theory review ("Those who have written about X have thought R, S, and T about it"). This will come from your current design document, modified by recent reflections, and will shamelessly set up your own research to be the *deus ex machina* that will resolve all remaining theoretical problems. Then comes your own theory—"We need first to define some important terms. . . ." The terms are your own controlled vocabulary, and setting them out will allow you to begin to clarify the problems in the literature, which will have used them quite chaotically. Then comes the roadmap: "In order to investigate the issues, we need to do the following things." The roadmap tells the reader the order in which you will establish your theoretical argument by showing its empirical power over your puzzle. The roadmap will be based on the organization you've chosen, which will as we have just seen be rooted in your crosswalk, your decisions about which are the most important dimensions of organization, and so on. After the roadmap can come a brief passage on sources, if it needs to be in the text rather than in footnotes.

Then you're ready for the main body of the paper. Assembling that out of the minianalysis write-ups, source descriptions, and other texts is really an endphase task. But you don't need my advice here. Once you've made the main decisions about how to linearize, you can turn to the many excellent books that give advice on writing. (That's why my endphase chapter is short.) Booth, Colomb, and Williams's *The Craft of Research* is the book that I happen to use in my courses, since it focuses on the problem of writing persuasive prose and has a very clear theory of that task. To be sure, I have my own strong views on writing (you know by now that I have strong views on most things), but writing—producing linear text—is not really the focus of the present book. This book is about making sure that you function well enough in the nonlinear research context in order to have what you need to write up the linear text at the end. As I have repeatedly stressed, that means you have to start writing little pieces of text long before the linear design and structure can be formed.

11 *Midphase Design*

As I said in chapter 4, design consists of four things: puzzles, conceptualization, general and specific research questions, and action lists. At any given time, these things are embodied in a design document, which is the current plan for the project. In the preliminary phase, this document shifts quite radically every week. Later on, it remains constant for longer periods.

Midphase design means two things: one is simple, one more complex. The simple part is keeping track of both completed and pending tasks and keeping an eye on minor shifts in specific research questions, controlled vocabulary, or other core parts of the project. These are handled easily, as you go along; you cross items off the action lists and note minor changes.

But from time to time you should step back from the research and review the overall project design to make sure you are still carrying out a coherent project and have not wandered into a new and tangential line of inquiry (or, quite the contrary, that your new line of inquiry may actually be more feasible and more coherent than what you had previously planned). You also need to appraise whether you are moving through your various research questions quickly enough to leave yourself sufficient time for writing.

The reasons for review are obvious. Your potential topics have no boundaries and limits. There will have been drift as you followed new leads in bibliography. Minianalyses may have undercut some pieces of your original empirical puzzle. New theoretical readings may suggest new directions. You must eventually react to these larger drifts and shifts, resettling the project again into a coherent, aligned structure running from design through bibliography to sources, materials, analyses, and, ultimately, writing. Remember, it's a nonlinear project that gradually turns itself linear by mutually adjusting all of its parts as they develop in parallel. So at any given redesign, you need to get it again into a (probably new) coherent structure.

How often to take stock is a function of the size of the project. Given half-time work (twenty hours a week), a graduate seminar paper, an MA paper, or an article of forty to sixty pages will take about three to five weeks in preliminary phase, from ten to fifteen or more weeks in midphase, and three to five weeks in endphase. A serious undergraduate thesis or BA paper, written over the course of senior year, would be on the long end of those ranges: five weeks, fifteen weeks, five weeks. A substantial library-based dissertation will take two years or more. A good rule of thumb is therefore that the shorter forms need a stocktaking every two to three weeks, while the long forms need one every month or two.

As I have mentioned throughout, specific moments of redesign define the transitions between the phases. "Transition to midphase" is just a shorthand for saying that (a) the design proposal has stopped changing radically every week, and (b) you can project some actual minianalyses based on that proposal, one of which will establish that your empirical puzzle really exists and really is a puzzle. "Entering midphase II" is a similar shorthand for the moment when that "establishment minianalysis" has given a positive verdict; your empirical puzzle has been shown to be an actual empirical fact, is still puzzling, and can be specified in its full complexity. Now you can settle into midphase II, the long, nonlinear middle of the project. You can now create a first crosswalk and think about the best order for the various necessary minianalyses.

The trigger for midphase III is that the minianalyses start to group themselves obviously into larger, coherent structures, suggesting possible organizations for a linear argument. At the same time the design document has begun to align with that structure as you have gradually elaborated your controlled vocabulary and crosswalk. You begin to expand the design document into a text introduction and to arrange the minianalyses into a fully organized flow of argument. Endphase arrives when that organization has become a solid linear outline. The writing itself now becomes the supervising force in the project. Because of this, certain research questions will be orphaned—their answers have no place in the linear design of your chosen rhetorical form.

I shall discuss midphase design along two dimensions: first, the temporal dimension of the phases, and second, the substantive dimension of the various aspects of design. This involves some repetition, but that's useful. Design is the aspect of library research that controls the others. It is therefore essential to master it. To be sure, mastery doesn't mean that you can design your way into a perfect paper. That's precisely what nonlinearity says that you cannot do. But it does mean that if you don't pay continuous attention to design, you will wander randomly.

1. Phases

A. PRELIMINARY

The preliminary phase takes you from a vague interest to a reasonably specific proposal. As I have said throughout, this means establishing empirical and theoretical puzzles, a conceptualization, general and specific research questions, and an action list. You will establish these over about four to twelve weeks, depending on the size of the project. Typically, you begin with the empirical and theoretical puzzles: something that's strange and a theoretical reason why that strangeness is important. You will discuss several versions of those puzzles with some peers and advisors before trying to imagine general research questions, because there's no point in imagining questions posed by puzzles that you're going to change next week. Presenting your ideas to others is absolutely necessary; we are all too easy on ourselves and our ideas.

Even while you are developing the puzzles, you are already reading background works and locating crucial bibliography (which may suddenly become uncrucial because the puzzles change or perhaps because something you accidentally encountered seems more interesting). You will probably also be seeking relevant primary materials, because their availability could decide the feasibility of research on any given puzzle. All four of these things (puzzles, questions, background and specific bibliography, primary material search) are in motion simultaneously.

As this summary suggests, there are some simple criteria for the tentative designs that you sketch as possibilities: interest, clarity, coherence, and feasibility. First, the puzzles need to be interesting. Of course, there's no point in doing a research project that you know doesn't really matter, but, more important, interesting puzzles will motivate you during the confusing stages of the project. Second, you need clarity because only clear puzzles will produce clear general and specific research questions which in turn tell you what needs to be done. It's rather like the parlor game of "telephone"; if each step isn't very clear—from empirical puzzle to theoretical puzzle to general research questions to specific research questions—there is little chance that the beginning and end will connect. Clarity means that you clearly understand what you're doing.

The third criterion—coherence—means that what you are doing makes sense. Not only is there a clear link from step to step, there is in fact a single continuous logic, one that links everything from empirical puzzles through to specific research questions. This means that at any given time the design document is linear, rigorous, logical. Ongoing research will continuously undermine this linearity, often in good ways. But because of that undermining, you must continuously reimpose linearity and rigor. That reimposition can mean changing any part of the logical sequence—even its very beginning in the empirical puzzle—as long as the result reestablishes linear coherence in the design document (possibly on a new basis, of course).

Finally, although feasibility is a homely criterion, it is often the most important. You can't accomplish a project if it will take too long or if it involves languages you can't read, documents you can't find, statistical expertise you don't have, and so on. (Every year, in my course, I have two or three MA students who start out with completely unfeasible projects.) Particularly for bachelor's and master's students, your advisor is the crucial judge of feasibility, since you may not know what is necessary to accomplish a given investigation. Ascertain feasibility early: even a very interesting project is hopeless if you cannot do it.

These four criteria guide your decision. Preliminary phase ends when you have a design document that is more or less stable, that proposes an interesting study in clear steps, and that gives a coherent design for a feasible project.

B. MIDPHASE I

This first design allows you to begin midphase I with a plunge into primary sources. Background reading recedes. Bibliography continues but grows out of minianalyses rather than general topics. Browsing—in primary sources, bibliographical tools, and materials related to minianalyses—introduces much more randomness into your project, and brachiations take advantage of that randomness. In short, you surrender to nonlinearity.

But the defining characteristic of this phase is the first set of minianalyses and particularly the "establishment minianalysis." As I have noted several times, it is usually not possible to know in the preliminary phase whether your empirical puzzle is actually credible. Therefore, one of your first minianalyses must be one that establishes your empirical puzzle more surely. As I noted in chapter 9, in my dissertation that establishment minianalysis succeeded only after a year of work on the definition and demography of psychiatry as a profession.

One is not always so lucky. I once tried to investigate the empirical puzzle of why each American profession seemed to acquire restrictive licensing before acquiring an ethics code. (I had a theory that professions always started with monopoly and only later worried about morals.) But after serious investigation, it turned out that licensing had been a longstanding movement across many occupations in the late nineteenth century, while most professions acquired ethics codes during a post–World War I project of Rotary Clubs to spread—you guessed it—commercial ethics codes. (Even the Carbonated Beverage Bottlers got an ethics code!) The observed sequence from licensing to ethics was not at the profession level at all but was a more general phenomenon, and one related to a specific social movement. My empirical puzzle was only an apparent reality, not an actual one.

When this happens, you have to shift your puzzle. In that case, I gave up the old empirical puzzle, and indeed I gave up investigation at the national level. I moved to the local level and to an individual profession (medicine) on which I knew I had data (feasibility!). The new puzzle was "Did local groups of professionals (doctors) start monopoly activities (issuing fixed price lists) before they created knowledge institutions (journals and discussion groups), and if so, why?" So I retained the theoretical alternatives of the monopoly theory of professions versus the purity theory of professions, but I redefined pure professionalism in terms of knowledge focus (which could be conceived and measured locally) rather than ethics enforcement (which could not).

In sum, close investigation may reveal that your original puzzle was wrong, or misapprehended, or ill-conceived. It may also reveal that that puzzle is too big for feasibility. Both things require that you quickly shift puzzles. In this example I had both problems: an incoherent mixture of national and local levels as well as too many professions for feasibility once I moved to the purely local level. Such a puzzle shift returns you to preliminary phase almost by definition.

But if your establishment minianalysis looks positive, you should undertake a design review. This means checking the design document for clarity and cohesion, and adjusting to any minor drifts and shifts that have recently emerged. In particular, the theoretical puzzles will be getting foggy at this point, because you will have spent a lot of time on other things, most of them empirical and substantial. So you should tighten up the theoretical puzzles. Indeed, it would not be unwise to begin expanding and specifying the theoretical section of the design document, a task facilitated by your controlled vocabulary, which should by now be growing.

At this design review, you should—if you have not already—create a first version of your question/source crosswalk matrix. The matrix arraying your various primary sources across your general and specific questions will tell you whether every question is addressed by some source, and hence by some minianalysis. Insert any that you think are newly important. Check off those that are done. Consider a best order in which to do those that remain. Make sure your sources are actually available.

C. MIDPHASE II

Once your empirical puzzle is established and you've resettled the project via a major review, you can enter the fully nonlinear part of the project—midphase II. Thanks to your design document you can tell an advisor or peer what you are doing and why, but you will actually be executing the research in an order dictated by source availability and convenience, by logical dependence among minianalyses, by the accidents of brachiation, and—to tell a secret—by excitement and interest. Since you have an overall control document, you can afford to surf around a bit.

There will be much brute-force primary source work in midphase II, and you will need the excitements of browsing, brachiation, and randomness to carry you through the dullness of that brute force. Minianalyses will grow into mesoanalyses, taking one or even two weeks of full-time work. At the same time, as the minianalyses are piling up, you will undertake your first writing: a biography here, a source note there, all the bits that were discussed in chapter 10.

Midphase II will also spawn a lot of just-in-time research. A small detail may stand between you and a page of writing, so you research the detail and finish the writing. A pending bibliographical task may suddenly become absolutely necessary, so you do it immediately. A set of minianalyses may make sense to do together, even though they cut across the logic of the project or the realities of source availability. Just do them.

During midphase II, you should be watching for such groups of mutually supporting minianalyses. Maybe they are all of the same "shape"; biographies, or organizational histories, or comparable cases, or whatever. Maybe they are linked by a particular actor or set of groups. Maybe they involve similar forms of quantitative or content analysis. These are incipient possibilities for linear pieces of a final text. Often, as we saw in chapter 10, there will be many such possible arrangements. But you should begin to see them as possibilities.

Midphase II can also be a good time for meditative reading. Chances are that you will have forgotten most of the general theoretical issues of the project in the flow of exciting details. Now may be the time to take a couple of days off from brute-force source work to read some related piece of theory at a snail's pace, now that your head is full of the project, its terms, its people, and its implications. You will be astounded by how rich that theory seems now that you have the empirical knowledge with which to interrogate it. You will see many new issues, and you may want to recast your theoretical puzzles or modify your controlled vocabulary.

Another useful time-off activity in midphase II is to review your files. Just read through all your substantive data so far. Perhaps you need new categories. Perhaps whole substantive areas need rearrangements. You will be surprised at the new ideas that emerge from rereading recent work and thinking about new connections you can draw.

Depending on the size of the project, you should review the design document every two (small paper) to eight (dissertation) weeks in midphase II. This is for the usual reasons: to take account of various shifts and drifts, to realign the various parts of the design document, to check off minianalyses in the crosswalk matrix. Indeed, as you work through midphase II, that matrix becomes less a matrix of specific questions across specific sources, and more a matrix of controlled vocabulary and theoretical issues across empirical substance. That is, it gradually frees itself from the practical management of nonlinear research to become more theoretical. This change will enable you to see the linear structures that could be made out of the mass of your research. (You can also maintain two different matrices, if that is easier. But the two are quite closely related, nonetheless.)

D. MIDPHASE III

Eventually, a midphase II review will reveal that large subparts of the project have started to agglomerate into units. You can now think seriously about alternative possibilities for aligning all your various materials as a linear argument and about using the design document to introduce that argument. Midphase III is that portion of the project where you consider the various possibilities for this alignment. Once you make your choice, the design document turns into the written introduction, and your emerging text takes control, telling you which analyses have to be done to fill out the text design, which bibliography items will be used as references, and so on. The move to text control will also stop your work on many aspects of the project; they are no longer relevant.

For me, midphase III is often short. Sometimes I'm constrained by the realities of conference and publication deadlines. More often I simply fall in love with a particular organization for my paper. You may be different. But it remains the case that midphase III is basically transitional. The design document is relinquishing control to the various possible write-up structures. When that has happened, you are in the endgame—back in the world of linearity, the world of texts.

E. ENDPHASE

Endphase is simply the execution of that linear design. In this phase, all aspects of research other than writing move onto a just-in-time basis. You search for bibliography only as needed. You scan and browse only to find a missing detail. You undertake only those minianalyses that are required by the design. You read nothing that is not immediately necessary. You use only the files that are needed and indeed occasionally rearrange them to meet the necessities of writing.

If you have been writing the bits on sources, people, organizations, methods, and minianalyses as you went along, a lot of the writing will be simple assembly. But arguments have their own logic, and you will find that little bits of research become necessary even at this point, just because paragraph X leads not directly to Z but to Z via Y: there's a detailed logic to writing that is not exactly the same as the abstract logic imposed by your organization of general and specific research questions. You will therefore do research in the endphase, but it will all be ad hoc. It will not feel like the fluid brachiation or strict brute force that dominates midphase II.

There will be a complete text, eventually. After it's done, you should set it aside for as long as you can: a few days for a BA paper, a month or more for a dissertation. Then you can edit it as an outsider, a person unfamiliar with it. A substantial portion of endphase should be dedicated to this defamiliarization. To make sure you have time for it, set a phony deadline well ahead of the real one. There will be many things to edit and improve.

2. Aspects of the Project: Design Proper

So much for the flow of work through the phases. We now turn to the particular issues that arise in various aspects of design—looking at design not

chronologically, but by substantive area. There are two broad families of issues here: issues involved in the design document itself and issues involved
with the various particular activities of library research. We look at design
document issues first.

In my experience, the best way to improve your design document is to
read the design documents of your peers. (For this purpose, I break my course
into mutual commentary groups of about four students each.) Peers' design
documents will provide both good examples and bad ones, even in the same
document. You may find that their empirical puzzles are foggy or not even
empirical. You may find that their theoretical puzzles are just very general
empirical puzzles or that their general and specific research questions are
unrelated to their puzzles. You may see that they take for granted things that
you as reader don't know. Of course you will make lots of gracious but critical
comments, but mainly you will immediately realize that you've made some of
the same errors and will fix them at once, whether others have noticed them or
not. You'll also see things that others did well and will figure out how to apply
those lessons to your own document.

A. EMPIRICAL PUZZLES

I should begin with explicit rules for good empirical puzzles. Then we can
worry about changes in them.

An empirical puzzle is nearly always of the form "Why is it that X is true?"
(or happened, or didn't happen, or whatever). That is, a good empirical puzzle
almost always a why question. Many students don't start out with why questions as their first empirical puzzles; students most often start with very descriptive puzzles—what or how questions. But most such questions can be
easily transformed into why questions, as we shall see.

Purely descriptive questions are not really empirical puzzles. That is,
questions like "What are the trends in the attitudes of Southerners to abortion?" are not really empirical puzzles. They are purely empirical questions,
to which there exist, presumably, fixed answers that can simply be found. But
nearly always they conceal a why question, for no one would ask "What are
the trends in attitudes of Southerners to abortion?" without wondering why
that trend had taken a particular shape. Thus, the better way to design a paper is to propose the puzzle "Why did Southern attitudes to abortion become
less liberal in the 1970s?" on the basis of tentative empirical evidence, and
then verify and complexify that puzzle in an early minianalysis. That allows
you to propose a variety of theoretical mechanisms for why the attitudes

might have changed. Thus a first possibility would be that Southern attitudes changed because *all* American attitudes to abortion changed, in which case we have the wrong unit of analysis. A second possibility is that migration brought new kinds of people to the South, with new attitudes. A third possibility might be that the South saw a particular rise in evangelical Christianity. All of these permit the descriptive analysis, but more important, they point us beyond description to explanation.

A variant of the purely empirical puzzle-that-isn't-a-puzzle is the "how" question. There are two versions here, depending on the two meanings of the word *how*. These are well illustrated in the following empirical puzzle, actually proposed in one of my classes: "I'm interested in how girls today are all wearing high heels." The word *how* here means simply "the puzzling fact that." This reduces the "puzzle" to a purely descriptive question of whether it is in fact true that girls are wearing high heels (a question with many subparts: all girls or just some? all the time or part of the time?). The other meaning of *how* is "the means by which," in which case the trivial answer is obvious: "on their feet" (this was my first reaction). But there are in fact a lot of serious extensions to that "how" question: With or without stockings or other garments? Only for certain kinds of occasions? That is, under the second meaning of *how*, we start to see some real empirical puzzles: Why do girls wear high heels for some occasions and not others? Have those occasions shifted (and why)? But in general the raw "how" question is not a good empirical puzzle.

Another set of empirical puzzles that aren't really puzzles are classifications and illustrations. One student proposed a study of sex-themed parties that are officially sponsored by universities, with an empirical puzzle of "Are they socially sanctioned rituals that carve out a liminal space?" This "puzzle" simply asks whether such parties fit into a certain category of social analysis. Worse yet, this category is not a general one, but rather comes from one particular theorist. (Anthropologist Victor Turner worked on liminal [transitional] situations in the 1970s.) The preferable version of the empirical puzzle here is "Why would universities officially sponsor sex-themed parties?" and that's the version with which this student went on to an excellent research project.

More generally, an empirical puzzle should never be of the form "Does X phenomenon illustrate Y's theory of Z?" Thus one student proposed analyzing a certain social movement with the puzzle "How do these events illuminate Bakhtin's theory of the carnivalesque?" The correct puzzle here is "Why were these events more like a carnival than like a practical social movement?" where Bakhtin's theory of carnival provides the mechanisms sustaining the first interpretation and the various social movement theories provide the mechanisms for the second. Note that in this study one could not use Bakhtin's theory to decide whether the events really were carnival-like, because that would just reduce the whole project to the original illustration-of-Bakhtin formulation.

Empirical puzzles should be clearly focused. One student recently proposed "What were the general social effects of financialization in the US?" This is a blueprint not for a short empirical paper, but for a lifetime of research. It's too vague and grandiose to sustain an actual project. Another way to test empirical puzzles is the seatmate test. Can you state your empirical puzzle in two sentences to the random person in the airplane seat (or bus seat or movie seat) next to you in such a way that that person (a) can repeat it back to you and (b) finds it interesting? A recent example, good although very ambitious (actually, it has become the empirical puzzle of a dissertation): "There were dozens of rebellions in nineteenth-century China; why did one of them manage to expand rapidly and powerfully when all the others didn't?" Note that that's a good empirical puzzle because even though there are books galore on the famous Taiping Rebellion, there are not books galore on all those other failed rebellions.

Note, too, that sometimes an empirical puzzle may involve absence. I had a student who was focused on the role of women as topics in newspapers in the United Arab Emirates, but then it turned out that the real puzzle was not so much why there was so much about women, but rather—given the potential security problems there—why there was so little about security. It turned out that the stories about women were consciously designed to be a distraction from the security issue.

B. THEORETICAL PUZZLES

Proper theoretical puzzles are the hardest part of design. For more advanced students, this is because theoretical framings are easy and cheap. Advanced students can easily produce four theoretical accounts of a given empirical puzzle in half an hour. Their problem is to choose the realistic alternatives.

For less advanced students, the situation is different. Often they don't yet know enough of the literature to propose questions that are properly theoretical, so their theoretical questions are often simply general versions of their empirical puzzles: "Why did Armenian immigrants assimilate in Los Angeles but not in New York?" at the empirical level becomes "Why is it that some immigrant groups assimilate and others do not?" at the theoretical level. A proper theoretical puzzle here would be "Some argue that assimilation depends on whether immigration flows continue from the sending country, while others argue that it depends on the current pattern of other migrant communities in the receiving cities." Then it might turn out that the contrast of the two cases of Armenian immigrant communities supported one or the other theory.

Proper theoretical puzzles are alternative theoretical accounts of why things happen, not simply larger categories of things happening. Sometimes, of course, it turns out that both accounts are right, and that the research shows either how they relate to each other, or why each dominates under different conditions, or that they are both surface expressions of a single underlying and hitherto unsuspected theory. In fact, the student fixed the Armenian puzzle by considering only Los Angeles and examining internal and over-time variation in assimilation there—an excellent paper.

Note that theoretical puzzles can sometimes pose alternative colligations of a situation, rather than different explanations. Thus, the Chinese rebellions puzzle above has two theoretical alternatives: on the first argument, rebellions succeed (or not) based on their internal characteristics; on the second, rebellions succeed (or not) because of the ecology of other rebellions around them (it is easiest to expand when you have no competitors). In this second case, the new theoretical claim is that the individual rebellion is the wrong unit of analysis; we should really be looking at the whole system of rebellions.

Loosely speaking, your empirical puzzle must involve variation if your theoretical puzzles involve claims about causality. So if you want to adjudicate between two theories explaining why something happens, you need different cases, or different periods in one case, or different subgroups in one case. The exception to this is a historical narrative, where it is considered legitimate to have alternative "causal accounts"—alternate narrations, really—of a given set of events. (Hence, in the recurring Ecuadoran example, we might argue, "Nature got rights in the Ecuadoran constitution because of things elites did rather than because of things indigenous peoples did." Such an argument invokes alternate groups within one case). Another theoretical use for a single case is to show that although previous theories provide satisfactory explanations, a new explanation is nonetheless equally plausible. (Given the strength of earlier scholarship, this can be an uphill battle.) But most often, you strengthen your theoretical puzzles by focusing on different subgroups or subperiods within your object of study, even when your project looks like a single case study.

Because the theoretical puzzles are the flimsiest part of the original design document, you need to rethink them often. However, this should happen almost automatically in midphase. As you categorize and recategorize your materials, you will build up your controlled vocabulary, and you should continually try to rephrase your theoretical puzzles in your newly clear terms. After all, your controlled vocabulary is your own conceptual machinery, the raw materials of your own "theory" of the data. As that becomes clearer, you should revisit the theoretical puzzles. You may find that your theoretical puzzles now sound like truisms and need to be rephrased or reposed.

For example, one student started with the following theoretical puzzle: "Was the history of the eugenics movement determined by 'resource mobilization' issues or by the 'political opportunity structure' or by questions of 'framing?'" (The three phrases in single quotes are the three principal versions of social movement theory.) That theoretical puzzle is in fact simply the statement "I want to figure out which category of theory will best let me tell the story of the eugenics movement." It is a category puzzle of the kind I rejected earlier. The improved phrasing was "Looking at the eugenics movement in detail will tell us under what conditions framing and political opportunities modify the impact of resource constraints on social movements." That is, instead of just sticking the eugenics movement into the proper explanatory pigeonhole, the writer could use the movement to tell us how we can rebuild the pigeonholes altogether. This example underscores the fact that you should always keep your empirical and theoretical puzzles closely related. This is particularly important for advanced students, who know the theoretical literature all too well and have a tendency to get lost in a forest of microtheories that are mostly distinctions without differences.

Note that you may have to bring something back into your theoretical armamentarium. Here's a note from the student working on Ecuador:

> The influence of indigenous politics on the idea of giving rights to nature had been staring me in the face all along, but I considered and dismissed it after initially studying the events around the time the constitution was drafted and learning that Ecuador's major indigenous organizations had not proposed the "rights of nature" language. But their political presence in progressive politics during prior decades clearly influenced how this rights idea was conceptualized and the very fact that it was introduced.

Two final words on changes in theoretical puzzles during the midphase. First, if you do shift your theoretical puzzles, remember that this sometimes affects your general and specific research questions. There may be new things you need to research. Most often, however, this will not be the case, because the theoretical changes usually come from minianalyses that accidentally provided answers to questions you hadn't proposed. A new theoretical frame usually means that some existing general and specific research questions are now irrelevant, and that the new ones have already been asked and answered.

Second, if you are a more advanced student, you know that you can do more than one theoretical thing with a particular project. You may need to make up your mind which of those you want to do. Often this is a question of "What literature do I want to address?" and it will be connected with your future career plans. Remember to make this decision consciously rather than simply drifting into a theoretical approach ad hoc.

C. CONCEPTUALIZATION

Ferreting around in the primary sources may have changed your conceptualization. There may be new dramatis personae. Old ones may have changed partners halfway through your time period. So you can't study babysitting by looking only at teenage girls; you have to look at grandmothers and others who babysit.

By far the most common change in conceptualization is that the unit of analysis or the setting of action was wrongly conceived. In the project that started out analyzing sex and opium in Thailand and Burma, for example, the original plan took the two national governments as the units of analysis and aimed to compare enforcement of two different kinds of policies. But it turned out that social problems like prostitution and drugs flow quite easily across international borders, particularly in the region along the Upper Mekong where Thailand, Burma, Laos, and China all come together, far away from the central authorities of any of those states. Enforcement was therefore completely dependent on policies in adjacent countries. (Tough enforcement in one country simply shifted the opium a few miles away to another country.) This Golden Triangle—and the flow of opium through it—became the new basic unit of analysis, with the states as subordinate actors carving it up in various ways.

For another example, the paper on Pap smears was founded on a theoretical puzzle about gendering. But of course gendering can't be studied with only one gender, so the paper had to broaden to include screening for prostate cancer. A project comparing Nebraska and Kansas changed into a paper on the plains areas of the two states versus the eastern/riverine regions. All of these examples involve a change of units and settings of analysis in order to sustain the empirical and theoretical questions the students proposed.

It is also quite possible that one of the major pieces of your conceptualization does not really exist. One student aimed to do a project on the neuroimaging of autism and the ways that neuroimaging had changed people's reactions to the disease. But it turned out that conceptions of the disease itself were so precarious—and diagnostic criteria for it so labile—that even the very definition of what was the disease was caught up in the shift to neuroimaging, and so the paper had to be reconceptualized completely to focus on those changes of definition, despite the scientific claims of the "discovery" of the "realities" of autism. The most peculiar version of this problem in my experience was a proposed student paper about the planning and creation of the city of Chandigarh, the capital built de novo for the Indian state of Punjab after the partition of 1947. It turned out that until quite late in the planning process, the city had no name. It was known only as "a city to be named later." So there was no keyword with which to search for documents! "Chandigarh" would retrieve only documents from late in the process, when the name had finally been chosen. So doing the research was almost impossible.

But of course any part of the conceptualization can shift—who, what, where, when, how. And so all of these things have to be checked out at each major design review—both for omissions of important things and for retention of things that are no longer important.

D. GENERAL AND SPECIFIC RESEARCH QUESTIONS

Your general research questions also need periodic review. As you go through the project, some of them get answered and can therefore be crossed off the list. Sometimes they are no longer real questions, either because you have found that they have well-known answers or because they are no longer relevant to your recast empirical and theoretical puzzles. They must therefore be discarded. Sometimes you have found that they are posed erroneously and need to be rephrased. And of course if you repose or change your empirical puzzle, they will all have to be changed altogether. But the most usual trajectory for your general questions is that they get shifted and refocused and specified and tightened up as you go through the project.

Given any list of general questions, feasibility is always an issue. If the general research questions are too many and too big, it's time to focus the empirical puzzle a bit. Often it will turn out that you need to lop off pieces of that puzzle: to go from studying a whole government to studying one ministry in particular; to go from studying a long time period to studying a short one with a crucial event in it. Sometimes, this will involve change of underlying design; the "sex-themed parties" paper mentioned earlier went from two cases—one of which lacked data—to a detailed "alternative interpretations" study of the one particular case for which there were spectacular amounts of data. Comparison is preferable, it's true, but the data availability made the decision necessary.

Change in specific research questions flows directly from change in the general ones. Specific research questions are not something most students find problematic. They simply involve laying out the details of the general questions: it is getting the latter correct that is the difficulty. But of course it is fun to check them off the list when you have answered them. And at any given time, you need to make sure that they will be not only researched, but also processed by some planned minianalysis.

In short, a design review makes sure that your current design document reflects whatever adjustments are required by the ideas and information flowing from your research itself. It verifies that your design document is current, that it is the design for the project as it now exists, not as it was originally planned. It makes sure that the current design meets the standards of interest, clarity, coherence, and feasibility. It tells you roughly what remains to be done, and perhaps tells you the best order in which to undertake that work.

3. Aspects of the Project: Task Areas

A periodic review also means you should check through the various tasks of your project.

Bibliography. Make sure your master bibliography is finite in size. Make sure the bibliography is well classified and has no giant categories. Move the dead and irrelevant materials to the dead bibliography file, so you can more easily focus on what is important. If there are any major holes, make plans to fill them.

Minianalyses and crosswalk. Any periodic review means making sure of your question/source matrix and the growing crosswalk matrix between your controlled vocabulary and your substantial issues. On the one hand, you need to be sure that you are marching through the minianalyses that the matrix requires—knocking off this or that specific research question. But on the other hand, substantial issues will be emerging as assemblies of minianalyses and as you start to see how certain minianalyses capture the main substantive relations between the theoretical parts of your controlled vocabulary: "These three minianalyses let me show how gender and age relate in my study contrasting genealogy versus woodworking as hobbies" and that sort of thing. That is, on the one hand, you need to keep up the routine tasks of completing your current plans, but on the other, you need to be open to the inklings of linear, substantive argument that inevitably start to appear as the research goes on. You have to stay in control but also be open to emerging solutions.

Controlled vocabulary (CV). It is very important to keep up on your CV. Your CV will be crucial for coding your data (the keywords you write on documents or apply as tags). But it is also central to a clear and concise understanding of your theory. What exactly do you mean by *legitimation* or *cohort* or *psychiatrist*? These are flexible words, and you need to have a precise sense of them if your theoretical puzzle is to be capable of resolution. Keeping your controlled vocabulary under control is thus an important part in maintaining coherence in the project—in making sure that the vocabulary of the theoretical puzzles is the same as the working vocabulary of the analyses (that you mean the same thing by *cohort* in both places!). So periodic review is important. You don't want to discover at the end of the day that you have proposed one kind of puzzle and then researched another. Yet this is very possible if you are not careful about the core language and concepts of your project.

Scanning, browsing, reading. There is no particular need to monitor your scanning, browsing, and reading at a midphase review. You'll be doing all of these all the time throughout midphase. As I've said earlier, midphase may be a time for some meditative reading. Taking a break from the pressure of brute-force source work and the excitements of brachiation can provide a chance to think about your project in a completely relaxed way. And making that reflection part of a design review is a good idea. But be sure to read something that is a little outside the ordinary; if you read at this point some piece of finished work central in your area, you'll just get depressed. During midphase II you can easily despair that the mess of material before you will ever turn into a carefully argued text. Reading somebody else's fully assembled final result is not a good idea at such a moment. So read something reflective, general, and slightly off-subject.

Writing. On the other hand, any midphase review should include a quick census of what you have written—which bits have been turned into text. You should also identify things that could be written—minianalyses, source notes, other bits. And obviously it is your writer's sense of the level of assembled minianalyses and their texts that tells you whether to start thinking seriously about final text design, making the move into midphase III.

Files and housecleaning. Any midphase review should involve a complete housecleaning. Any of the shifts discussed above in empirical and theoretical puzzles, in CV and crosswalk, have implications for your current filing. It may be time to combine files, to separate files, to set files completely aside. You may need to make new distinctions or to consolidate unnecessary ones. All of this is part of rethinking your project itself, of course, and rethinking the controlled vocabulary and the theory that sustain it. However you do it, revisiting your files—and the data in them—is a central part of any design review. As always, a crucial issue in filing is the size of the units. One of my recent students sent a note:

> Of the two skills I must develop, the second is working with an electronic file structure that changes. It's clumsy to reorganize information in a way that crosscuts the files themselves. Physically, this is a bit easier because the basic unit is the sheet of paper, which can be torn apart, taped together, etc. So in retrospect, I should have done this project with a lot more physical files—they are easier to change.

Action list and suspense issues. There may be materials you are waiting for but have forgotten in the rush of other things. They may be planned minianalyses that were put off for one reason or another. To the extent that you can do so, checking on these things at a design review is useful. As I noted earlier, despite my obsessionalism, I eventually lose control of my projects (usually just in time to swing into writing them up!), and I think it is my failure to maintain any central to-do or action list that brings this about. Eventually, in midphase II, I just fall in love with the excitement and the action and start to let the project run itself. As usual, you need to undertake as much organization as is necessary and no more. I get by without keeping up on my housecleaning, but because of that I not seldom have the experience of receiving an important interlibrary loan item after I have sent off the final write-up of a project. Or I notice after the fact an important set of analyses that I have forgotten to put into the final text. Such is life.

ULTIMATELY, THE BASIC RULE FOR DESIGN REVIEWS IS TO USE THE aspects of your project that are both firm and well-developed to support your attempt to further develop some other and less certain area. If the theory is looking like the weakest link, then use the empirical puzzle, the conceptualization, and the results of the minianalyses to try to focus it. If one general research question doesn't seem to be working, then use the others to decide where it fits, whether it can be rejected, and so on. By following this rule you will always be basing your effort on the strongest current parts of the project and applying that effort to the project area where it can have the highest payoff. You will discover that fixing one area will reveal the weaknesses of others, which can move you along to those other tasks, until you have a complete overhaul.

And remember that this whole "midphase design" thing is a helpful checklist, not a rigid plan. You need enough design work to keep from getting lost, but it's not necessary in its own right. Its only purpose is to make sure you get to midphase III—the moment of linearization—and to make sure that when you arrive there you have everything you need to write a brilliant text. The amount of design you need is whatever amount will accomplish that goal.

12 Endphase

As I have emphasized, your design document and the various disciplines of midphase get you through the nonlinear period of library research. Endphase arrives when linearity returns. Your writing takes over direction of the project, and your guiding lights become the canons of structured exposition and linear prose. In a book focused on nonlinearity, there would seem to be little place for detailed discussion of writing. I've already referred the reader to Booth et al.'s *The Craft of Research* for such a discussion.

Advice on writing may be futile for another reason, one I know well after supervising hundreds of course papers, BA papers, MA papers, and PhD dissertations. When drafts are not explicitly required by an advisor, papers are usually written at most a few days—and sometimes only a few hours—before their deadlines. Partly, this happens because nonlinear research is dauntingly complex. But it also happens because students caught up in research underestimate the time and effort required to create a text out of their materials.

If you have followed the disciplines of this book so far, this second problem will matter less, to be sure. You will have written most of the introduction as you go along. You will have drafted many short bits about sources, people, minor topics, and so on. You will have begun in midphase to assemble linear chunks by combining minianalyses. You will have at hand organized files, a clear set of puzzles, a solid working vocabulary, and a clear logic leading from puzzles to analysis. All that means that you won't face a mountain of disorganized material with no way to fashion it into a text.

All the same, the approach to research portrayed here does entail an approach to writing. Research that has been well done deserves good writing, and so I shall say a few words about style. I won't say much about the overall organization and structure of the text. That will have grown naturally out of decisions discussed in chapters 10 and 11. But I will say a few things about clarity, logic, and elegance. You may already have inferred some of them from the discussion of reading in chapter 7: the style of writing I think best is the style that is best for mastery reading.

1. Style.

At the end of the day, you win the reader with prose. You can have done the best library research possible. You can have brilliantly returned from nonlinear research to linear argument. But if you do not write sentences and paragraphs that readers want to read, your message goes unheard.

The fundamental problem of modern prose mechanics is the same for everyone—professors and students alike. Most of us type so fast that our written texts are simply recorded talk. If you try to write a paragraph longhand, you will understand this fact at once. Before you have finished writing down your first version of a longhand sentence, you will have thought of two or three better ways to write it. That's what real writing feels like—very different from speaking.

But while word-processors have made today's writing much closer to speaking, we read just as we did before. Extracting meaning from a written text remains fundamentally different from extracting meaning from speech. In the oral context, we have gestures, expression, vocal tone, prosody, emphasis, and other paralinguistic cues to assist our meaning. We can say the one word "Right!" and determine by the tone of our voice whether our listener hears "I agree" or "Nobody but a fool would agree." In reading, there is no such paralinguistic repertoire; emoticons have not yet come to academic prose. The text itself must convey all our meaning to the reader. Therefore, words must be chosen very carefully, syntax must be precise, and ambiguity can be deployed only with clear intention. Put formally, writing means turning the natural communication of speech (talk plus paralinguistic cues) into a conventionalized text that conveys an unambiguous and complex message to a reader in our absence.

But in the current environment, we all write on computers, and in doing so we produce natural, spoken texts whose sentences are vague and telegraphic and whose larger structure is meandering and repetitive. We expect the reader (whom we imagine as a listener) to supply the logic, for we assume that any false assumption on the reader's part will be easily corrected in the next exchange, forgetting that in writing there will be no next exchange. Think about how easy misunderstanding is on e-mail or in texting, and you'll see why this argument is correct.

Real writing must therefore be very precise. The logic must be clear. Ambiguities must be foreseen and handled preemptively. Moreover, all this must be done in a linear text, in which the preemptive handling of ambiguity cannot be mistaken for the main line of the argument. That is why writing is full of directive constructions: "One might think X, but . . ."; or "One argument might be X, but I shall argue Y."

All this is clear enough, but it is still difficult to execute. Most of the text you have written earlier in the project—your minianalyses, source notes, and other bits—will have been written in the spoken style. All these bits must now be translated into real prose. Luckily, the design document will be written fairly well by the time you reach endphase. If you have discussed it extensively with others, they will have forced you to make your assumptions and logic clear in the newer versions.

But there is a larger problem. Most students have little practice in writing formally. Their image of finished prose is often stilted: long sentences, weighty jargon, elaborate constructions. It is a style simultaneously heavy and unclear. Moreover, the pressure of deadlines leaves students unused to editing. They seldom finish texts with time to spare for serious editing. Yet editing should be a drastic business. For example, the original draft of this book was twice as long as this published manuscript. That's what editing means.

Here then are four short notes on writing prose, dealing with this difficulty of creating an effective linear text out of your first, "spoken" versions of the project.

A. READING

The first step to writing good prose is reading good prose. We write what we read. And since you need some breaks from library research, spend them reading good prose.

You won't find it on the web. As any good web designer will tell you, general-purpose web pages are optimized at about the sixth-grade reading level. Indeed, Internet prose exaggerates the vices of newspaper prose: simplified arguments, vague generalities, limited vocabulary, reliance on graphics. Its model is indeed speech rather than writing, and its most characteristic form—the blog—recreates in written form the flaccid oratory of the nineteenth century. Sadly, academic prose is often little better. Humanistic writing is often filled with big words, coy puns, and foggy reasoning. On the other side of things, flavorless scientism turns the quantitative social sciences into the prose equivalent of Melba toast—noisy but tasteless.

It is best then to read classic literature. Let's name some names. Read great fiction stylists like Fitzgerald, Conrad, Austen, Hemingway, Woolf, Wharton, Lessing, and Updike. Read the great essayists like T. S. Eliot, E. B. White, and V. S. Naipaul. Read the modern poets like Anne Sexton, Derek Walcott, and W. H. Auden. These are people who make words do wonderful things. Jane Austen's characters may speak an English that no real human being ever spoke; but her books are uniquely readable for all that.

As for academic prose, read history and anthropology, especially from the period before the writers in those disciplines got lost in the Foucauldian fog (about 1980). Historians include many great writers, not only the overly self-conscious prose stylists of the Samuel Eliot Morison stripe, but also modern specialty historians like Charles Rosenberg, Lawrence Katz, Natalie Davis, and Samuel Haber. The English historians of midcentury—men like A. J. P. Taylor, G. R. Elton, and Hugh Trevor-Roper—were great stylists. But there are fine writers throughout the social sciences—Robert Dahl in political science, Harvey Zorbaugh and Howard Becker in sociology, Keynes and Joan Robinson in economics, and many others. Ask your advisors—they will be happy to tell you their favorites.

Good academic writing in English is clear and concise. Its logic flows ineluctably: sentence to sentence, paragraph to paragraph, section to section. Forced to choose, it prefers argument over elegance. But it prefers to avoid the choice, achieving the one by perfecting the other. Let me say a little bit about each of these.

B. CLARITY AND CONCISION

Often our arguments are highly complex. Therefore, they must be voiced in precise words, with clear definitions—given gracefully in text if need be. Syntax and word order make a big difference. In the name of clarity, many speech idioms are forbidden in prose. Three of them are endemic in the student prose I receive, so I will mention them here.

The first problem involves quantifiers like *only*, *some*, *not*, and so on. In speech we clarify the meaning of such quantifiers by emphasis, but in writing they must be located correctly. "Not all men passed the exam" does not mean the same thing as "All men did not pass the exam." In speech, we would often say the second of these to mean the first, but would make our meaning clear by emphasizing "all." But printed text has no such emphasis, so we must rely on precise word order. The same thing occurs with *only*; "Only I saw the book" is not "I only saw the book" is not "I saw only the book."

The second problem concerns reference. An obvious example is *this*. In speech we use *this* as a freestanding subject at the beginning of sentences to refer to some unstated aspect of what we have just said. ("This is what I've been talking about all along.") We don't repeat that aspect itself because we know we can clear things up if our listener takes *this* to refer to something other than what we meant. But in writing, there's no possibility of correction, so a freestanding *this* invites misinterpretation. In writing, therefore, one always repeats (or states, if it has been unstated) the substantive to which the *this* refers: "This idea," "This argument," "This style of thought." (Hence, "This problem of reference is what I've been talking about all along.") The reader shouldn't have to guess what *this* refers to. And reference is a problem with many other words as well. Make sure the reader clearly knows the referents of demonstrative pronouns (*this*, *that*, etc.), relative pronouns (*who*, *which*, *whose*, etc.), and personal pronouns (*it*, *its*, *them*, *theirs*, *whose*, etc.).

The third problem is the verb "to be." Using the verb "to be" usually betrays incomplete thought. "Bureaucracy is an important trend in contemporary organizations" means little or nothing. "Modern organizations proliferate useless managers and paperwork" says something quite definite. The verb "to be" can also be confusing because we use it for normative as well as descriptive statements. "The United States is a democracy" can mean that the nation has a certain list of properties (elections, secret ballot, universal suffrage). But it can also mean "The United States is a good place and I approve of it." To avoid both of these dangers (vagueness and normative ambiguity), go through your text circling every *is* and *are* and try to replace every occurrence with some verb that makes a stronger and more specific assertion.

These and many other aspects of prose style flow from the need for coherence and clarity, qualities you have built and maintained through the many revisions of the design document. Don't let vagueness creep in at the end through careless writing.

C. THE FLOW OF LOGIC

A linear text has an argument. Let's be clear about what I mean by "an argument." I recently asked a class of first-year students to tell me Adam Smith's argument in the first five chapters of *The Wealth of Nations*. They gave me a list of ten assertions (all of them indeed made by Adam Smith), but did not give those assertions in any order or with any logical connection. But such a list of bullet points is not an argument. An argument is an ordered set of assertions each of which follows logically from its predecessor(s). Your text has to make an argument, and that argument needs to be clearly and continuously—if unobtrusively—underscored. Each sentence should therefore grow directly out of its predecessor. If your prose is not full of words and phrases like "however," "nonetheless," "to be sure," "although," "correlatively," "similarly," "on the other hand," and so on, you are not making your argument clear enough. You're just giving a list.

Obviously, you don't solve this problem by scattering these words on the text like pepper on a salad. Put in the logical posting that is appropriate. But remember that you can't assume the logical posting will be pulled from your expression and emphasis as it would be in speech. In speech, we communicate much of our logic with head shakes, ironic tones of voice, and so on. You don't have those resources in writing. Be clear.

Your paragraph structure must also be clear. Each paragraph concerns one idea. No idea takes more than a double-spaced page, and most take less than half a page. If a paragraph is more than about 200 words it is probably too long. Begin most paragraphs with a sentence that links to the preceding paragraph clearly (using a demonstrative like "these ideas" or a logical marker like "on the other hand") and that makes clear how the new paragraph will advance your argument. Similarly, end most paragraphs with a transition sentence implicitly summarizing the paragraph and foreshadowing what comes next.

Just as paragraphs should not be lists of sentences, sections should not be lists of paragraphs. If you must have list-wise paragraphs (suppose you must talk briefly about the economy, social structure, and culture of several countries), use a parallel structure and order the things within the list from simple to complex or in some other semi-logical mode. Lists are boring to read; give them the appearance of logical flow even if they don't have it.

Use clear signposts. Do say "In the second place . . ." or "My third argument is . . ." Make sure readers knows exactly where they are. Don't be obtrusive about this, but if you must err, err on the side of clarity. Better that readers be annoyed with your overposting than that they be lost.

The final test of paragraphs is that you should be able to summarize each paragraph as a single sentence such that your larger argument is completely clear in this shortened form. Your entire paper, in fact, should be so condensable.

Above the paragraph level, a paper should fall into sections which have roughly the same structure as paragraphs. Each section should begin with an introductory paragraph saying what is coming, in what order, and why. Each section should end with a clear summary of what was said, how it goes

together, and what those arguments imply must come next. Transitions between sections should be absolutely clear. To be sure, none of this means that
your text cannot be elegant, as we shall see. But the reader should always find
a rock-solid organization underneath the gracious surface.

D. ELEGANCE

Elegance in writing comes with practice. But even well-practiced writers edit
very heavily. No one writes beautifully the first time: not you, not me, not
Mario Vargas Llosa. Cultivate the habit of continually improving your prose.
Reread, edit, wait, reread, edit, etc. The "wait" is central; you must forget a text
if you want to improve it seriously. The bigger the text, the longer you need
to be away from it. For professionals, this defamiliarization is built into the
rhythm of peer review. By the time a piece comes back to us for revision, we
have forgotten it and are more willing to see its flaws of structure and style.
But until you become a professional, you must learn to program these breaks
into your own practice of writing. It's the only way you can read your prose as
a reader, not as its writer.

Of course, the writer of a term paper does not have the time to do this.
Most term papers are written the day before they are due, by chatting into
the machine. (They read like chat, too; that's why I almost never assign them.)
But if you have written a genuine research paper, give it the respect of serious
editing. From a scheduling point of view, this means finishing the final draft
at least a week before it is due. Then you can be away from it for a few days and
edit it for real. Being away for two weeks would be better, but then you might
see so many needed changes that you would get discouraged.

2. A Final Note about Change

One thing about library research is certain. There will be continuous change
in the tools: their corporate homes, their availability, their interfaces, perhaps
even their internal workings. I should therefore close the book with advice
on how to deal with change. That advice is important for another reason, too.
There are many specific areas in library research I haven't covered in detail—
archives and government documents, for example. In those cases, too, you
will need to apply for yourself the general lessons of this book.

There are really four fundamental lessons. The first is that library research
is not about discovery but about creation. For all the rhetoric on the web pages
of the research tools, library research is not about finding things. Nor will it

be in the future. The whole discourse of "finding" and "discovery" is wrong. In library research—indeed in all forms of real thinking—we find information to help further our thoughts. But creative thought is humans' business, and finding information is merely one part of that activity. Far, far more important is figuring out what to look for. The tools will not tell you that, no matter how elaborate they become.

Of course, people will claim that the machine can tell you what to look for. The same claims were made for canned statistical programs, tables of integrals, microfilm, and various other commodifications of knowledge, just as they are now being made for related records listings in citation databases. But just like all those other commodifications, the new developments will mainly help those who use the tools to expand and complexify their decisions about what they will look for, not those who surrender those decisions to the machines.

The second lesson of this book is about nonlinearity. I have argued throughout that library research is a nonlinear process. I have contrasted that with the linear system that most of us have been taught at one point or another. Nonlinearity is also not going to change. It is enforced by the very practice of research with found data, as I argued in the opening chapter. The Internet has not changed the fundamental social situation of research with found data. It must still be a parallel process, advancing on many fronts at once.

You should therefore be suspicious of claims that library research has been turned into a linear procedure, even though the librarians, among others, have believed in the linear concept of research for nearly a century, and the information scientists are taking up the same belief today. But scholars have not, and the immense productivity of twentieth-century scholarship is obvious evidence that they were right. Moreover, my claim that library research is nonlinear is not only correct, it is also far too modest. As my quantitative colleagues know quite well, the vast majority of quantitative research in the social sciences is nonlinear, too. Quantitative scholars quite commonly submit grant proposals to do research when they are in fact well into the midphase of that research, aiming to use the granted funds to start their *next* project. A grant application for truly future research inevitably includes so many imponderables and unforeseen circumstances that it looks too tentative and risky by comparison with research that is carefully laid out in linear form. But only research that is mostly done can be laid out in linear form. So applications for truly future research seldom get funded.

The third lesson of this book is that quality matters. It matters that your sources be the best that you can find; that your bibliography contain the best writing on a topic; that your research tools be the most effective you can find; that your reading be subtle and creative. Your aim in research is to create something admirable and excellent, something worth knowing. There are to be sure many varieties of excellence—many disciplines, many methods, many canons. But each of those has its own forms of rigor, and your research should not only follow them, it should also make use of tools that follow them.

The immediate implications of this third lesson are simple. More is not better; better is better. Faster is not better; better is better. Quantity and speed are not the criteria of your research nor should they be the criteria for your tools. As new tools come into existence and old tools change, you must always judge them in terms of quality. Are they actually doing what they claim to do? Do they really have a controlled vocabulary or is it just an old thesaurus used as a keyword listing? Do they really have current data or are their databases full of unidentified (and uncritically accepted) migrated material? Are the differences revealed by a tool real differences, or do they stem from the accidents of OCR and other forms of reprocessing? Is a tool truly universal or is it simply a garbage can? Is it stable or will it be modified without notification to users?

These are the questions you must ask of every new tool you find. They are indeed the questions that have motivated my judgments of tools throughout. They guarantee that you will find tools that will be most likely to find reasonable and necessary amounts of the best material with the smallest amount of work.

These three lessons—about creativity, nonlinearity, and quality—will be your guides to dealing with the inevitable changes of the tools and repositories with which we work. My fourth lesson is of a different kind. It concerns the morals of library research. By this I don't mean avoiding plagiarism, reporting sources truly, seeking truly representative data, not playing favorites with your favorite hypotheses, and so on. All these things I take for granted. Nobody who did not care about them would bother to read such a book as I have here written. They are the morality of all rigorous thinking.

My moral point is rather about your stance toward your subject of research. It captures comments that I have often made in supervising particular projects, but that don't belong in any one particular place in this book. The fourth lesson is this: A library researcher must combine doubt and critique with a profound sympathy for his or her subjects. At the end of the day, all library research projects bring some other social world to life: its people, their friends and their enemies, their successes and their failures, their triumphs and their tragedies, their sainthood and their evil. They may be people from long ago or far away, or they may be people from now and close at hand. What matters for your research is that they did not live their lives in order to make a subject for your paper, or to exemplify some famous theory, or to provide a suitable object for anachronistic moralizing. You must address them with skepticism and critique, to be sure, but at the same time you must recognize them as people just like yourself: not cardboard cutouts, not the good guys and bad guys of the various -*isms*, but men and women struggling to make sense of this puzzling thing we call human existence and to live lives they found meaningful. They may have done it in strange and unfamiliar ways. They may indeed have done things that seem evil or wonderful beyond all comprehension. But your research and writing must translate their world into your own world in such a way that your readers find in that translated world some meaning, some new complexity that speaks to their own lives.

Your guide here should be Kant's categorical imperative. Do your research and write your text in the frame of mind in which you yourself would want to be researched and discussed. Read manuscripts the way you would like someone to read your e-mails or analyze your Facebook page. Interpret your subjects' intentions the way you would like your own intentions to be understood by skeptical peers. Pass only those moral judgments to which you hold yourself accountable. You assume an immense responsibility in doing library research: to portray one world of experience for those who live in another. It is a great trust. Do it well.

Glossary

Note: In the following list, the initials P and D stand for physical and digital. Thus "allusions" are the physical analogy of "hyperlinks," so the list has "allusions (P)" and "hyperlinks (D)."

ALA. American Library Association. The professional association of American librarians and organizer of many major collaboratively produced reference tools. Its most important publication is the *Guide to Reference Books*, in eleven physical editions from 1902 to 1996. The *Guide* has been in electronic format since 2008.

allusions (P). Physical-era hyperlinks requiring knowledge in the reader to be recognized. Hence *Stranger in a Strange Land*—the title of a famous science-fiction novel by Robert Heinlein—is actually a phrase from the Bible. So is Martin Luther King's "Let my people go." Sometimes allusions are whole phrases, as in "It was the best of books, it was the worst of books," where *books* replaces *times* in the opening line of Dickens's *Tale of Two Cities*.

archive. Usually the word *archive* means a repository containing physical material that is utterly unique: institutional records, manuscript collections, image collections, and so on. Sometimes it is used purely for institutional or organizational records, other such unique material being called "manuscript collections." (Hence, "the Harvard University Archives.") Archival material is almost always not published. Occasionally the word *archive* is used to denote a uniquely complete collection of unusual published material in a particular area such as jazz recordings, magazine covers, and so on. Increasingly, archival material is "born digital."

ASCII. American Standard Code for Information Interchange. The actual list of binary codes (128 in the simple version) that encode nearly all computer information at the level of machine code. (It's now part of a broader system that reaches across all languages, the UTF/Unicode system). For example, capital D is ASCII 68, binary 1000100.

bibliographer. A person who makes up lists of books. In most libraries, the "subject bibliographers" (or simply "bibliographers") are the people who decide which books to buy in a particular area as well as which specialty online databases to rent. They thus have immense knowledge of and power over a library's resources, both physical and digital. Once you have gotten deep into your project, subject bibliographers will be more helpful than reference staff, because their knowledge is more specific.

bibliography. The task of finding materials relevant to a project. Librarians also speak of "descriptive bibliography," the creation of precise records of particular items. "A bibliography" on a particular topic is a list of materials relevant to that topic. These were standard assignments in library schools in the old days, and the LC Z classification is full of them. "National bibliography" means a definitive listing of all books published in a particular nation, possibly in a given era. "The bibliography" of an article refers to the listing of items cited in that article, often called the "reference list."

catalog. The collection of records identifying and locating the materials held in a library. Traditionally, there are three kinds: author, title, and subject. In small and medium libraries, these were interfiled in the physical card catalog, but larger libraries often separated author/title and subject catalogs. Online, all three are indistinguishable. Most important for the researcher today is a browsable subject catalog—an alphabetized list of clickable subject headings, rather than a keyword subject catalog. Hundreds of important print-era catalogs have themselves been printed and are very useful bibliographical tools, usually for highly specialized areas.

citation (PD). A reference to a supporting document, typically done in one of two formats: scientific (author, date, and [possibly] page given parenthetically in text, with a reference list giving full bibliographical information at the end of the text) or humanistic (full bibliographical information given in a footnote at first mention of a source, then abbreviated information in later footnotes). In the digital era, citations are often live links, which has the advantage of quick reference to supporting material and the disadvantage of reducing the likelihood that a given text will be read as a whole unit.

clipping service (P). A clipping service was a hired group of newspaper readers who would "clip" from any newspapers items of interest to the client. The client specified areas of interest and the service reviewed the newspapers, periodicals, etc. The digital analog is a feed (D).

concordance (P). A printed keyword index, usually containing all words in a text other than *a, an,* and *the*. Normally, a concordance did not include the text of a line containing the keyword, but simply its location. Most dictionaries of quotations are concordance-indexed. Concordances to the Bible have existed for centuries.

controlled vocabulary (P). An indexer's name for a rigorous system by which ambiguous subject terms are reduced to a single term (e.g., *magic* for *sorcery, magic, witchcraft, occultism,* etc.). Normally a hierarchical structure in which terms are clearly related as broader and narrower, but often with some degree of cross-referencing. Failure to cross-reference sufficiently is the chief problem of controlled vocabularies; they favor clarity over linkage.

cross-references (P). Print-era hyperlink instructions, of the form "for United States Department of State see US Dept. of State." Used in physical catalogs and indexes to organize ambiguous terms, variant spellings, changing names, etc., into single locations. Especially important with government agencies, whose names tend to change arbitrarily. Card catalogs were full of these, and they can still be useful tools.

digitization. *See* OCR.

disambiguation (PD). Distinguishing between multiple individuals or groups or other items with the same name. In physical indexes, this was generally handled with birth and death dates for the individuals, and with geographic identifiers for places. Disambiguation is often a problem, in both settings, for common titles. (My university's online catalog has twenty-four distinct items with the title *Science*, most but not all distinguished by publication dates.) In part this reflects the fact that titles cannot be copyrighted.

draft (P). In the mode of academic production enabled by the typewriter, texts had succeeding "drafts," by which was meant a clean retyping of an edited manuscript. Since typing was arduous and often expensive, writers rearranged and inserted new text with marginal comments, arrows, and balloons, and even by cutting up and reassembling manuscripts with Scotch Tape and staples (cut-and-paste preceded tape-and-staple). Only once the resultant "manuscript" had become almost illegible was it retyped. This meant that papers had very clear successions of versions, typically three or four for an important piece of work. In computer-based production, updating is of course continuous.

EBSCO (D). EBSCO is a large conglomerate. EBSCO Information Services is a subset of this conglomerate. EBSCO Information Services is an amalgamator of databases and information services. It recently (2011) purchased the H. W. Wilson Company (q.v.), developer of most of the major indexing tools of the twentieth century. As of this writing, it is not yet clear what the implications of this purchase will be for the functionalities of the old Wilson databases.

endnotes (PD). *See* footnotes.

ephemera. A librarian's word for those materials that are literally *ephemeral*, that is, expected to vanish. Includes pamphlets, broadsides, handouts, postcards, mimeographed magazines, roadmaps, and a million other things. Collections of ephemera are useful for research on popular attitudes, since formally printed media usually arise in particular parts of society. In the digital era, many ephemera—e.g., Facebook pages—are perpetually archived, if not necessarily easily available.

facets (PD). Different aspects of a text or artifact, typically title, author, date, publisher, publication location, ISBN, etc. By extension, subject headings are sometimes called facets. All of these can be used to narrow a search.

feed (D). An automatic download or attention line issued to a subscriber by a site. These are not subject- or interest-screened, other than by the user's choice of the site that is doing the automatic notification. *See also* clipping service (P).

finding aid (PD). A document summarizing the contents of a particular set of archival materials, often containing a biography or history of the archive's subject as well as a detailed inventory of materials, down to the box or even folder level. Many of these are online.

footnote (PD). A piece of information justifying or extending a text but not integral to it, and therefore placed at the foot of the page. Endnotes are "footnotes" placed at the end of a manuscript, because in the print era, text composition could become unduly complicated with footnotes. From a scholarly point of view footnotes are clearly preferable to endnotes, because the reader can find immediate clarification on the page. In the print era, endnotes were also favored by some publishers on aesthetic grounds, footnotes being thought to disfigure the page.

govdocs. Short for "government documents," the branch of the library (and possibly a branch of its collection) associated with the cataloging of and access to documents from all forms of governments. Of these (some of) the national documents are now well indexed and available online. State documents are available online for some wealthy states. However, most state documents and nearly all local documents are available only in print. International govdocs are their own arcane specialty. Navigating govdocs is nearly always a task for specialists.

Guide; Guide to Reference Books. See ALA.

hyperlink (D). Clickable reference from words or phrases in one text to another site. They have the advantage that they do not require knowledge in the reader, and the disadvantage that they thereby discourage the acquisition of that knowledge, which is the foundation not only of research, but also of all forms of expert knowing. *See also* allusions (P); citations (PD).

International Index. See Wilson, H. W.

JSTOR (D). A site amalgamating most scholarly periodicals of any importance in the humanities and social sciences. Founded in 1995 by the Mellon Foundation and thus a not-for-profit organization. Although there is a complicated history (JSTOR is now part of a larger not-for-profit called ITHAKA), JSTOR continues to operate more or less as before. In some cases, publishers create a "moving wall" which prevents access through JSTOR to the most recent issues of their journals (in which case you must find those journals through your catalog). The aim of JSTOR was to enable broader access to journals, but a major unforeseen result has been to enable scholarly libraries to throw out most of their physical journals. This saved some money but also prevented the kinds of fast scanning possible only with physical materials.

keyword (D). Technically, a subject heading assigned to a work by the author of that work. Later generalized to mean any word in a text, either standing alone (KWOC = keyword out of context) or in association with other words (KWIC = keyword in context). Modern keyword indexing is KWIC when more than one word is used, KWOC otherwise.

KWIC. Key word in context. A form of indexing, in effect, by two-word pairs, based on simple word searches in text.

KWOC. Key word out of context. The original name for what is now called keyword indexing: one-word, concordance-type indexing of texts.

LC. Library of Congress. Although sometimes used to refer to the library itself, this term usually denotes the Library of Congress Classification System, the dominant classification system for books and monographs in American libraries.

Library Literature. See H. W. Wilson.

MARC (PD). Machine Readable Cataloging. The MARC rules are the conventional rules that govern cataloging of books, serials, and other items. As the name suggests, they are driven by the need for standardized formats for input to universal cataloging systems in all languages. The centralization of cataloging enabled by the Internet has removed the local information that card catalogs often provided, and while increasing the bibliographic exactitude of catalog records, has generally reduced their scholarly content.

MLS. Master of library science.

National Union Catalog (NUC). A somewhat fictitious entity, gradually turned into a reality over the twentieth century. This phrase originally referred to the entire card holdings of the Library of Congress, which long covered only a minority of all books held in US libraries. Various grants brought the collection closer to completion and a first printed version was sold in the 1940s under the title *Catalog of Books Represented by LC Printed Cards*. From the 1960s to the 1980s an enormous effort produced a 750-volume *NUC* of all imprints before 1956 held in US libraries. This is the present definitive national bibliography, it being assumed that everything since 1956 is cataloged in the current LC master files.

OCLC (PD). Originally the Ohio College Library Center, a collaboration of Ohio libraries on cataloging, acquisitions, and related matters. The cataloging initiatives led to an early foray into computers and the eventual morphing of OCLC into the Online Computer Library Center (same acronym). OCLC supports WorldCat and a wide variety of other tools. It is (as of this writing) a nonprofit, which makes it more user-friendly than the Googles and EBSCOs of the world.

OCR. Optical character recognition. Capturing data by creating a graphical representation of the page (e.g., a digital photograph of the page, pixel by pixel) and then applying algorithms to decide what characters appear on that graphical representation. Texts created by OCR are opposed to truly digital texts, texts created by digital processing. The latter are error-free by definition. Confusingly, "digitization" is used in some contexts to denote any form of reduction of analog information to digital information, thus including OCR as a subcategory.

periodical (PD). A source that emerges periodically, usually meaning journals and magazines. *Serials* is a broader term, since it embraces materials that are printed over time, but possibly at irregular intervals.

Readers' Guide. See Wilson, H. W.

reference. Traditionally, the reference desk was the place where librarians advised users. In the print library, the major reference tools were located near the reference desk. These tools were usually divided into "ready reference," the most central few shelves of material, and "reference stacks," which might include the national bibliographies, extended biographical tools and indexes, catalogs of government publications, disciplinary handbooks, and other finding aids for print materials. If you are fortunate, these are still in place somewhere near the center of your library. Most current reference departments use only online materials. *Reference* can also mean "a citation," with *reference list* meaning the list of items cited by an article or book.

reprint (P). A physical copy of a single article or book chapter. In predigital and pre-Xeroxing days, scholars worldwide kept in touch through "reprint requests" via postcards. A publishing author typically bought a hundred or so reprints to send to scholars beyond the reach of journal subscriptions. The digital equivalent would be the download, but in downloading, the downloaded author does not know the downloader's identity.

serial (PD). Something issued at intervals, such as a journal, government report, or annual. Traditionally, newspapers were not considered serials, but were treated separately.

stacks (P). The portion of a library in which are located the main book collection and, in most libraries, also the back volumes of the periodical collection. In libraries from the interwar period, the stacks are a peculiar iron/steel construction with low ceilings, bare lightbulbs, opaque glass floors, and a somewhat Gothic feel.

subject heading (P). A topic assigned to a particular text. Thus, in digital terms, a formally assigned tag. Unlike tags, subject headings are generally taken from controlled vocabularies.

surfing (D). Surfing the net is allowing a random trail of hyperlinks to take you to new places and ideas. Although this kind of practice was possible in the physical era, other random practices were more common. One was the scanning of physical issues of periodicals relevant to one's area. Another was the equivalent scanning of a range of stack shelves or of a new-book shelf. These were of course actually forms of professional browsing. For intellectual adolescents of the print era, the equivalent of surfing was reading encyclopedias.

tags (D). Labels assigned by users to texts and other online artifacts. Although these can be shown to converge gradually to "folksonomies," they are usually at a much more abstract and general level than the average controlled vocabulary and prone to ambiguities that the latter was designed to avoid. Controlled vocabularies are essentially regimented tag systems without the problems of ambiguity and vagueness.

union list (P). A combined list of holdings, WorldCat being the ultimate example. The first and most famous of these, long called simply the *Union List*, was the three-edition *Union List of Serials in Libraries of the United States and Canada*, first published in 1927. For each serial, this work gave a complete history (still useful, because it traces the various renamings of journals, often unavailable online) and the actual holdings at every major library in the US and Canada.

Web of Science (WoS). Currently a Thomson Reuters product. Often known as ISI, for Institute of Scientific Information, its original owner in the print era. The first large-scale electronically-generated bibliographical tool, with comprehensive coverage in the sciences, and later the social sciences (Social Sciences Citation Index [SSCI] from the early 1970s), and the humanities (Arts and Humanities Citation Index [AHCI] from the later 1970s). Covers articles only, although currently moving into books. Introduced citation indexing, a feature which makes it by far the most useful bibliographical tool on the market. All of its indexing is by keyword, and before the era of electronic journals all of its data entry was by OCR, with all the usual issues.

Wilson, H. W. (P). A company that provided indexes and general reference tools to librarians throughout the twentieth century. Many online indexes are descendants of Wilson indexes. As of this writing, the legacy Wilson tools are owned by EBSCOhost. The most important of the Wilson indexes is the *Readers' Guide to Periodical Literature*, which dates from 1902. Also important is the *International Index*, a scholarly spinoff from the *Readers' Guide* in 1919, and itself divided into *Humanities Index* and *Social Sciences Index* later in the century. The *Essay and General Literature Index*, another Wilson tool, was the only index to edited volumes until WoS (and to some extent Google Scholar) started to do such indexing in recent years. Wilson himself took the lead in such general efforts as the production of the original *Union List of Serials*.

WorldCat (D). A compilation of catalogs from thousands of libraries worldwide, created by OCLC. WorldCat is merely a compilation, not a magical perfect list to all the world's libraries, as its name implies and as most students assume. As of this writing, there is no attempt to quality-control the records, which were simply input by libraries themselves. (Later libraries tended to simply download the records already in WorldCat, which meant, since the well-funded libraries came later, that weaker records tended to drive out stronger ones.) Nor are the acquisition holdings continuously updated—one can find something in World-Cat that proves no longer to be in the collection that claims it. Nonetheless, WorldCat is an extremely useful tool for long-shot bibliographical questions.

Index

Note: This is not a keyword index, but a subject index based on a controlled vocabulary. It is shorter and leaner than a keyword index, including only those occurrences of concepts that I thought necessary to call to a reader's attention. Major discussions appear as groupings of three or more continuous pages. Cross-referencing is minimized; phrases are listed under the main substantive noun in the phrase unless the phrase is an obvious unit (e.g., design document).